I0810375

IMAGES
of America

TRAPPE AND COLLEGEVILLE

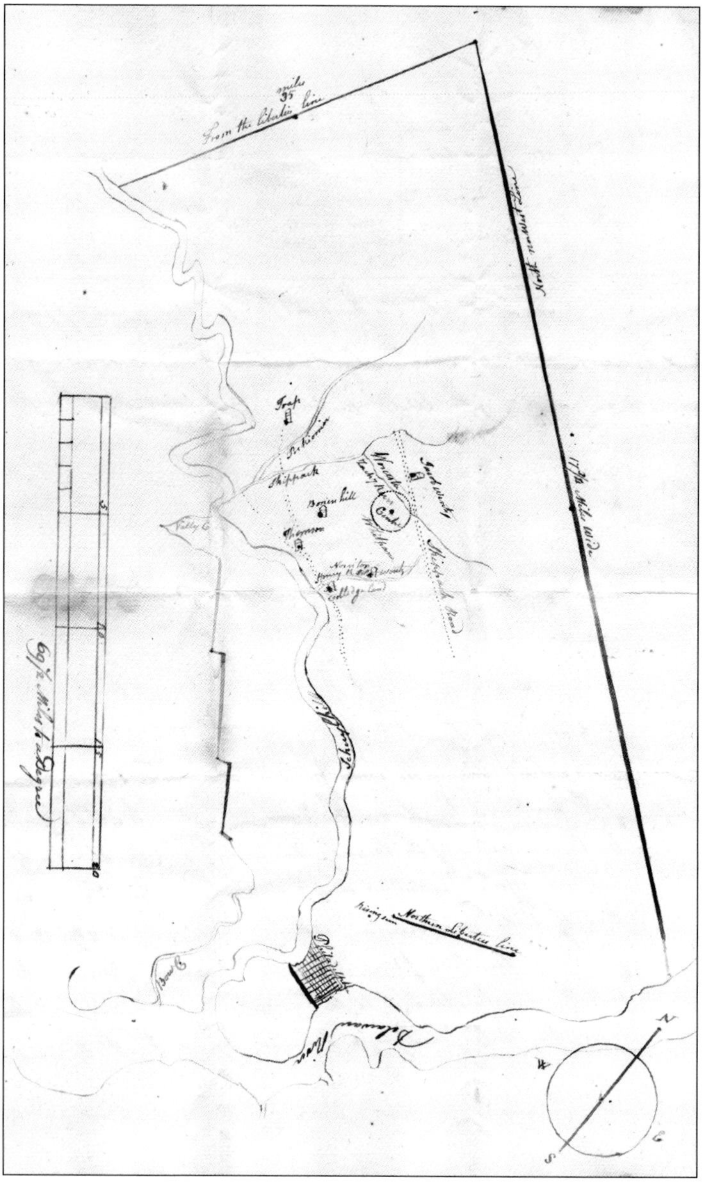

MAP OF MONTGOMERY COUNTY, C. 1784. The earliest map of Montgomery County, which was subdivided from Philadelphia County and established on September 10, 1784, suggests that Trappe (then spelled Trap) was considered as a possible location for the county seat. This was likely due to the presence of Frederick Muhlenberg, who was appointed the county's first president judge, register of wills, and recorder of deeds. Although Norristown was ultimately chosen as the county seat, a courthouse was not built there until 1787, and thus Muhlenberg's house at 151 West Main Street in Trappe served as a de facto seat of county government for several years. (Courtesy of the Historical Society of Montgomery County.)

ON THE COVER: On August 19, 1899, Francis and Margaret Clamer of Collegeville hosted the local community for a Harvest Home festival at their Glen Farm estate. Guests were greeted by an enormous arch made of fruits and vegetables. (Courtesy of the Historical Society of Trappe, Collegeville, Perkiomen Valley.)

IMAGES
of America

TRAPPE AND COLLEGEVILLE

Lisa Minardi

ARCADIA
PUBLISHING

Copyright © 2017 by Lisa Minardi
ISBN 978-1-4671-2448-5

Published by Arcadia Publishing
Charleston, South Carolina

Printed in the United States of America

Library of Congress Control Number: 2016950072

For all general information, please contact Arcadia Publishing:
Telephone 843-853-2070
Fax 843-853-0044
E-mail sales@arcadiapublishing.com
For customer service and orders:
Toll-Free 1-888-313-2665

Visit us on the Internet at www.arcadiapublishing.com

This book is dedicated to residents of Trappe and Collegeville—past, present, and future.

Contents

Acknowledgments		6
Introduction		7
1.	People	11
2.	Main Street	27
3.	Churches	43
4.	Transportation	53
5.	Business and Industry	67
6.	Schools	91
7.	Ursinus College	103
8.	Community Life	117
Bibliography		126
About the Organization		127

Acknowledgments

In 2011, Trappe and Collegeville celebrated the 300th anniversary of the birth of Henry Melchior Muhlenberg, patriarch of the Lutheran Church in America and longtime Trappe resident. Shortly thereafter, local history buffs realized that, in 2017, Trappe itself would turn 300 years old. A community-wide effort soon got under way to plan for this momentous occasion, and the Trappe 300 Steering Committee was born. From the very beginning, one of our major goals was to produce a book about the history of Trappe and its adjacent borough, Collegeville, because of their long and intertwined historical connection. Many people aided in this effort. Anne Grasberger made the rich photographic and archival collections of the Historical Society of Trappe, Collegeville, Perkiomen Valley accessible and scanned hundreds of images for this book. Jen Cianci provided assistance during the early stages, and Antonio Aloia and Manni McNeil helped with the research and scanning. Kate Minardi and Barbara Wentz shared their extensive knowledge gleaned from years of research into local land records, maps, and early newspaper advertisements. Carolyn Weigel provided access to the Ursinus College Archives, which yielded a treasure trove of images from which Andy Prock made dozens of scans.

Many current and former residents, as well as Ursinus alumni, shared memories and images, including Richard Allebach, Robert Brant, Bruce Clark, Walt and Bridgie Daller, Dave Duryea, Richard Holcombe, Mary Lou Weaver Houser, Rev. Martha Kriebel, Chip and Katharine Levengood, Jim Moyer, Pat O'Hara, Mayor Connie and Bob Peck, Kitty McHarg Spickard, Terry Stagliano, Mary Stevens, Stephen Weaver, Matthew Wismer, and Gene Zvarick. Augustus Lutheran Church kindly granted permission to use many historical images of the church's buildings, and Barry Rauhauser of the Historical Society of Montgomery County provided an image of the earliest-known county map. Denae Zvarick helped verify street addresses and took photographs on demand when vintage versions could not be found. Rick Bates and Kurt Bell offered insights on the Perkiomen Branch of the Philadelphia & Reading Railroad and the Collegeville train station, while Mike Szigalyi shared his research on the trolley line operated by the Schuylkill Valley Traction Company. Jerry Chiccarine commented on drafts of the manuscript and shared dozens of postcards and other items from his collection. Donald R. Brown, an Ursinus graduate and founder of the Institute of American Deltiology, also kindly shared postcards from his collection. Together, these and many other individuals contributed far more than what could be presented in a single book.

INTRODUCTION

The adjacent boroughs of Trappe and Collegeville share a rich and fascinating history. Located in the heart of the Perkiomen Valley, this area was first settled by the Lenape people. The name "Perkiomen" derives from a Lenape word meaning "the place where cranberries grow," and as late as 1910, there were reports of cranberry bogs along the Perkiomen Creek. In 1684, William Penn purchased "all the land lying on the Pahkehoma," or Perkiomen, from Lenape chief Maughaughsin for "two Matchcoats, four pairs of Stockings and four bottles of Sider." The creek was identified as the Perquaminck on Thomas Holme's 1687 map of Pennsylvania. At nearly 40 miles long, the Perkiomen Creek is the longest in Montgomery County and drains into the Schuylkill River near the town of Audubon. Supported by its namesake creek, the Perkiomen Valley was a fertile region that beckoned newly arrived European immigrants to settle there by the early 1700s. The area's location—about halfway between Philadelphia and Reading, along a major thoroughfare once known as the Manatawny Great Road—also made what would eventually become Trappe and Collegeville a frequent stopping place for travelers and spurred the rise of numerous inns and taverns.

One of the earliest settlers in the region was Edward Lane. In 1698, Lane acquired a tract of 2,500 acres that straddled the Perkiomen Creek and included the present-day towns of Trappe, Collegeville, and Evansburg. By 1701, Lane had established a tavern on the west bank, near a shallow stretch of the creek that soon became known as Philip's Ford. He bequeathed the tavern, along with all of his land west of the Perkiomen, to his son Samuel in 1708. For more than three centuries, this tavern served weary travelers in need of food and lodging. After the completion of a major stone-arch bridge over the creek in 1799, it became known as the Perkiomen Bridge Hotel.

About a mile west of Lane's tavern, a German immigrant named Johann Jacob Schrack Sr. established a tavern in 1717. It was advertised in 1760 as having "the sign of the Three Crowns, but commonly known by the name of the Trap." Schrack was instrumental in the 1742 arrival of Lutheran minister Henry Muhlenberg in Pennsylvania, having written several letters to Germany requesting a pastor, although Schrack died just months before Muhlenberg arrived. According to Muhlenberg, the nickname of the tavern and its immediate locale came about as follows:

> Joh. Jacob Schrack and his wife, Eva Rosina, who came to this country in 1717 . . . built themselves a makeshift hut and dug a cave beside it, in which they did their cooking, and then established a small shop and inn for travelers. Once, when an English inhabitant stayed too long in the cave, came home late, and had a row with his wife, he made excuses and said that he had been in the Trap. From that time on the section was called Trapp, and is known all over America.

Muhlenberg went on to note that the Schracks "would tolerate no disorderliness or vice, so that their inn came to have the best of names among respectable inhabitants . . . and did not deserve the name of Trapp." In 1777, he wrote, "In my time they were the most prominent family in Providence." The Schracks were highly important to the area's early development. Jacob and Eva Rosina had at least nine children: John, who took over the tavern; Jacob Jr., a blacksmith; Christian and Philip, both tanners; Nicholas; Eva Barbara; Elisabeth; Catharine; and Anna Maria Sabina. Jacob Schrack Sr. owned nearly 470 acres of land, which covered portions of what is now Trappe and Collegeville. It was distributed among his sons after his death in 1742. A quarry located on the tract where Philip Schrack lived, along what is now Clayhor Avenue, provided the stone for many of the oldest houses along Main Street, including 201 West Main Street (built between 1750 and 1755 for Jacob Schrack Jr. and owned by Henry Muhlenberg from 1776 to 1787) and 151 West Main Street (built in 1763 for John Schrack and owned by Frederick Muhlenberg from 1781 to 1791).

The tavern passed from Jacob Sr. to his eldest son, John Schrack, in 1742, then to Johannes Ried after John's death in 1772. Matthew Brooke Sr. of Limerick Township bought the tavern at a sheriff's sale in 1784, and it remained in the Brooke family until 1806. In 1788, it was known as the Sign of Dr. Franklin. The last innkeeper was Gabriel Kline, who offered the tavern for sale in 1810 and described it as a "large and commodious stone dwelling-house, being the oldest stand as a tavern in the place." Unable to find a buyer, Kline later sold the property to his son-in-law John Longstreth in 1842. Henry A. Hunsicker, who grew up in the house known as Fircroft at 930 East Main Street in Collegeville, recalled in 1906 that he well remembered the "old stone house which was kept many long years ago by John Jacob Schrack, which gave a name to 'The Trap.' The old building was torn down by John Longstreth." Longstreth built a new house on the property, which passed to his son Isaac Longstreth, then to his daughter Katharine Longstreth Stearly, and finally to her son H. Douglas Stearly. That house was razed in the late 1980s for the construction of the Trappe Shopping Center.

The village that began to develop around Schrack's tavern was also soon referred to as the Trap or Trapp, although it was officially named Providence, which was also the name of the township in which it was located (subdivided into Upper and Lower Providence Townships in 1805). Until 1784, when Montgomery County was formed, this area was part of Philadelphia County. In 1762, Samuel Seely purchased 150 acres of land on the west side of what is now Main Street in the upper end of Trappe. He divided it into 57 lots of 66 by 165 feet each and named the town Landau, but it never took off, and the area remained known as the Trap or Trapp. Long before Henry Muhlenberg's journals with his account of the tavern were translated and published in the 1940s, an alternate theory was put forth by Gov. Francis Shunk on the origin of the name. Shunk argued that "Trappe" was derived from the German word *Treppe*, for steps or staircase. According to Shunk, the Schrack tavern had a steep staircase that an early patron tripped on, causing him to exclaim, "*Verdamt die Treppe!*" or "Damn the steps!" In February 1835, local residents gathered to determine the proper spelling of the town's name. Shunk and Matthias Haldeman advocated strongly for Treppe or Trappe, while Wright A. Bringhurst and Jacob Fry argued for Trap or Trapp. The meeting concluded that Trapp was the proper spelling, but by the mid-1800s, it had been changed to Trappe.

Collegeville also has a long and complex history of changing names. After the completion of the magnificent stone-arch bridge across the Perkiomen Creek in 1799, its environs became known as Perkiomen Bridge. When Freeland Seminary was founded in 1848, about midway between Trappe and Perkiomen Bridge, the surrounding area was soon referred to as Freeland. For a brief period, newcomer Samuel Townsend of Philadelphia led an effort to rename part of the area with his surname, even bribing a mapmaker to use Townsend rather than Freeland on the *Map of Bucks and Montgomery Counties and the Consolidated City of Philadelphia* published in 1857. A lawsuit ensued when Henry A. Hunsicker, who had paid for the name "Freeland" to be used on the map and to include an engraving of the Freeland Seminary buildings, refused to pay for his $45 order. The mapmaker sued Townsend for unpaid bills and damages and won. That, along with Townsend's death in 1860, soon put an end to the name "Townsend." After the Pennsylvania Female College was chartered in 1853, yet another name came into use—Collegeville—due to the presence of multiple colleges. The controversy was finally settled by the Philadelphia & Reading Railroad, which constructed a railroad station there in 1868 and named it Collegeville. It was not until 1869 that Ursinus College was founded, and thus the name of the town predates Ursinus. Freeland continued in use for some years, however, as the 1877 atlas of Montgomery County depicts Trappe, Freeland, and Collegeville as separate towns.

Education has long been highly important to Trappe and Collegeville. In 1743, Henry Muhlenberg helped found the first school in the immediate area at Augustus Lutheran Church. In 1838, Henry Prizer opened the Trappe Boarding School at what is now 360 West Main Street. It was later renamed the Washington Hall Collegiate Institute and moved to a four-story brick structure built in 1853 at what is now 550 West Main Street, where it was run by Abel Rambo for many years. Collegeville also had its share of schools. In 1832, Andrew Todd donated the land on which a stone schoolhouse was built near his house at what is now 801 East Main Street. It became the Freeland Public School in 1844. In 1848, Rev. Abraham Hunsicker established Freeland Seminary, where more than 2,000 young men studied during the 21 years the school was in operation. Three years later, Dr. J. Warrene Sunderland and his wife, Luanna, founded the Montgomery Female Institute, or Seminary, which was chartered as the Pennsylvania Female College in 1853. More than 1,000 young women were educated at the college before it closed in 1880. These institutions were subsumed by Ursinus College, which was founded in 1869 and became coeducational in 1881. Nearly 150 years later, Ursinus is a top-rated liberal arts college with a total enrollment of nearly 1,700 students and more than 60 majors to choose from.

Trappe and Collegeville were officially incorporated as independent boroughs in 1896, but remain connected in numerous ways. In 1936, the two municipalities joined together to form the Collegeville-Trappe Water Authority; today, there is both the Collegeville/Trappe Joint Public Works and the Collegeville/Trappe Municipal Authority. In 1938, the Collegeville-Trappe School District was established, which later merged with Skippack in 1955 to form the Perkiomen Joint School System, now the Perkiomen Valley School District. Perhaps most remarkable of all is the two-mile-long Main Street that runs seamlessly through both boroughs. Other than some small signs at the borough line and a shift in the house numbers from West Main Street to East Main Street as one moves from Trappe to Collegeville, there is no major demarcation between the two boroughs. How appropriate, then, that the following pages offer a pictorial overview of their intertwined history.

Despite the many changes wrought by modernization and the loss of some important historic structures, Trappe and Collegeville retain much of their historic character and small-town charm. Local residents rallied in 1973 to save the Dewees Tavern from being razed, again in 1989 to safeguard the Henry Muhlenberg house, and yet again in the early 2000s to rescue the Frederick Muhlenberg House, now known as The Speaker's House. The old Fountain Inn, today known as the Trappe Tavern, continues to welcome both travelers and locals in search of a hearty meal. The sturdy Perkiomen Bridge, nearly 220 years old, is used daily by thousands of vehicles. Heritage tourism is thriving as local residents and out-of-town visitors alike regularly visit the four historic buildings in Trappe that are open to the public for tours: Augustus Lutheran Church, Dewees Tavern, the Henry Muhlenberg House, and The Speaker's House, as well as the Philip and Muriel Berman Museum of Art at Ursinus College. Agriculture also remains an important part of the local heritage, exemplified by the longevity of Keystone Grange No. 2, founded in 1873 and the second-oldest grange organization in the state, and Northern Star Farm, a 230-acre family-owned and -operated farm located at 97 East Third Avenue. History is happening in Trappe and Collegeville!

One

PEOPLE

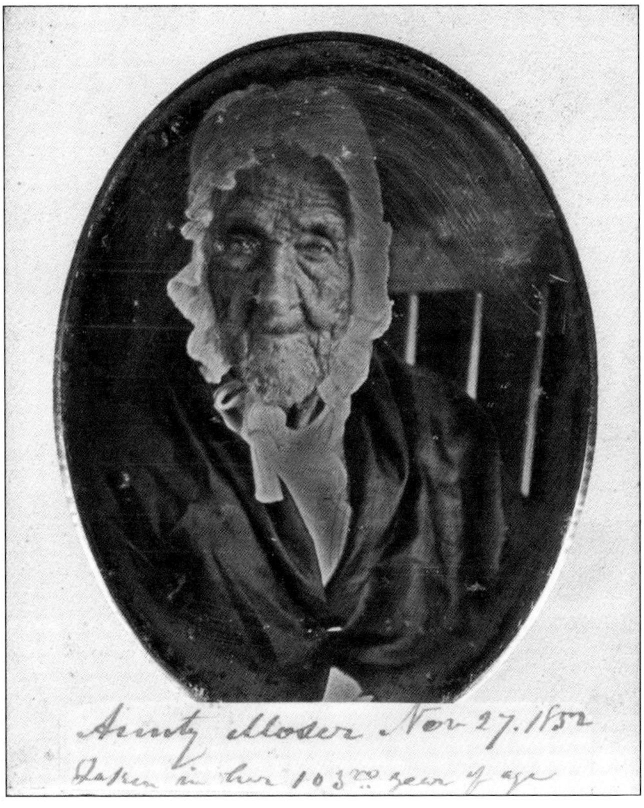

MARGARET "AUNTY" MOSER, 1852. Margaret Laver was born in 1750, and at age 102, she was one of the earliest-born Americans ever photographed. She married George Moser, a German immigrant, teamster, and soldier in the American Revolution. According to family tradition, George was called to war before he could finish shingling their new barn, so Margaret climbed to the roof and completed the work. She died in 1854 at age 104 and was buried in the Augustus Lutheran Church graveyard. (Author's collection.)

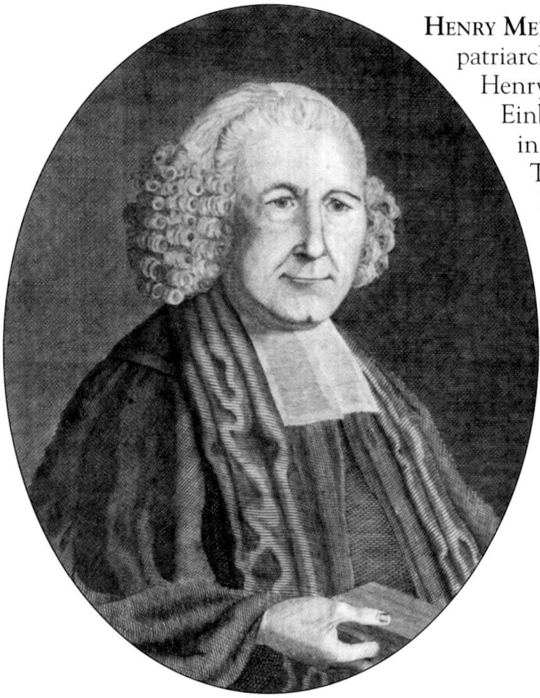

Henry Melchior Muhlenberg. Known as the patriarch of the Lutheran Church in America, Henry Melchior Muhlenberg was born in Einbeck, Germany, in 1711. He immigrated in 1742 to Pennsylvania, where he settled in Trappe and served as pastor of Augustus Lutheran Church. He founded the Pennsylvania Ministerium in 1748 and served as its president until his death in 1787. Muhlenberg lived in Trappe from 1745 to 1760 and 1776 to 1787. (Author's collection.)

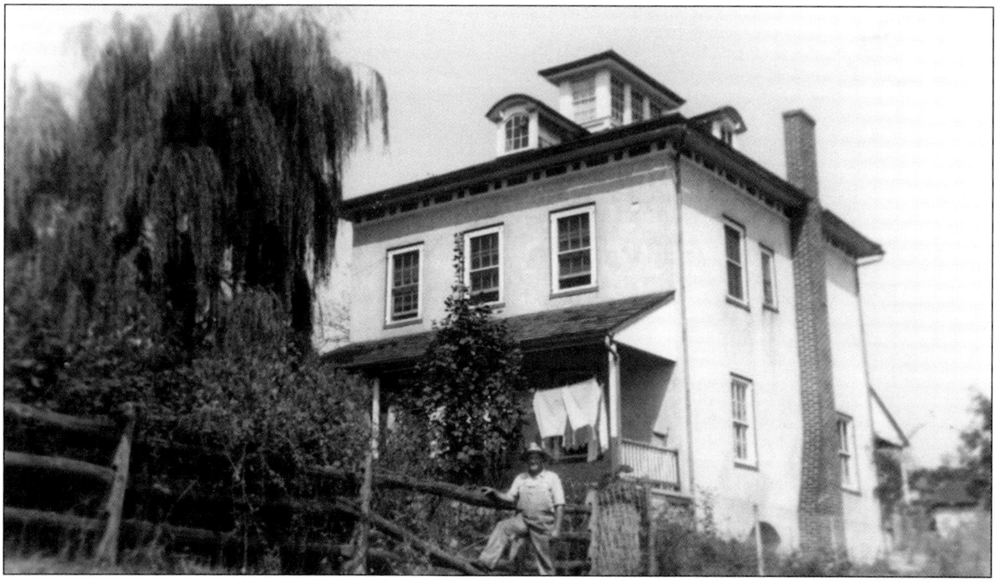

Muhlenberg Parsonage, 1942. Built for Henry Muhlenberg in 1745 soon after his marriage to Anna Maria "Mary" Weiser, this stone house was the birthplace for eight of the Muhlenbergs' eleven children. It also served as the unofficial parsonage for Augustus Lutheran Church until the Muhlenbergs sold it in 1763 and moved to Philadelphia. Charles Heebner, a marble merchant, bought the house in 1850 and renovated it, adding the hipped roof with glass observatory. The house was stuccoed sometime in the late 1800s. A small area near the upper right window was left uncovered, exposing the initials "iL" that are carved into the stone—possibly those of the stonemason. The parsonage still stands at 160 East Seventh Avenue in Trappe. (Photograph by Andrew Steinmetz; courtesy of the Historical Society of Trappe, Collegeville, Perkiomen Valley.)

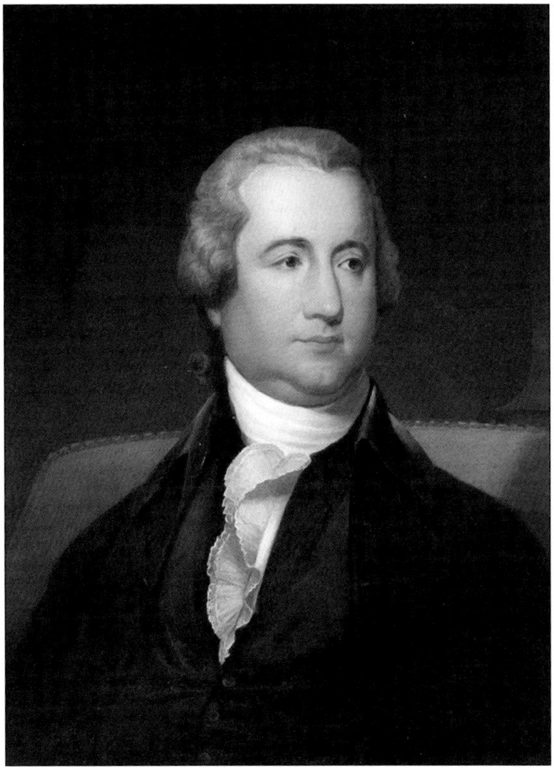

Frederick Augustus Conrad Muhlenberg. The second son of Henry and Mary Muhlenberg, Frederick Muhlenberg was born in Trappe on January 1, 1750. Sent to Germany for his education in 1763, Frederick returned to America in 1770 and was ordained as a Lutheran minister. In 1779, he became a member of the Continental Congress, and from 1780 to 1783, he was speaker of the Pennsylvania General Assembly. When Montgomery County was established in 1784, Frederick was appointed as the first recorder of deeds and register of wills, in addition to serving as a justice of the peace. In 1787, he presided at Pennsylvania's constitutional convention. Elected as a representative to the first Federal Congress in 1789, Frederick Muhlenberg was the first speaker of the US House of Representatives. His house still stands at 151 West Main Street in Trappe and is currently undergoing restoration. (Courtesy of The Speaker's House.)

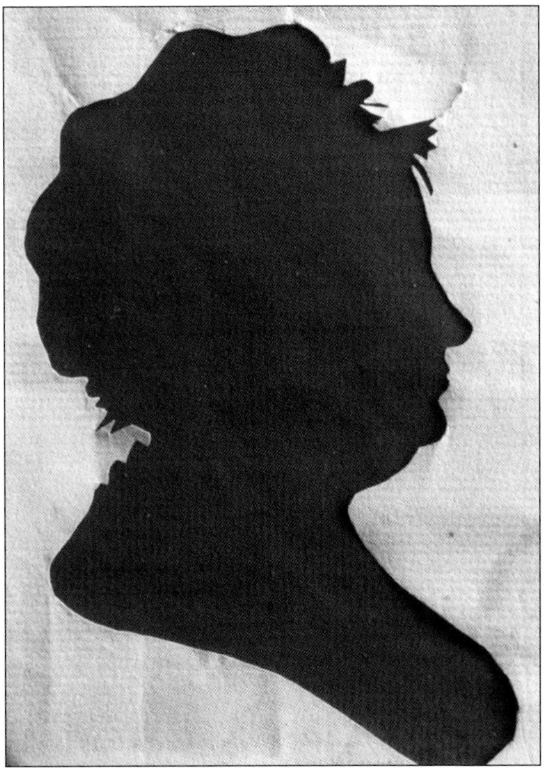

Maria Catharine Muhlenberg Swaine. The third daughter of Henry and Mary Muhlenberg, Maria Catharine "Mary" Muhlenberg (1755–1812) married Irish immigrant Francis Swaine in 1775. Four years later, while living with her parents in Trappe, Mary gave birth to their first child, George Washington Swaine. The Swaines had three more children, but all died during childhood. Mary worked as a nurse and midwife, helping her mother to recuperate after she was severely scalded in a kitchen accident in 1781. After Frederick was elected speaker of the US house, he sold his Trappe property to the Swaines and moved to Philadelphia in 1791. The Swaines lived there until 1800, when Francis was made prothonotary of the court of common pleas and the couple moved to Norristown, the county seat. Twelve years later, he was elected the first burgess (mayor) of that town, and in 1815, he became the first president of the Bank of Montgomery County. (Author's collection.)

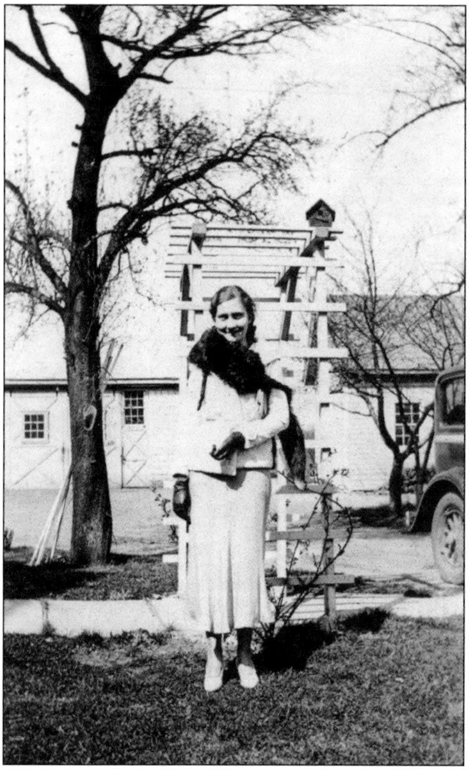

Kathryn McHarg. The Muhlenbergs' second home in Trappe, at 201 West Main Street, was purchased by the McHarg family in 1895. There, Kathryn "Kitty" McHarg was born and raised. She was the daughter of John S. and Mary Viola (Shainline) McHarg and a member of St. Luke's Reformed Church. In 1942, she married Ralph G. Spickard. (Courtesy of the Historical Society of Trappe, Collegeville, Perkiomen Valley.)

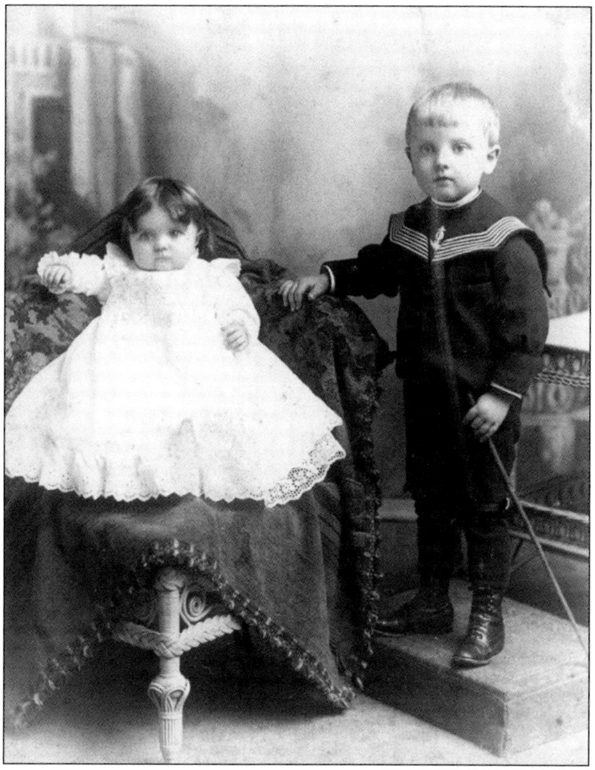

Betty and Paul Fry, c. 1901. Siblings Betty and Paul Fry had their photograph taken at Saylor's New York Gallery on North Sixth Street in Reading, Pennsylvania, around 1901. Paul was born in December 1897 and Betty in 1900 to Jacob E. and Idella G. Fry, who are listed in the 1900 census as residing in Perkiomen Township in the household of Idella's parents, Jacob and Lizzie Fuss. (Courtesy of the Historical Society of Trappe, Collegeville, Perkiomen Valley.)

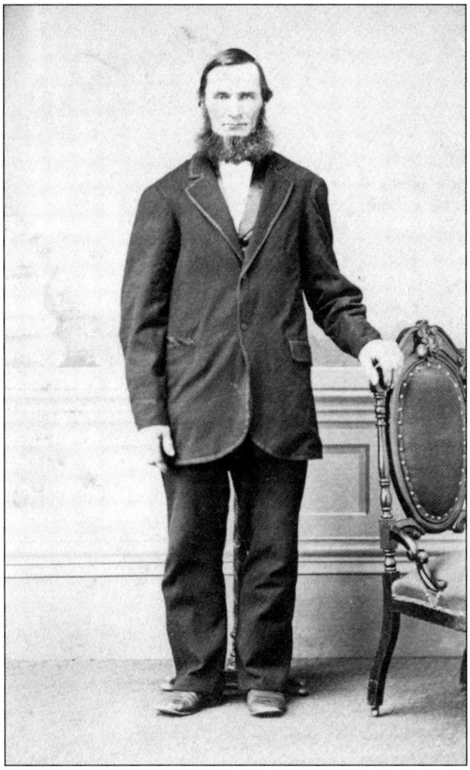

GOV. FRANCIS SHUNK. Francis Rawn Shunk, the 10th governor of Pennsylvania, was born in Trappe in 1788. A Jacksonian Democrat, he was elected to the governorship in 1845. Shunk was reelected in 1847 but resigned on July 9, 1848, and died 11 days later of tuberculosis. He was buried at Augustus Lutheran Church, where his grave is marked by a large obelisk dedicated by the citizens of Pennsylvania on July 4, 1851. Shunk took a keen interest in the history of his hometown and theorized that the name of Trappe was derived from the German word *Treppe* for staircase. On one side of his tombstone, there is a carved image of a staircase. (Right, courtesy of Kate Minardi; below, courtesy of the Historical Society of Trappe, Collegeville, Perkiomen Valley.)

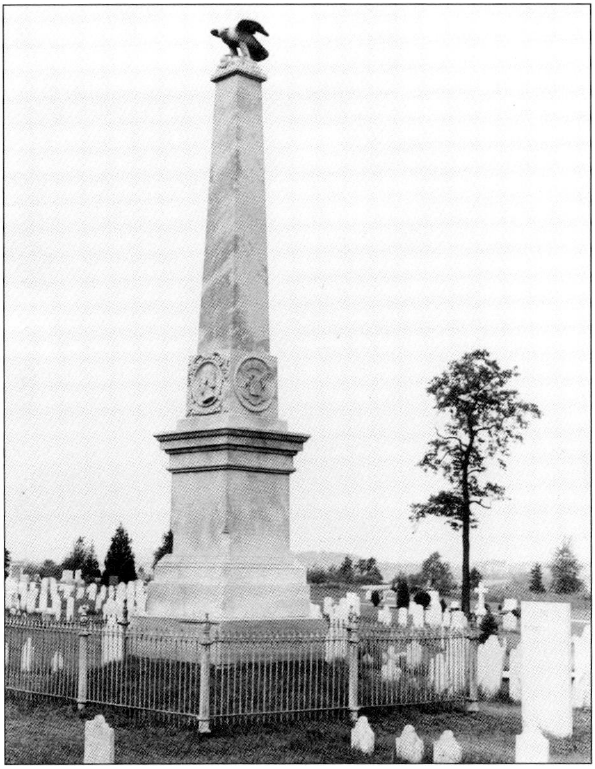

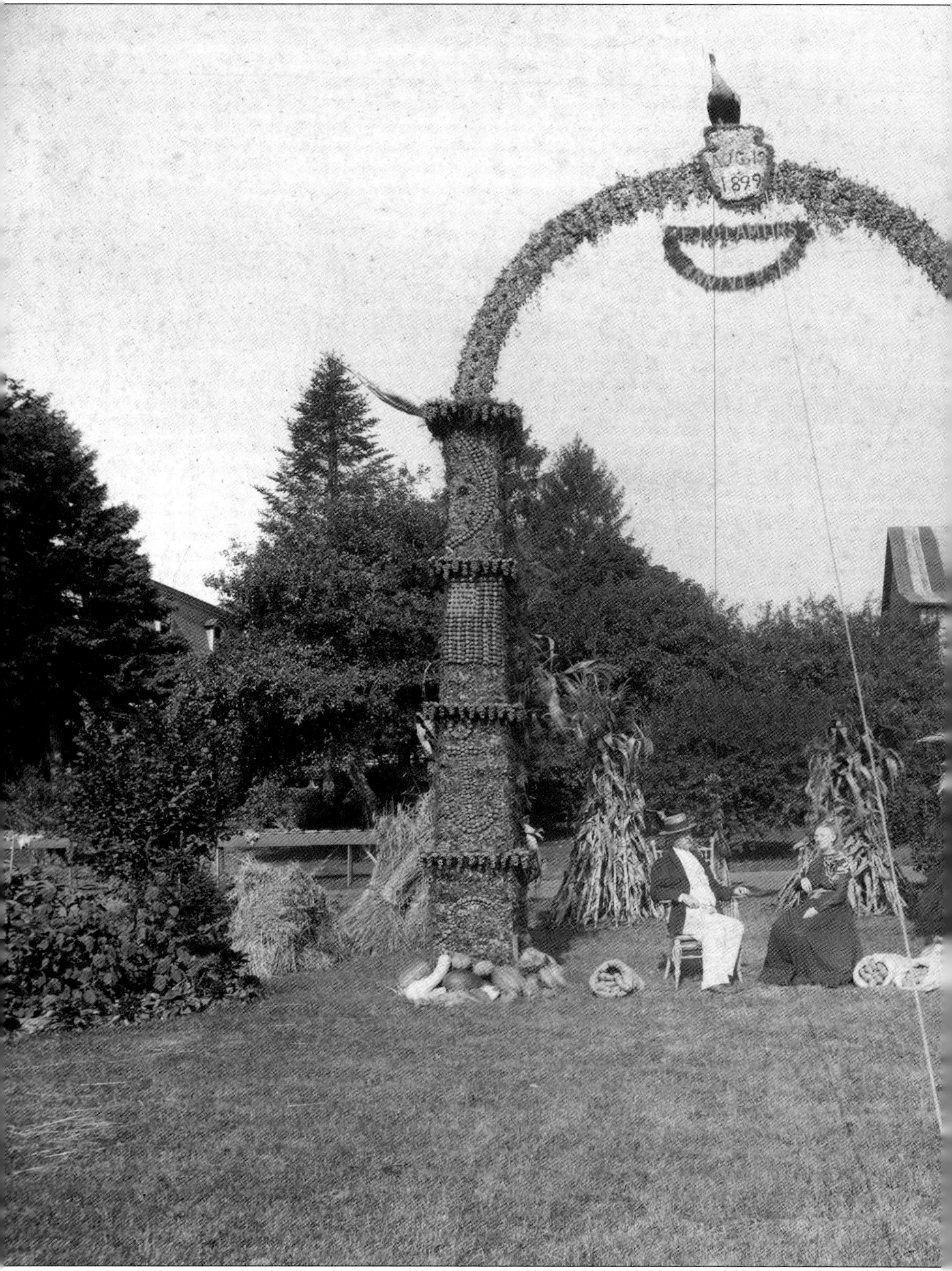
1899

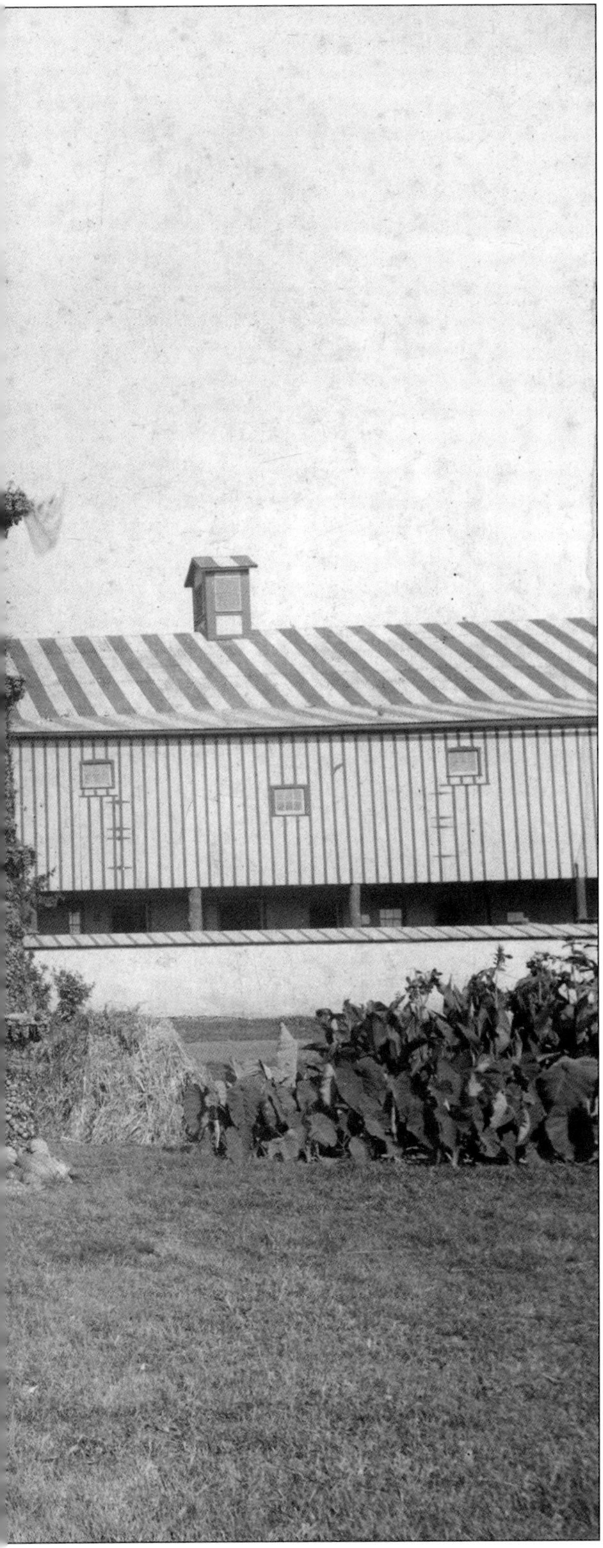

Glen Farm, 1899. Francis and Margaret Clamer of Collegeville hosted a community-wide Harvest Home festival at their Glen Farm property for many years. Guests were greeted by an enormous arch made of fruits and vegetables; a keystone-shape pendant at the top of the arch bears the date August 19, 1899. Born in 1841, Francis emigrated from Germany in 1852 and married Margaret Dietrich in 1864. He became a renowned chemist, metallurgist, inventor, and co-owner of the Ajax Metal Company, enabling him to retire at age 55. In 1888, he purchased Glen Farm from Prof. J. Shelly Weinberger of Ursinus College. After the Clamers died, the property was sold and later became the Oakwood Farm housing development. Glen Farm was located at the east end of Ninth Avenue, near the intersection with First Avenue, or Gravel Pike. (Courtesy of the Historical Society of Trappe, Collegeville, Perkiomen Valley.)

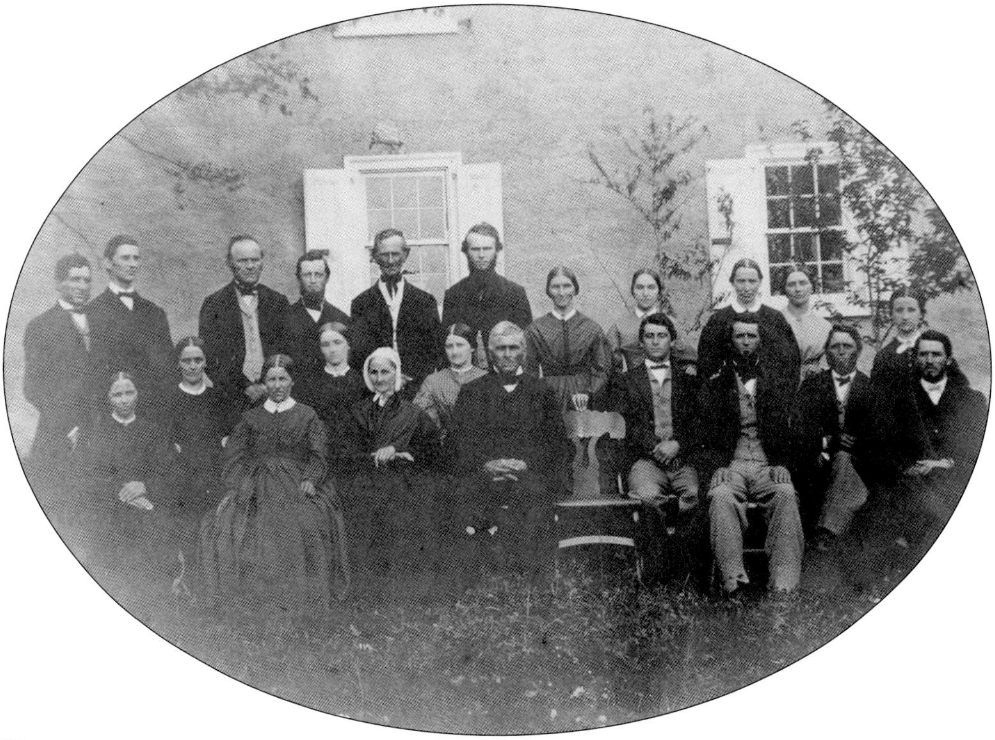

Hunsicker Family, c. 1870. Rev. Abraham Hunsicker (1793–1872) married Elizabeth Alderfer (1798–1898) in 1816. They lived in a stone house known as Fircroft, still standing at what is now 930 East Main Street in Collegeville. In 1848, Hunsicker founded the Freeland Seminary. A former Mennonite bishop, Hunsicker broke with the church and founded the nondenominational Christian Meetinghouse at Freeland in 1854. The congregation later became known as Trinity Reformed Church. (Courtesy of the Ursinus College Archives.)

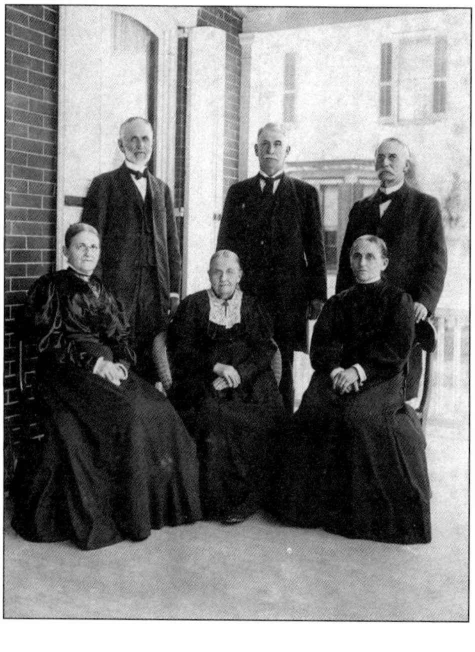

Hunsicker Family, 1909. On April 22, 1909, the six surviving children of Rev. Abraham and Elizabeth (Alderfer) Hunsicker met in Collegeville and posed for this photograph. From left to right are (seated) Mary A. Preston, Esther Fetterolf, and Catherine Hendricks; (standing) Henry A. Hunsicker, Elias A. Hunsicker, and Horace M. Hunsicker. (Courtesy of the Historical Society of Trappe, Collegeville, Perkiomen Valley.)

Rev. Joseph Hendricks. A native of Upper Providence Township, Joseph Hendricks (1834–1905) enrolled in Freeland Seminary in 1851 under the direction of Rev. Henry A. Hunsicker (son of Rev. Abraham Hunsicker, founder of the seminary). He served as pastor of what is now Trinity Reformed Church in Collegeville from 1862 until his death in 1905. Hendricks married Catharine Hunsicker, a daughter of Rev. Abraham Hunsicker, in 1858. (Courtesy of the Historical Society of Trappe, Collegeville, Perkiomen Valley.)

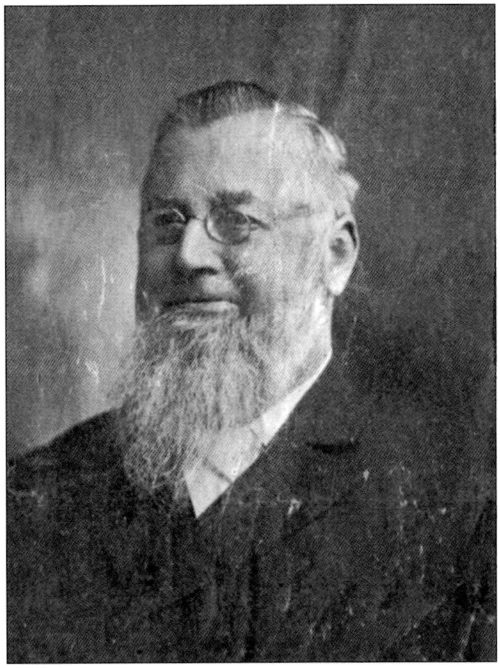

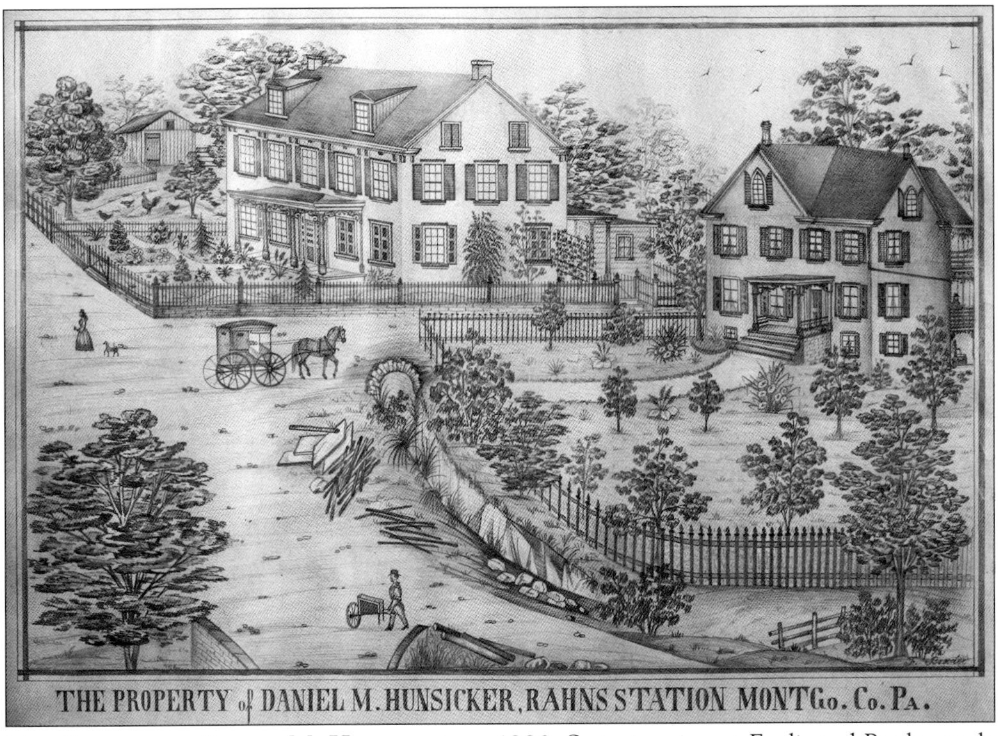

The Property of Daniel M. Hunsicker, c. 1880. Swiss immigrant Ferdinand Brader made this intricate pencil drawing of the property of Daniel M. Hunsicker (1847–1911) in the village of Rahns, about a mile and a half northeast of Trappe. Daniel was a great-nephew of Rev. Abraham Hunsicker, and is buried at Trinity Reformed Church in Collegeville. (Courtesy of a private collection, Boston.)

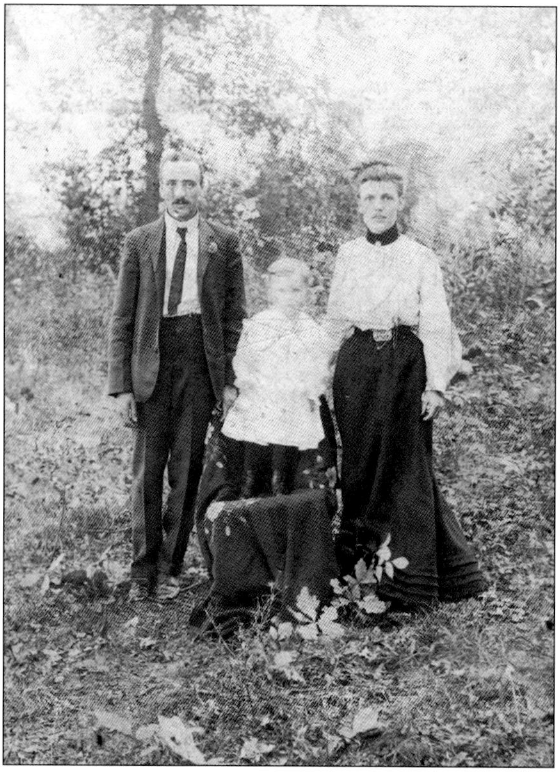

Hiram and Katie Poley, c. 1915. This photograph shows Hiram Willard Poley (1880–1962) and Katie Nora (Wisler) Poley (1879–1942) posing with one of their children (probably Leonard, born in 1912). The Poleys were members of the Grace Evangelical Association Congregational Church of Trappe, founded in 1841. Hiram's ancestor Hans Georg Bohlig immigrated to Pennsylvania in 1754 and settled in Trappe. (Courtesy of the Historical Society of Trappe, Collegeville, Perkiomen Valley.)

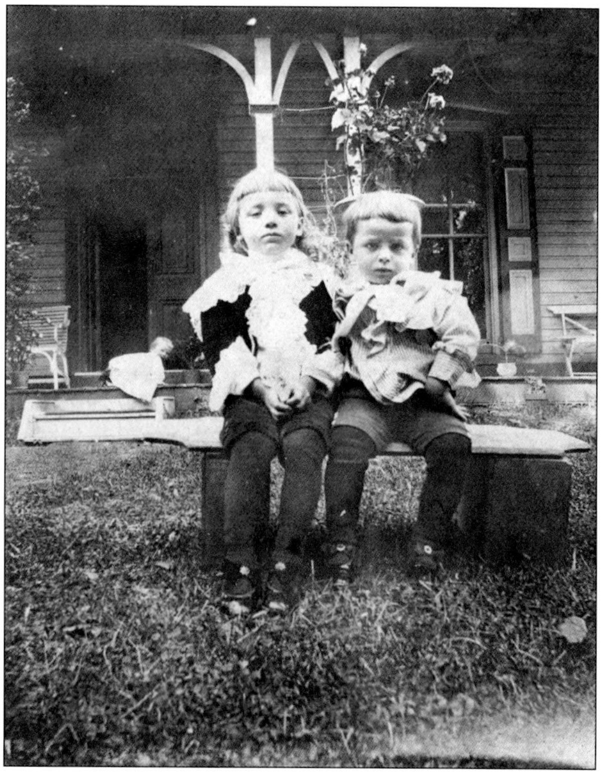

Leidy and Frank Poley, c. 1902. Siblings Leidy M. Poley (1898–1972) and Frank J. Poley (1899–1980) sat on a bench in front of their house for this photograph, taken around 1902. A baby, probably a younger sibling, crawls on the front porch in the background. Frank fought in World War I as part of the 103rd Signal Battalion, then returned to the Trappe area; after his death, he was buried at St. Luke's Reformed Church, along with his sister Leidy and their parents, William H. and Andora L. Poley. (Courtesy of the Historical Society of Trappe, Collegeville, Perkiomen Valley.)

Frank and Jennie (Poley) Shalkop. Anna Jane "Jennie" Poley was born to Hiram Corson and Sarah Ann (Buckwalter) Poley of Trappe in 1875. She married Frank Webster Shalkop in 1894 at age 19. Anna died in 1944 at age 69 and was buried at Augustus Lutheran Church. Frank was an undertaker and also served as Montgomery County treasurer from 1924 to 1928 and register of wills from 1932 to 1936. He sold the undertaking business to Charles J. Franks Sr. in 1929. Franks moved it to a newly built funeral home at 21 West Main Street, the first of its kind in Trappe or Collegeville, in 1934. After Charles Franks died in 1958, his widow, Mildred, sold the business in 1960 to Norman D. Holcombe, whose son Richard A. Holcombe continues to operate it. (Right, courtesy of the Historical Society of Trappe, Collegeville, Perkiomen Valley; below, courtesy of Jerry A. Chiccarine.)

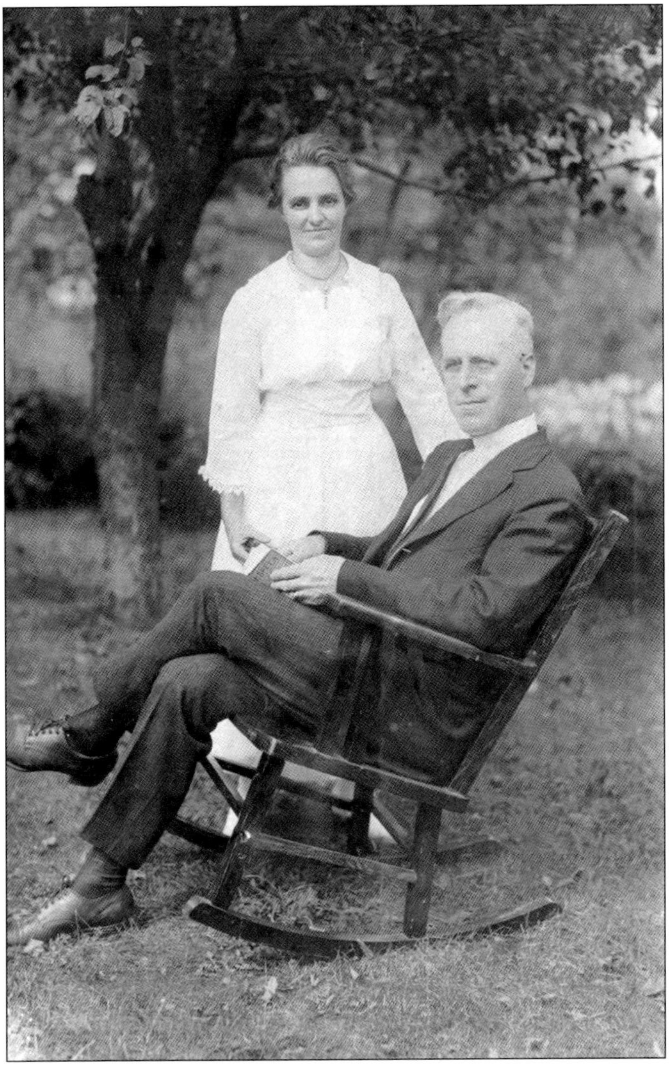

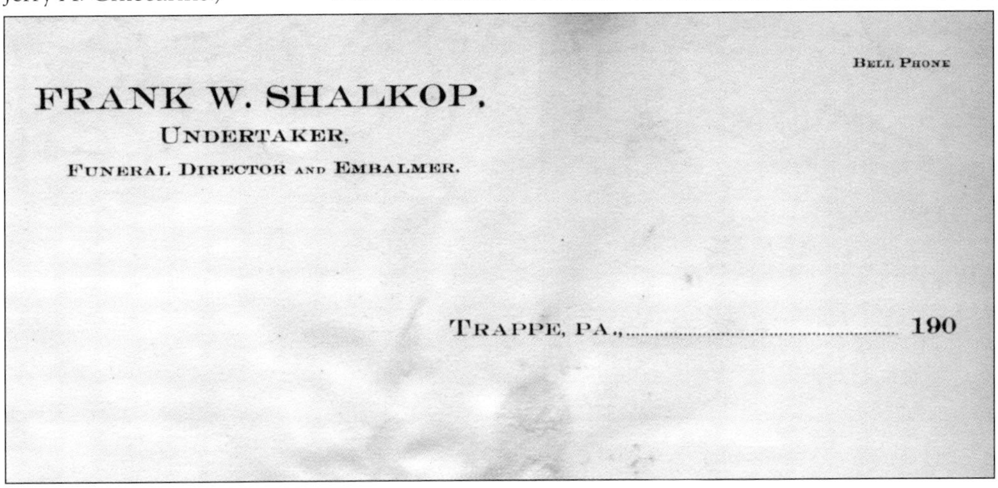

Bell Phone

FRANK W. SHALKOP.

UNDERTAKER,

FUNERAL DIRECTOR AND EMBALMER.

TRAPPE, PA., ... 190

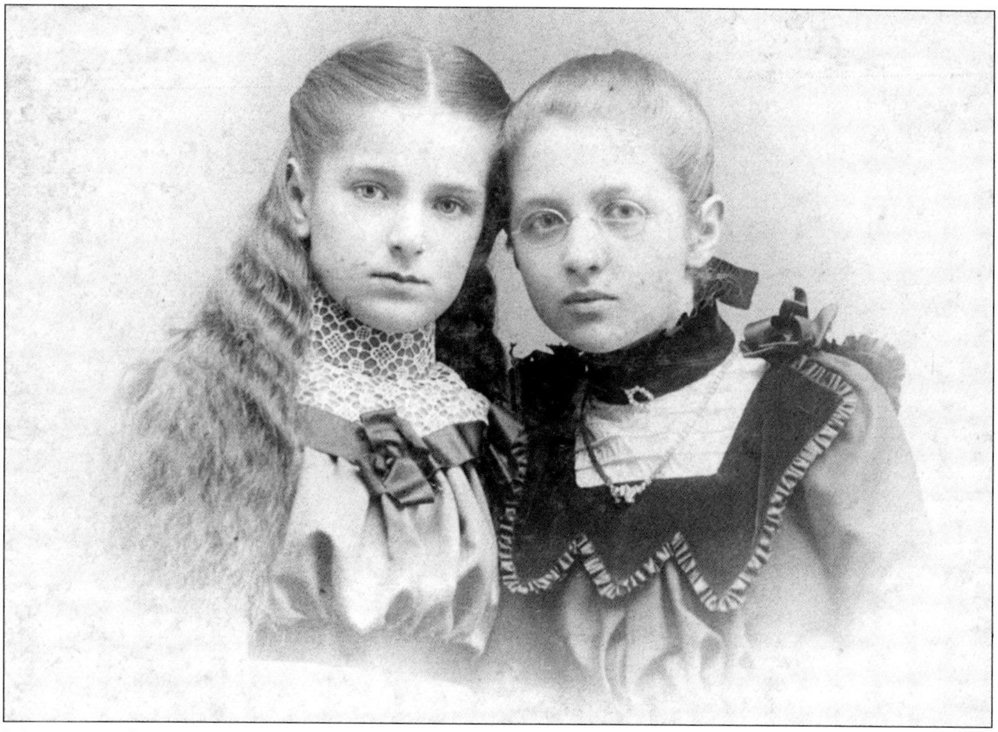

Mary and Anna Weikel. Sisters Mary (left) and Anna Weikel were frequently photographed together, both in formal studio portraits and candid shots such as the one below of the two girls in a horse-drawn carriage. Their parents were Erwin and Mary (Walker) Weikel, who owned a farm in Trappe. (Both, courtesy of Matthew G. Wismer.)

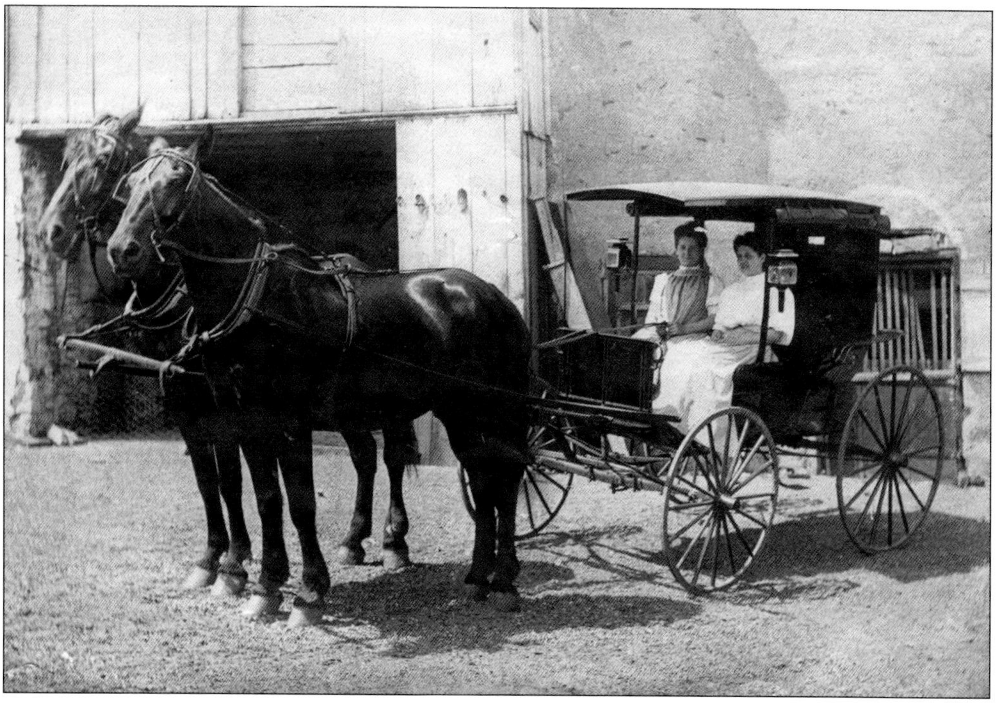

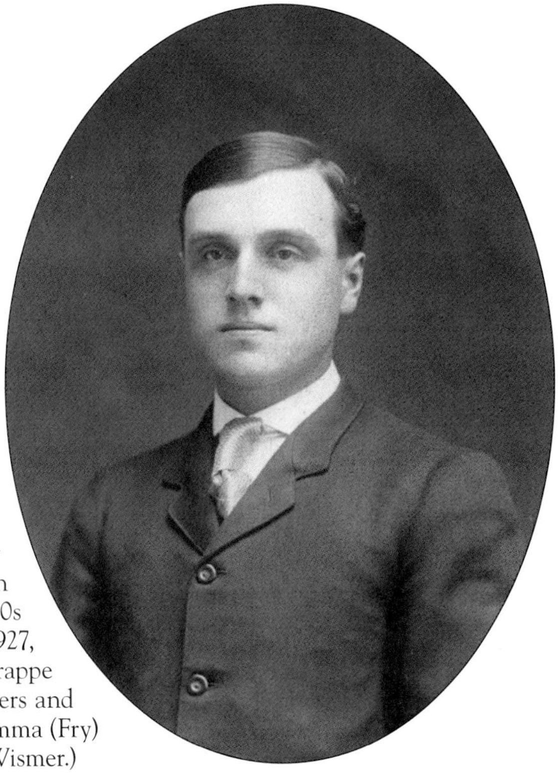

CHARLES AND ANNA (WEIKEL) WISMER SR. Anna Weikel (1890–1975) married Charles E. Wismer Sr. (1887–1968); they were the first full-time residents of what is now the Northern Star Farm at 97 East Third Avenue in Trappe. Descended from a 1680s German immigrant, Charles grew up on a farm in nearby Graterford, which was seized by eminent domain in the 1920s for the construction of a state prison. In 1927, Charles and Anna purchased a farm in Trappe and moved there with their three daughters and his elderly parents, Christian and Mary Emma (Fry) Wismer. (Both, courtesy of Matthew G. Wismer.)

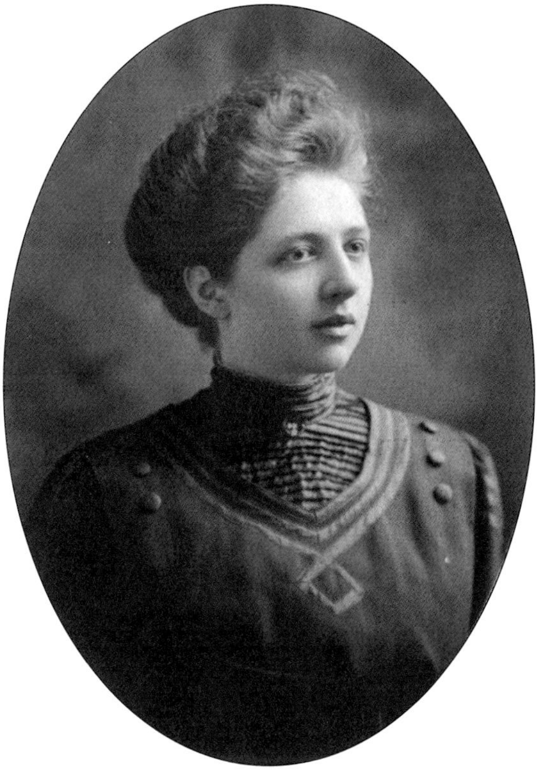

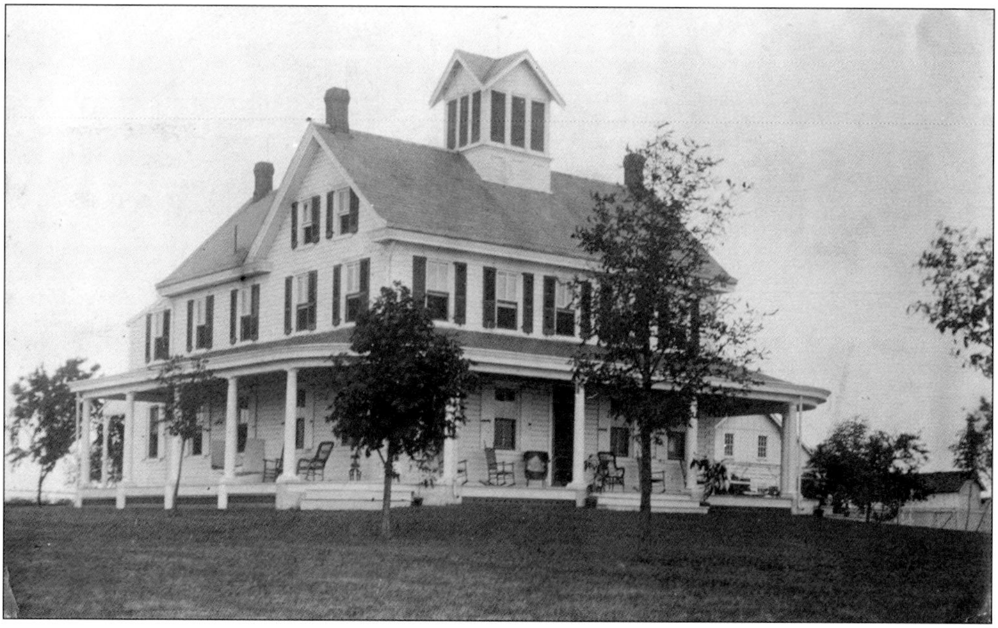

Royer-Wismer Farmhouse. Built in 1895 for Dr. Lewis Royer, this elegant dwelling was his summerhouse in the countryside. It was bought by Charles E. Wismer Sr. in 1927 and remains in the Wismer family to this day. The farmhouse was once topped by a massive cupola, which provided visual interest as well as superior ventilation through the house. Difficult to access and maintain, however, the cupola was prone to leaking and was removed during the 1930s. (Courtesy of Matthew G. Wismer.)

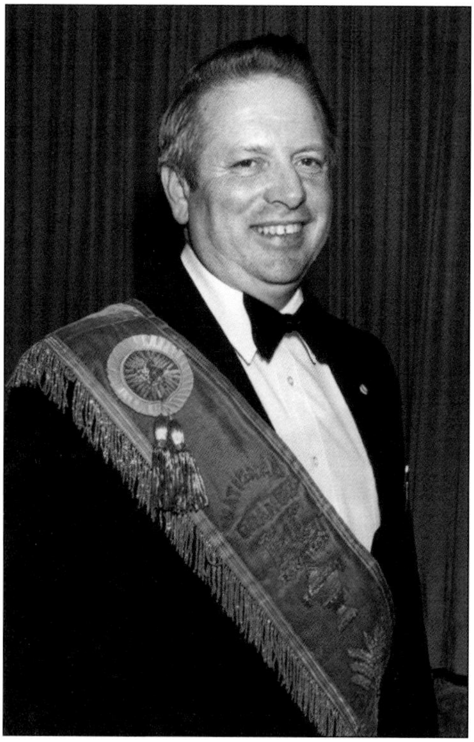

Charles E. Wismer Jr., 1983. A lifelong Trappe resident, Charles E. Wismer Jr. (1933–2006) purchased his parents' dairy farm (now known as Northern Star Farm) in 1964. Over time, he expanded its holdings to a total of 230 acres—located entirely within the borough of Trappe and protected by conservation easements to ensure its preservation. In the 1980s, his only son, Matthew Guy Wismer, became a partner in the dairy business, enabling Charles to pursue a variety of civic activities, including serving as Trappe's mayor and as chairman of the borough's 275th anniversary commission in 1992. A longtime leader of Keystone Grange No. 2, Charles also served as master of the Pennsylvania State Grange. (Courtesy of Matthew G. Wismer.)

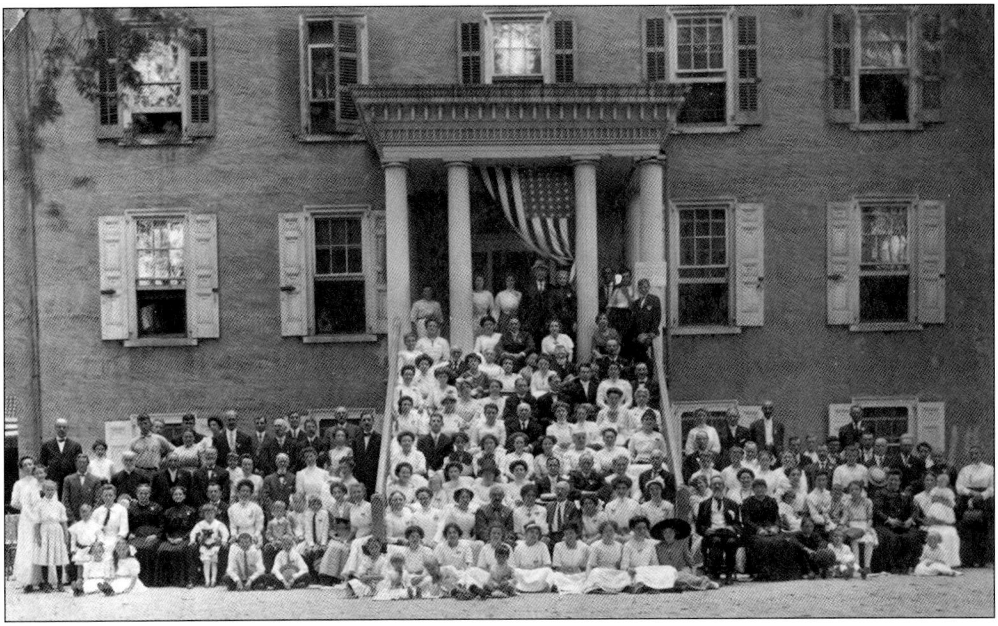

SPARE FAMILY REUNION. Descendants of the Spare family, including Leonard Spare and his son Nathan, who was an early Trappe resident, gathered in Collegeville for a family reunion in the early 1900s. This group photograph was taken on the front steps of the old Freeland Seminary building, by then part of Ursinus College, sometime before it was remodeled in 1913. (Courtesy of the Historical Society of Trappe, Collegeville, Perkiomen Valley.)

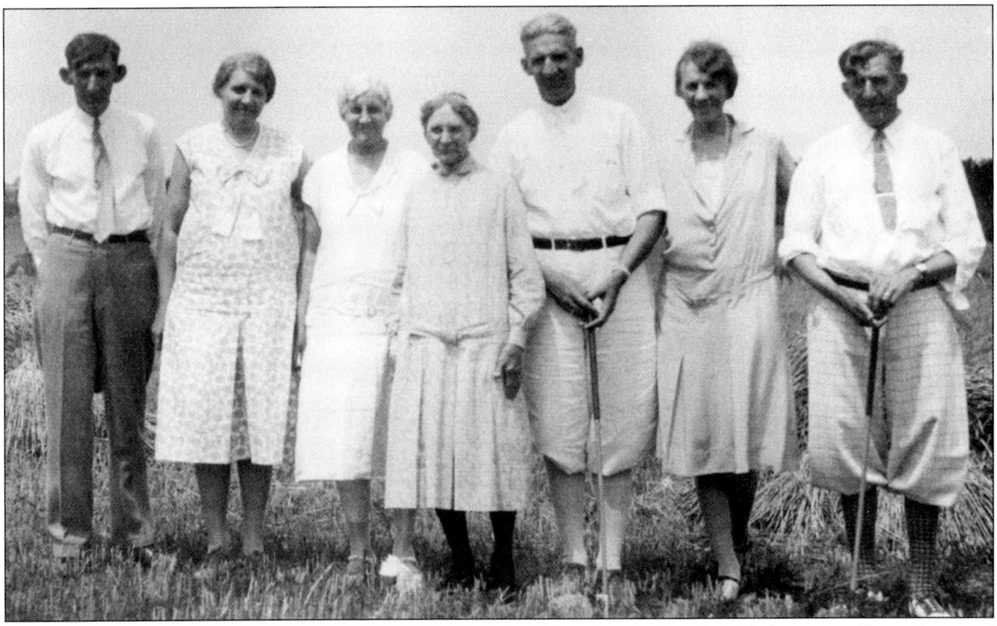

MOYER FAMILY, 1907. From left to right, siblings Robert, Nan, Bertha, Arlington, Dorothy, and Otto Moyer pose with their mother, Josephine Kohl Moyer (1849–1948), for this photograph taken at a family picnic on July 4, 1907. Brothers Arlington and Otto (the two men holding golf clubs) operated the Moyer Brothers general store in Collegeville, located at 331 East Main Street, during the early 1900s. (Courtesy of Richard K. Allebach.)

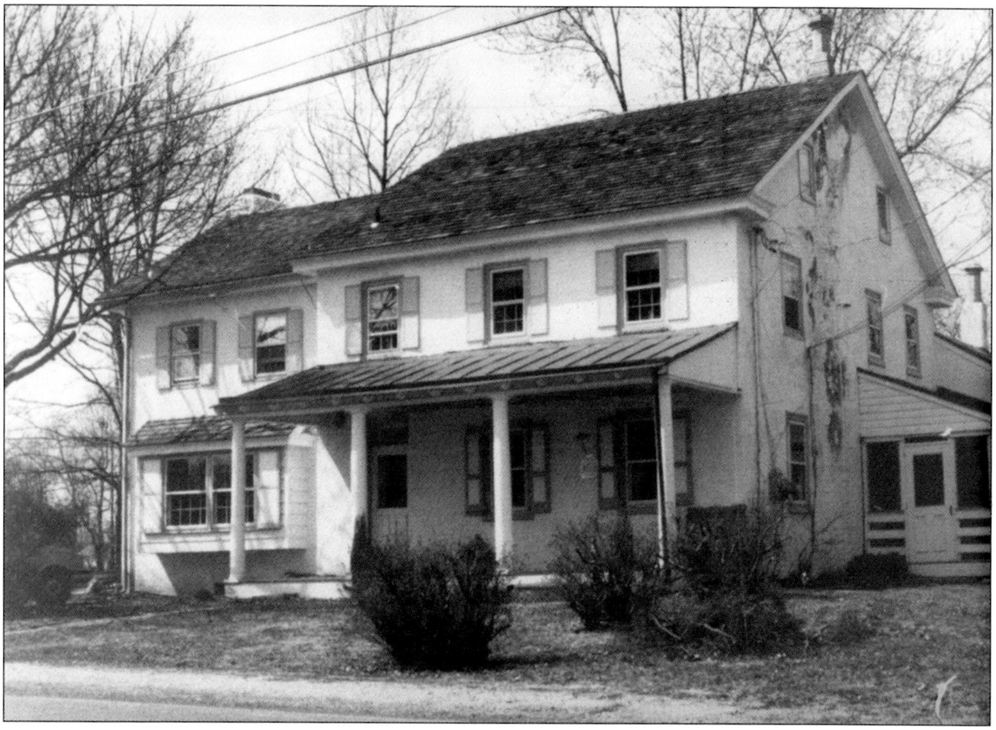

Zvarick Farm. In 1921, Slovak immigrant Henry Zvarick purchased a 55-acre farm at 901 Clayhor Avenue in Collegeville. It passed to his son and daughter-in-law, Albert and Loretta Zvarick, after their marriage in 1949. Both were active members of Keystone Grange No. 2 in Trappe and St. Eleanor Catholic Church in Collegeville. (Above, courtesy of the Historical Society of Trappe, Collegeville, Perkiomen Valley; below, courtesy of the Zvarick family.)

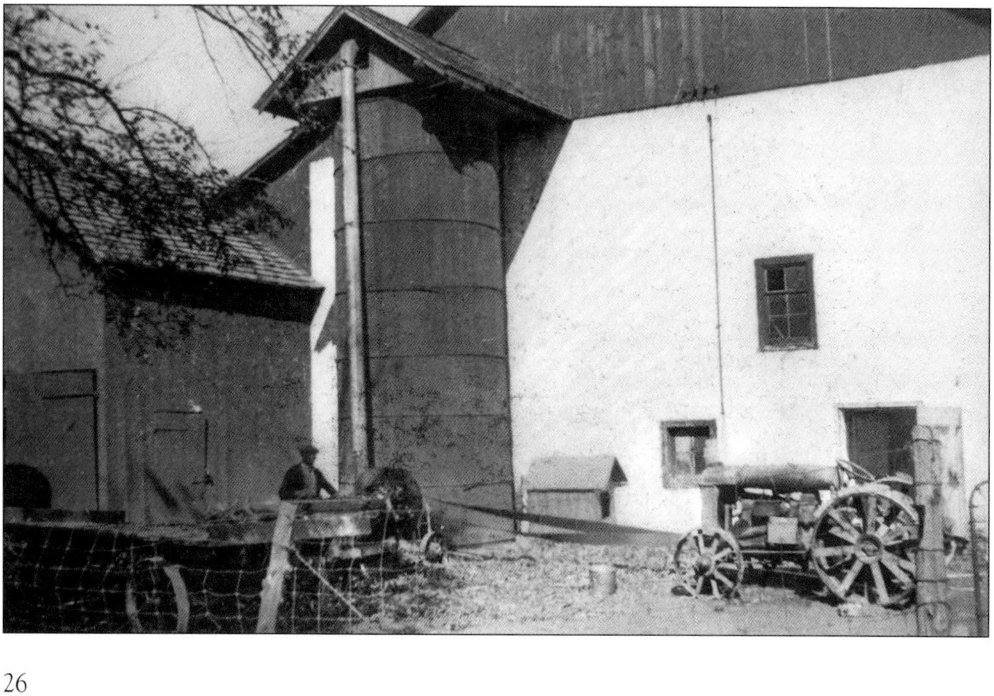

Two

MAIN STREET

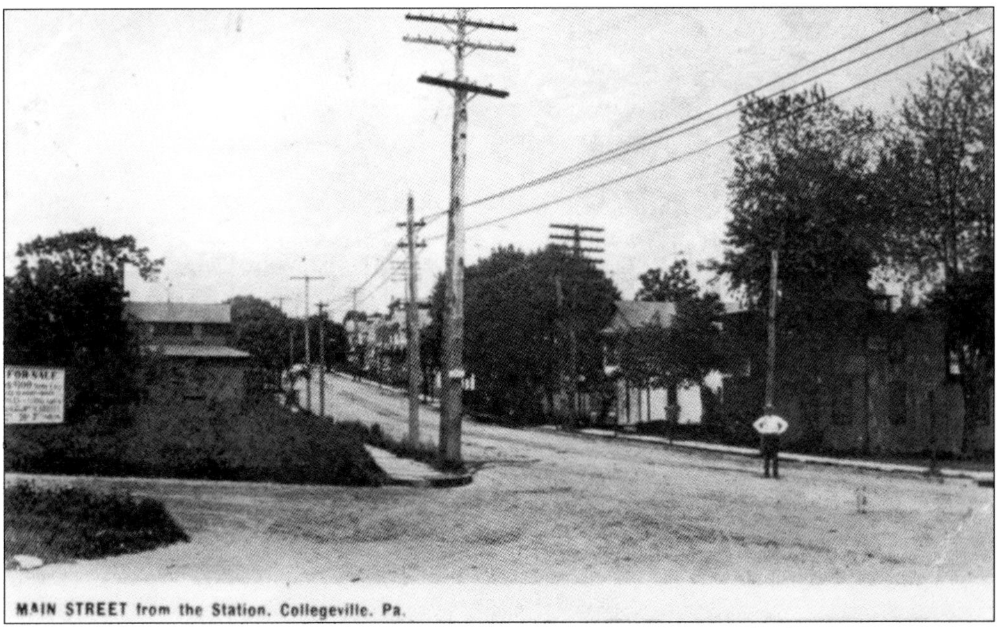

MAIN STREET, COLLEGEVILLE, C. 1909. This postcard depicts the view looking up Main Street from the train station near the intersection with Third Avenue. The building at right was the headquarters of the *Independent* newspaper, at 307 East Main Street. Its distinctive pyramid-roofed tower is hidden behind the trees. The man standing in the street with his hands on his hips may be Elwood S. Moser, who founded the newspaper in 1875 and printed it until his death in 1935. (Courtesy of Jerry A. Chiccarine.)

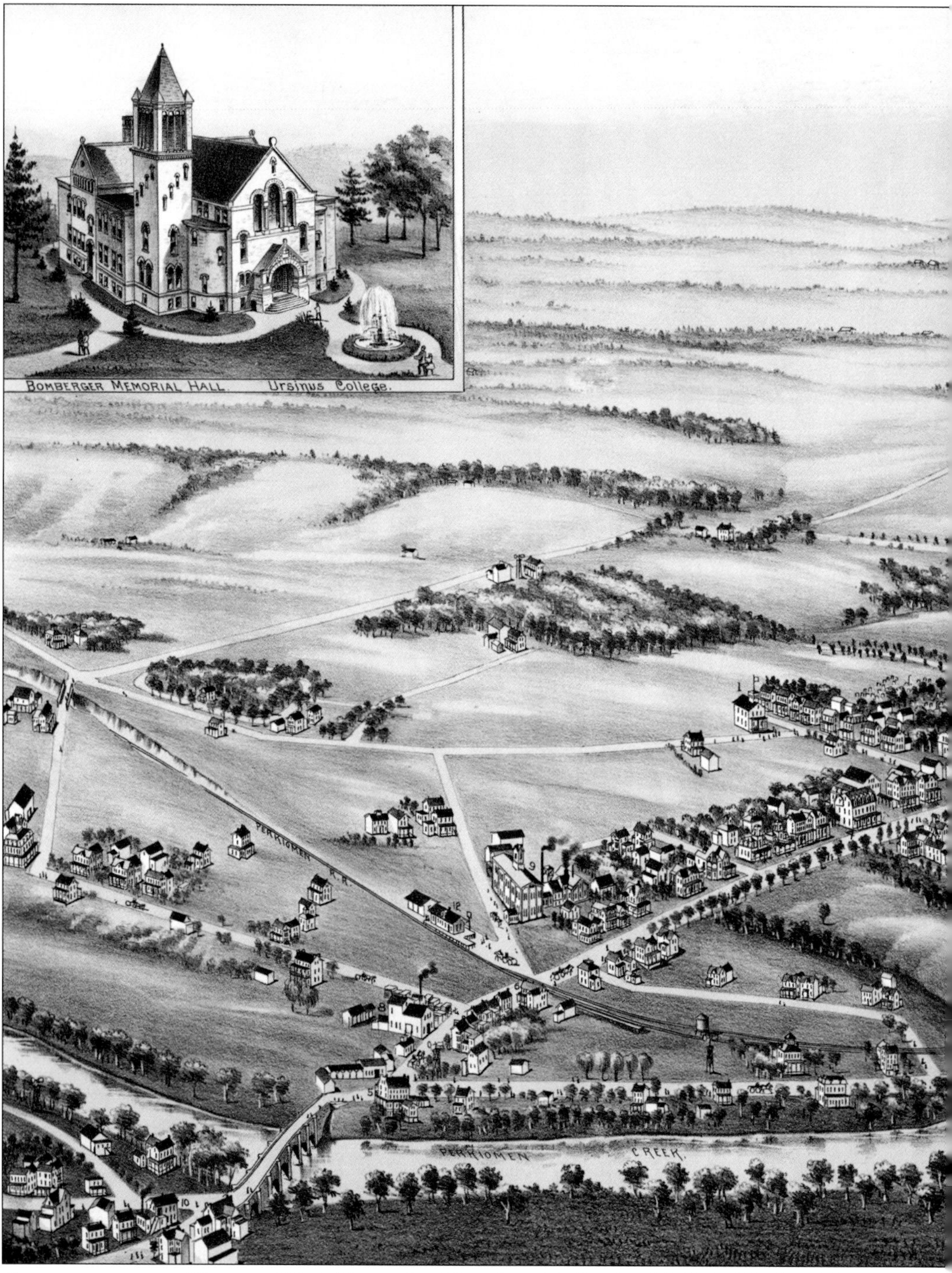

COLLEGEVILLE AND TRAPPE, 1894. Drawn by Thaddeus M. Fowler (1842–1922), this 1894 map offers a bird's-eye view of Collegeville and Trappe from the southeast. At top left is a large inset of

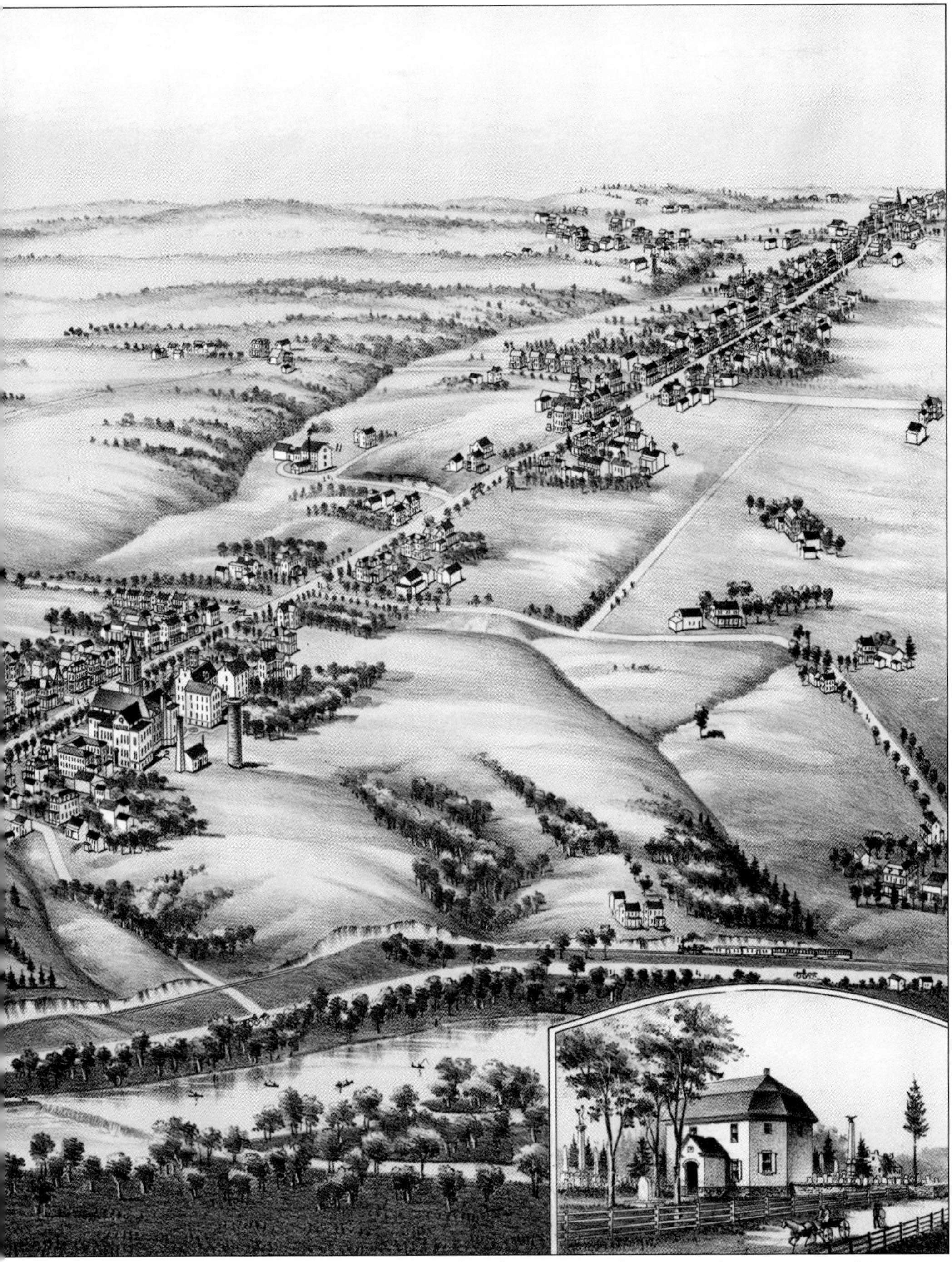

Bomberger Memorial Hall, which was completed in 1892. At bottom right is an inset of Augustus Lutheran Church. (Courtesy of the Library of Congress.)

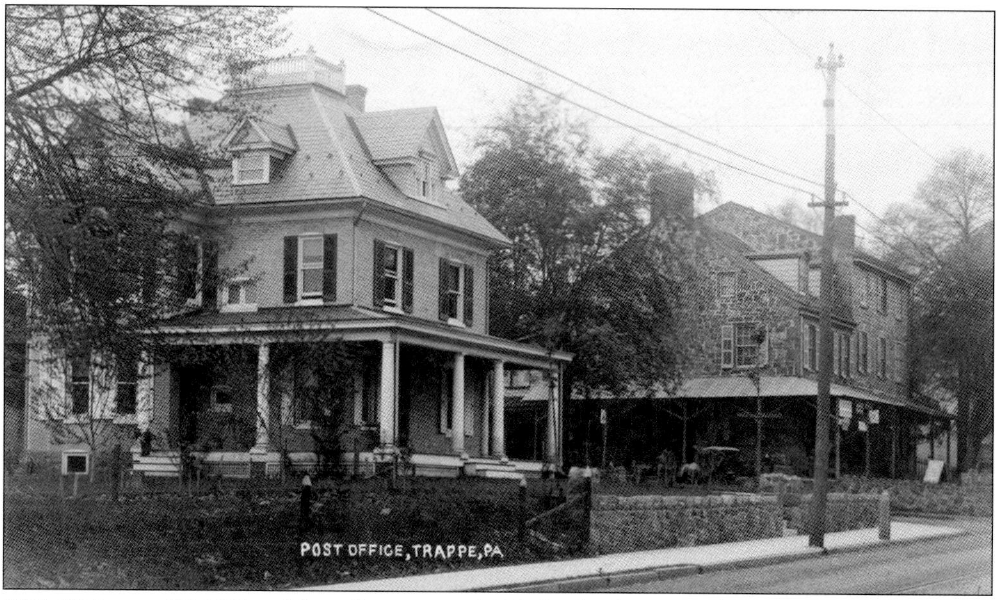

608, 702, AND 704 WEST MAIN STREET, C. 1910. In the foreground is 608 West Main Street, sold by Dr. Joseph Warren Royer to Jacob Wisler in 1908. The three-story stone house at far right was built for Dr. Royer's parents, Judge Joseph Royer and Elizabeth Dewees, who were married in 1818. The adjacent two-story wing served as a general store and post office. Judge Royer was a descendant of German immigrant Johann Carl Reyer (1711–1780), who settled in Trappe and became active in Augustus Lutheran Church. (Courtesy of Jerry A. Chiccarine.)

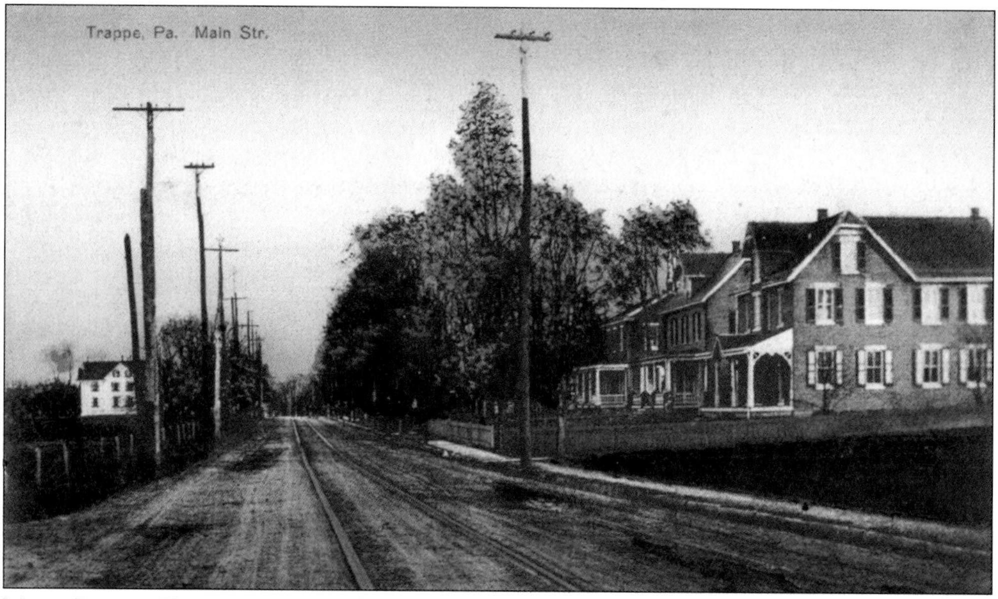

MAIN STREET, TRAPPE, C. 1910. This view is looking east toward the intersection of West Fifth Avenue and West Main Street. The houses on the right are 562, 568, and 572 West Main Street, all of which still stand today. Trappe's first ordinance, enacted on June 14, 1897, was to straighten and widen Main Street to a uniform width of fifty feet, with eight feet per side to be used as a sidewalk. Three years later, the borough approved spending $10,000 to macadamize Main Street. Utility poles were authorized in 1905. (Courtesy of Jerry A. Chiccarine.)

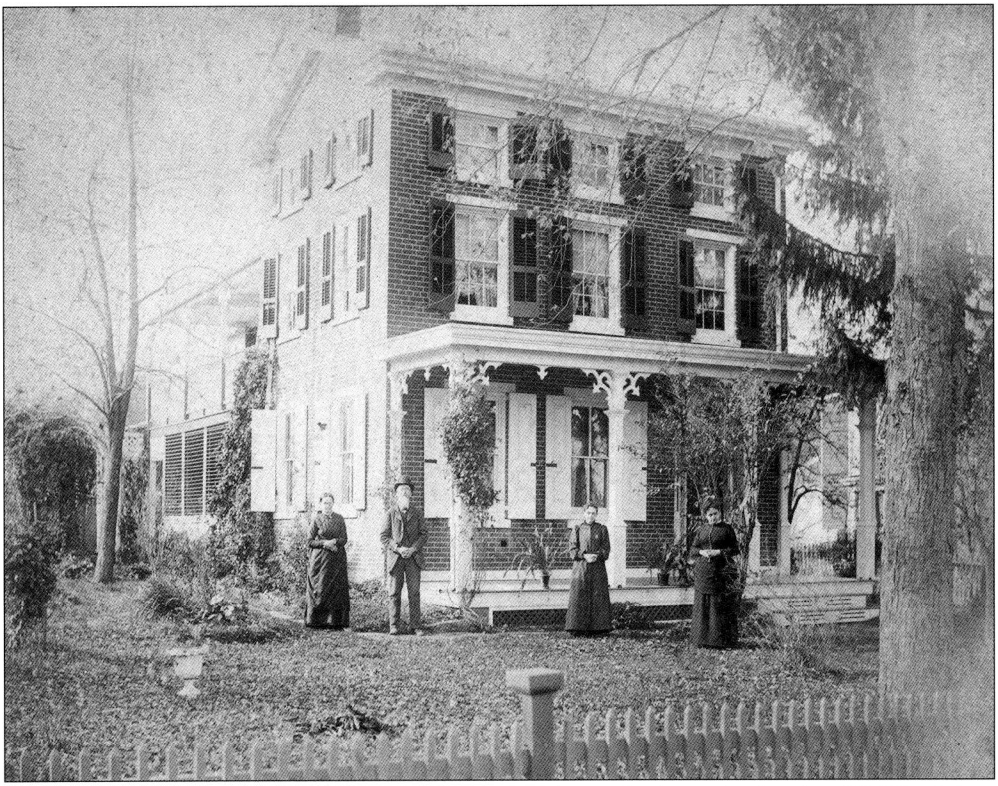

532 West Main Street. John K. Beaver (1824–1906), a tailor by trade, lived at 532 West Main Street in Trappe for many years. He operated a general store at 538 West Main Street, which was later taken over by his son-in-law Edwin G. Brownback. The photograph above shows John Beaver, his wife Mary (née Shellenberger), one of their two daughters, and a niece standing in the front yard. The photograph below shows the same house with a small boy hiding among a profusion of potted plants in the yard. (Both, courtesy of Mayor Connie and Robert Peck.)

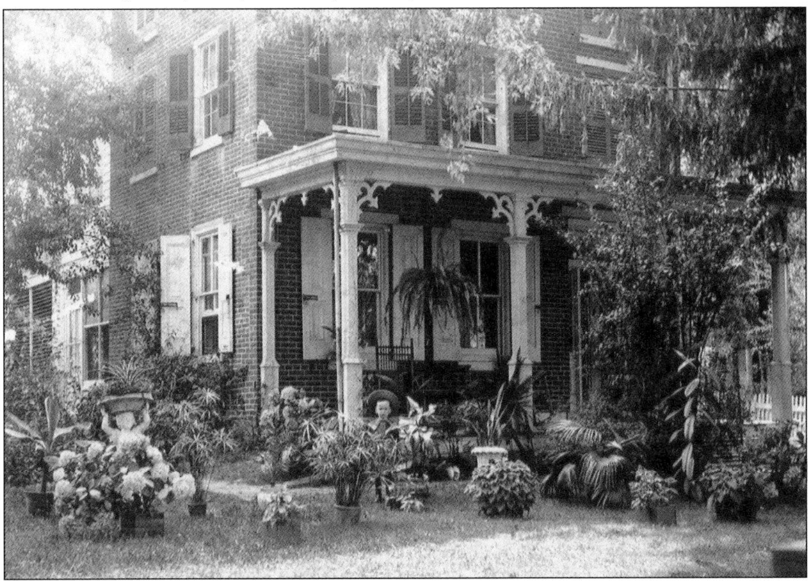

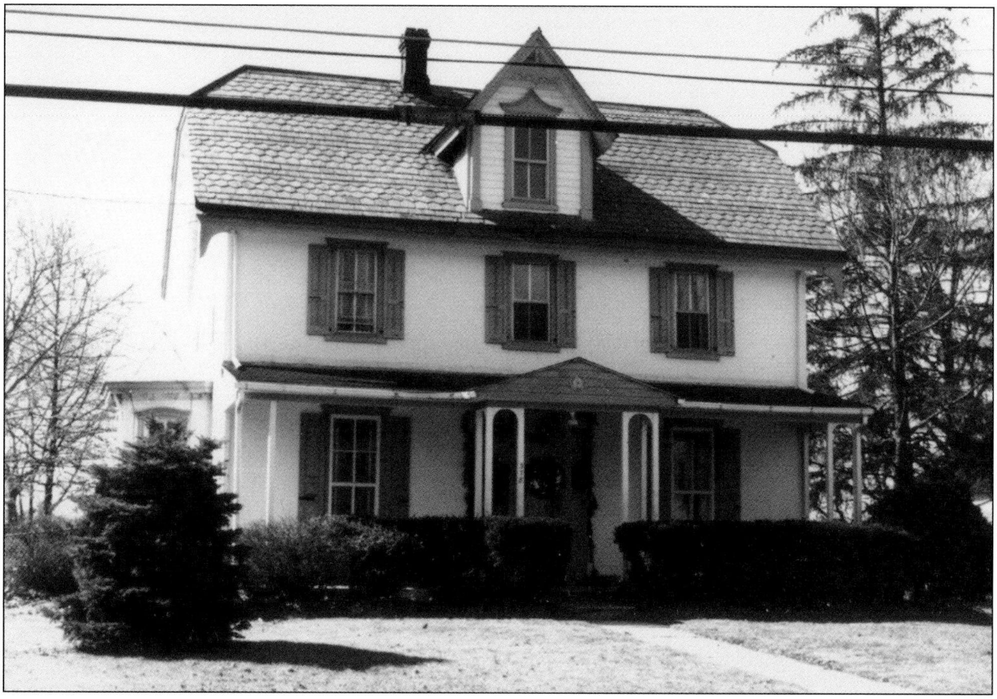

378 West Main Street. This house was built in the mid-1800s for Henry W. Kratz (1834–1917), who entered politics in 1862 and served as a justice of the peace for many years. He moved to Norristown in 1889, and five years later was elected to the Pennsylvania House of Representatives. The small frame building below once served as Kratz's office. It was also used variously as a post office, as the headquarters of the Perkiomen Mutual Fire Insurance Company from 1872 to 1889, and as the first borough council room after Trappe was incorporated in 1896. (Both, courtesy of the Historical Society of Trappe, Collegeville, Perkiomen Valley.)

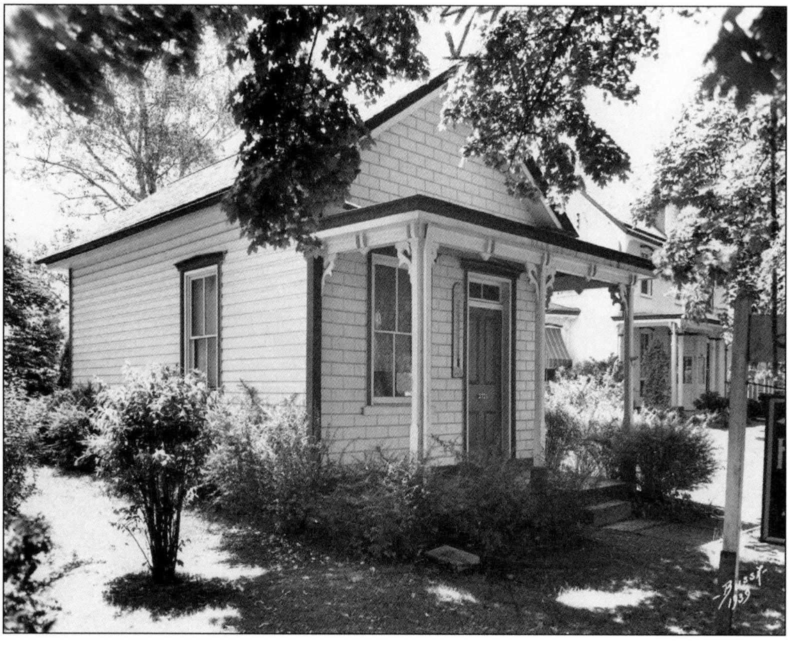

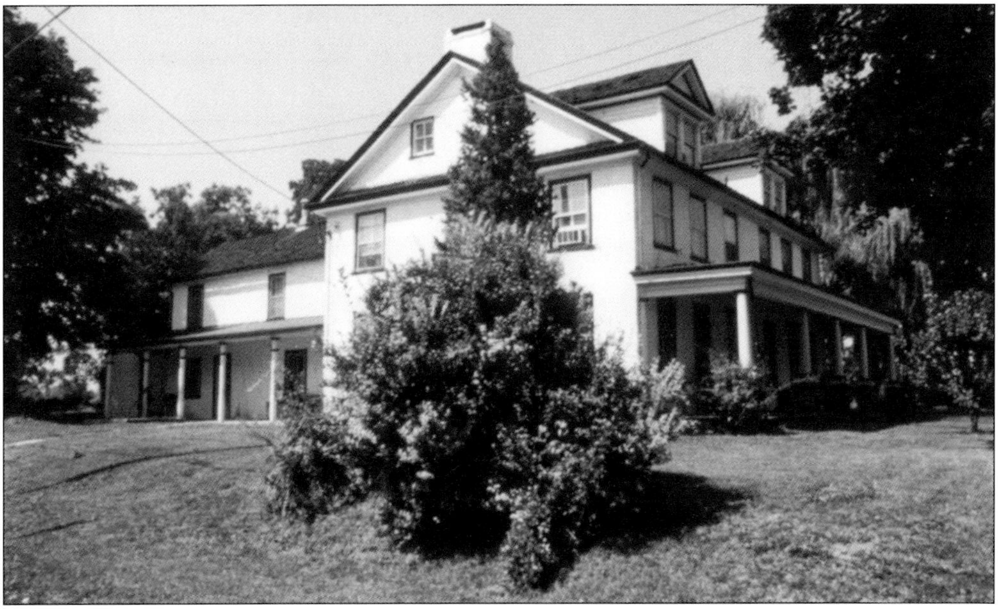

306 West Main Street. Built before 1800 for William Moore Smith, this house was later owned by Israel Bringhurst, who ran a store there, and then by his son Wright A. Bringhurst (1799–1876). Wright was a successful businessman and politician who left $100,000 in his will to "build houses of moderate size, to be rented to poor persons, according to their circumstances." The houses were to be built in Upper Providence Township, as well as Norristown and Pottstown boroughs. Four houses were constructed on West Third Avenue in Trappe with some of the Bringhurst funds and remain standing today. The Bringhurst mansion itself was badly damaged in a tornado that struck Trappe on June 7, 1961, and was torn down on December 5, 1971. It was replaced by a Getty gas station and service center, which closed in 2013. (Courtesy of the Historical Society of Trappe, Collegeville, Perkiomen Valley.)

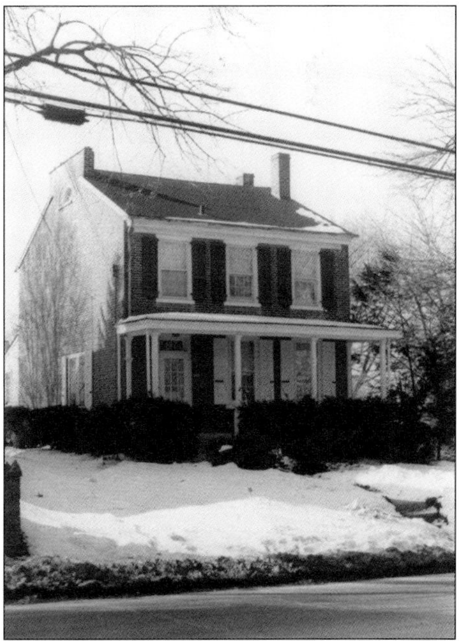

212 West Main Street, c. 1988. This two-story brick house was built shortly after 1851 when James Rambo purchased a tract of land from the estate of Mary Bringhurst. Ten years later, it was owned by Rev. Engelbert Peixoto, whose daughter Rosamund was a milliner in Trappe. During the 1870s, it was owned by Philip Williard, a noted civic leader who was trained as a Reformed Church minister. (Courtesy of the Historical Society of Trappe, Collegeville, Perkiomen Valley.)

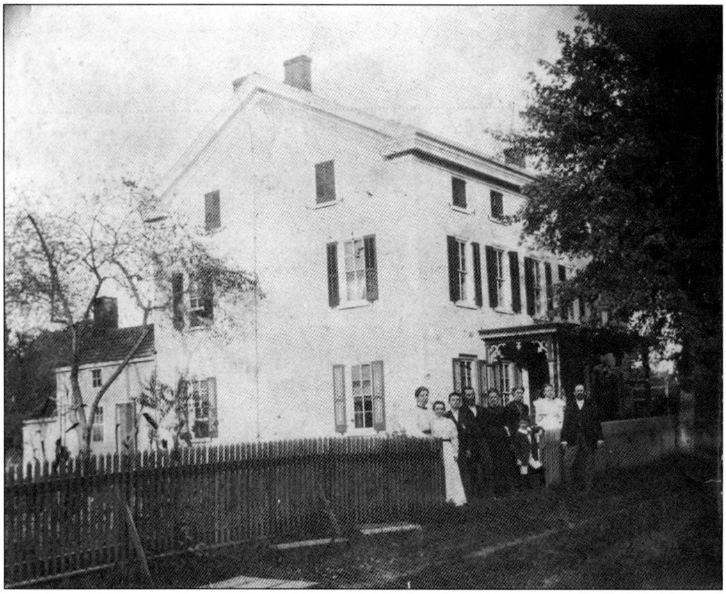

201 West Main Street, c. 1890. This photograph shows the west side of the house where Henry and Mary Muhlenberg lived from 1776 to 1787. Around 1863, the roofline was raised four feet to add a third story to the house. The people seen here are probably members of the Hunsberger family, who owned the property from 1848 to 1895. (Courtesy of the Historical Society of Trappe, Collegeville, Perkiomen Valley.)

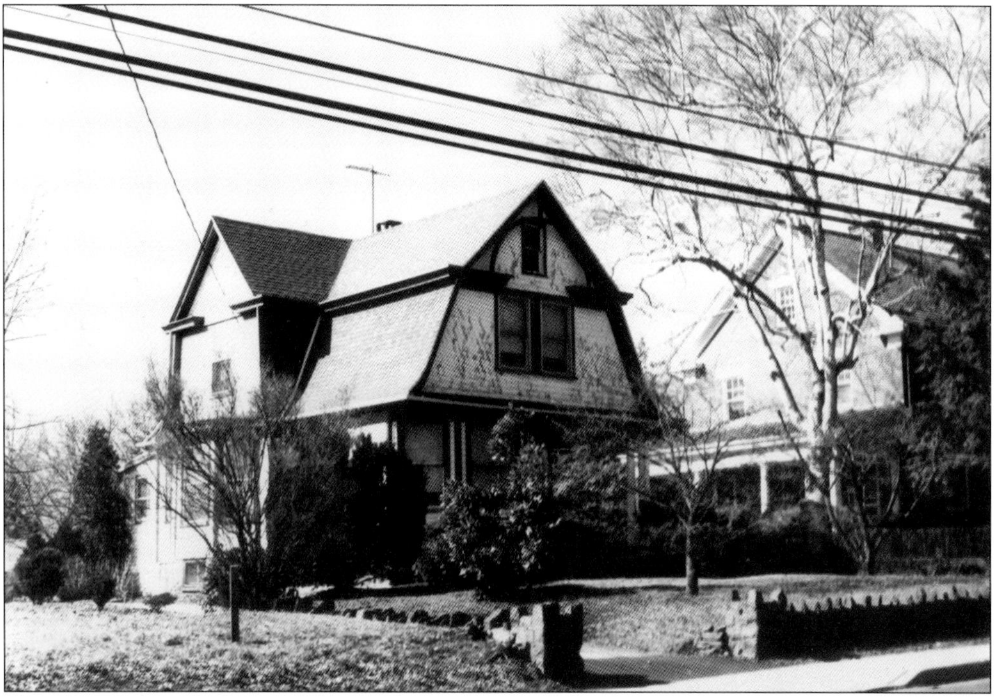

178 West Main Street, c. 1988. Built around 1905, this shingle-sided house retains its original Arts and Crafts–style interior. For many years, it was the home of Dr. Charlotte Witmer (1921–2013), a renowned biochemist and toxicologist. She was also a longtime member of the local historical society, serving on its board from 1964 to 2003. (Courtesy of the Historical Society of Trappe, Collegeville, Perkiomen Valley.)

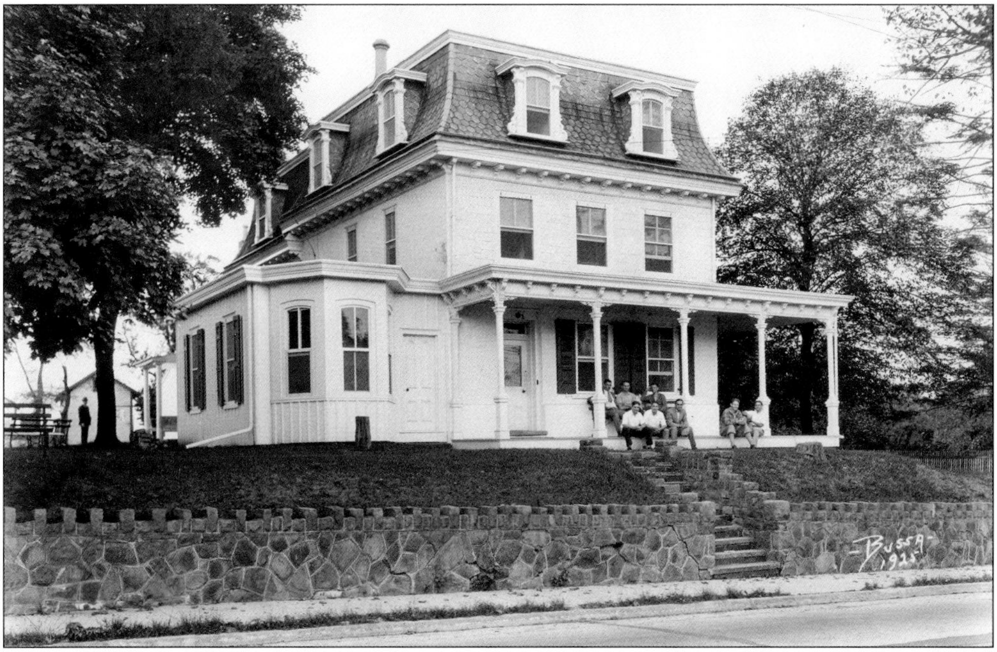

151 West Main Street, 1925. The front section of this house was built in 1763 for John Schrack, the eldest son of Trappe's founder. In 1781, it was bought by Frederick and Catharine Muhlenberg. They sold it in 1791 to Frederick's sister, Mary, and her husband, Francis Swaine, who owned it until 1803. In the late 1800s, the house was owned by Dr. Lewis Royer, who extensively remodeled it, and then by Ursinus College from 1924 to 1944. During the college's ownership, the house was used as a men's dormitory named Highland Hall. It later became the home of the college's athletic director, Russell C. "Jing" Johnson, a former pitcher for the Philadelphia Athletics. After the college sold it, the house once again became a private residence and later an apartment building. It was nearly torn down in the early 2000s, but a group of local citizens rescued it and formed a nonprofit organization known as The Speaker's House. (Both, courtesy of the Ursinus College Archives.)

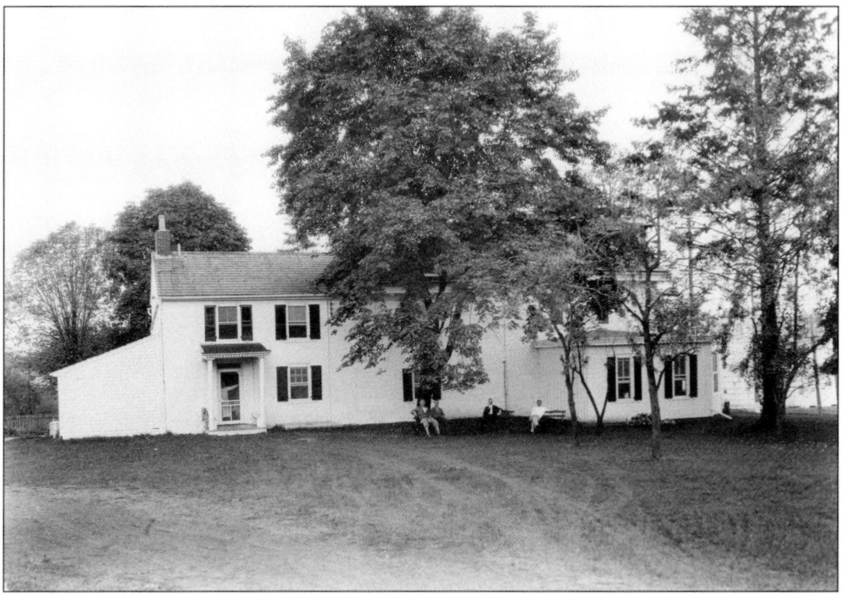

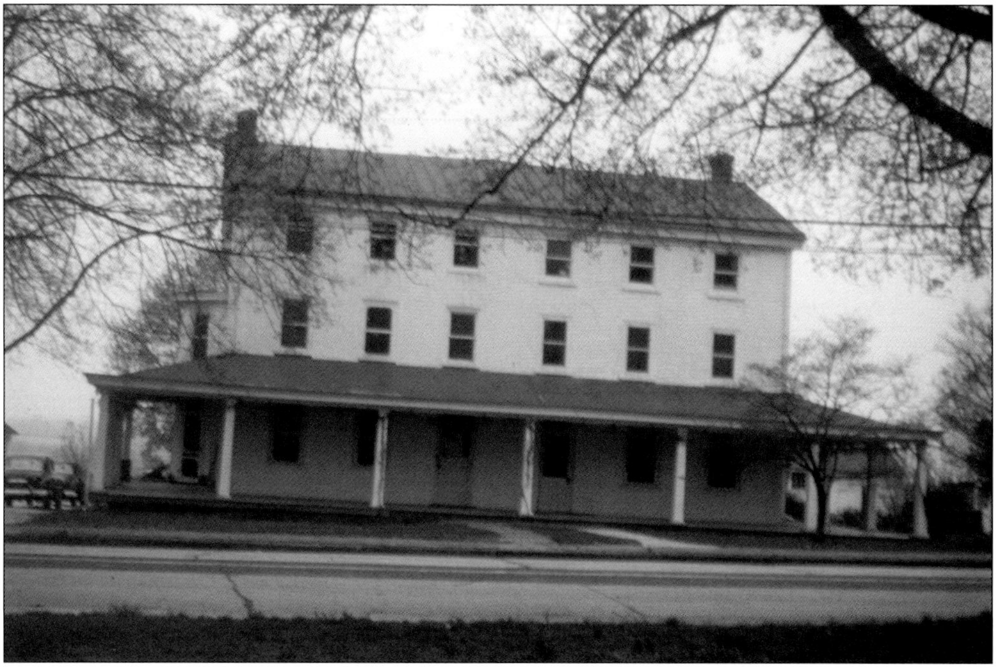

STEARLY FARM, 1958. The original Trappe Tavern was located where the Trappe Shopping Center now stands. The last innkeeper was Gabriel Kline, who offered the tavern for sale in 1810 and described it as a "large and commodious stone dwelling-house, being the oldest stand used as a tavern in the place." Unable to find a buyer, Kline held on to the property and sold it in 1842 to his son-in-law John Longstreth. In 1906, Henry A. Hunsicker, who grew up at 930 East Main Street, recalled the "old stone house which was kept many long years ago by John Jacob Schrack, which gave a name to 'The Trap.' The old building was torn down by John Longstreth." Longstreth built a new house on the property, which passed to his son Isaac Longstreth, then to his daughter Katharine and her husband S. Walter Stearly, and finally to their son H. Douglas Stearly. After five generations of ownership in the Kline-Longstreth-Stearly family, the farm was sold and the buildings were demolished to make way for the construction of the 125,000-square-foot Trappe Shopping Center, which opened in 1989. (Both, courtesy of Richard A. Holcombe.)

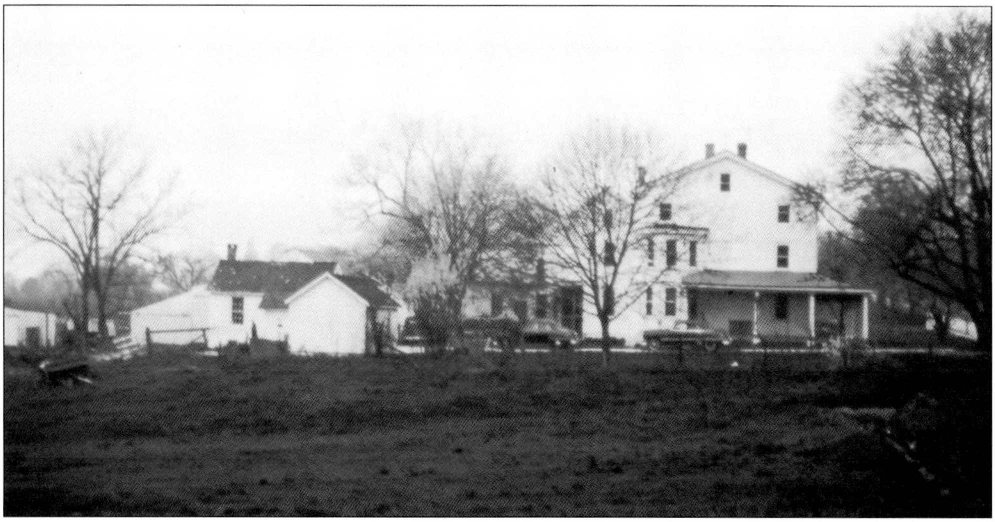

930 East Main Street. Known as Fircroft, this house was built around 1835 for Rev. Abraham Hunsicker, a Mennonite bishop and the founder of Freeland Seminary. It contains elements of an earlier stone house built for Christian Schrack, the son of Trappe's founder and a tanner by trade. Fircroft was later owned by the Vanderslice family and then in 1926 by Sara E. Ermold, who worked for Ursinus College from 1907 to 1942. Upon her retirement, Ermold gave Fircroft to Ursinus in memory of her mother, Ella Ermold. (Courtesy of the Historical Society of Trappe, Collegeville, Perkiomen Valley.)

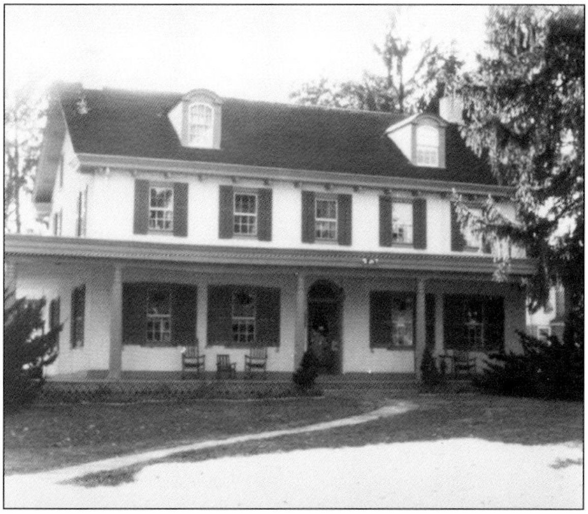

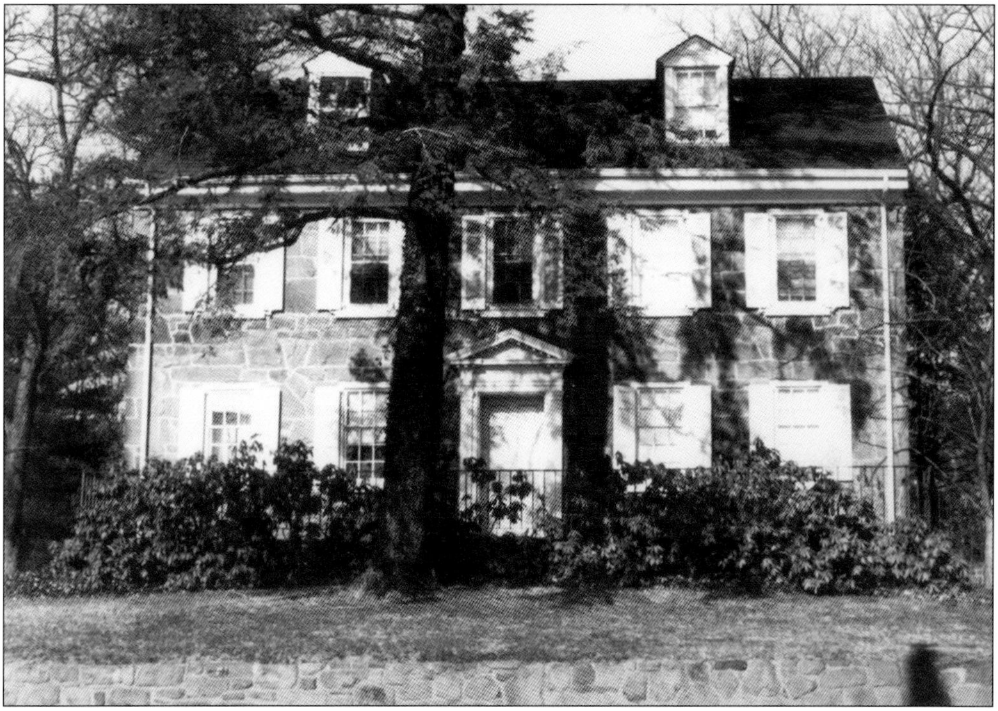

801 East Main Street, c. 1988. One of the oldest houses in Collegeville, this stone dwelling was owned by Andrew Todd, who donated the land for a one-room stone schoolhouse in 1832. After Todd's death, it was owned by his son John Todd and later by Dr. James Hamer and his wife, Flora G. Hunsicker, who were married in 1879. Tragedy struck there five years earlier on February 23, 1874, when Flora's brother Abraham L. Hunsicker, then a freshman at Ursinus College, was accidentally shot to death by a classmate while rehearsing for a play. A pond near the corner of Ninth Avenue and Main Street, known for years as Hamer's Pond, was a popular spot for ice-skating until 1945, when it was filled in. The house was acquired by Ursinus in the 1960s and is now known as Isenberg Hall after Rev. James M.S. Isenberg, who was vice president of the college from 1925 to 1930. (Courtesy of the Historical Society of Trappe, Collegeville, Perkiomen Valley.)

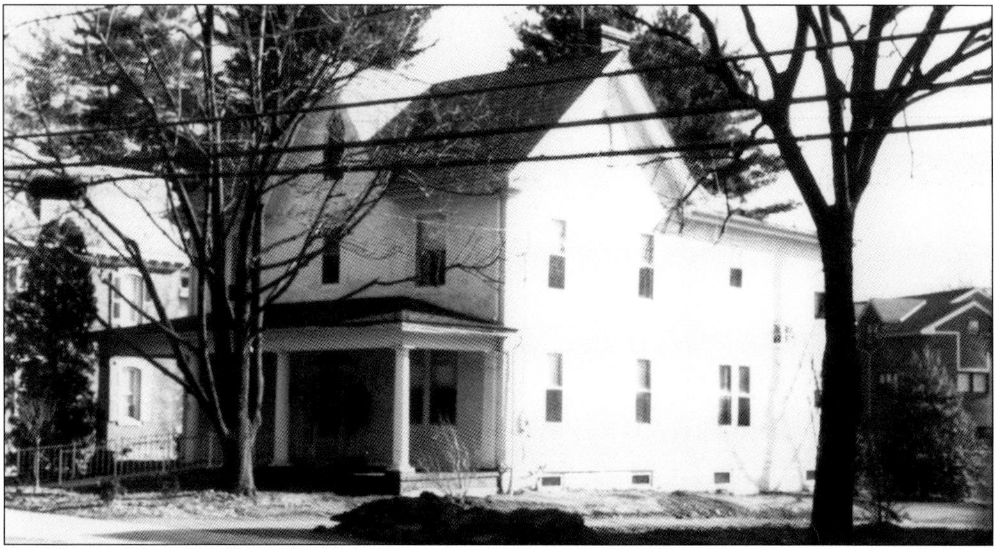

620 East Main Street, c. 1988. Built during the mid-1800s as a private residence, Zwingli Hall retains much of its original charm, including a large front porch. It is named after Ulrich Zwingli, a Swiss theologian and Reformation leader. Paul and Elisabeth Levengood lived here from about 1950 until they sold it to Ursinus College in the early 1960s and moved to 155 Ninth Avenue. Paul was the second owner and publisher of the *Independent*. (Courtesy of the Historical Society of Trappe, Collegeville, Perkiomen Valley.)

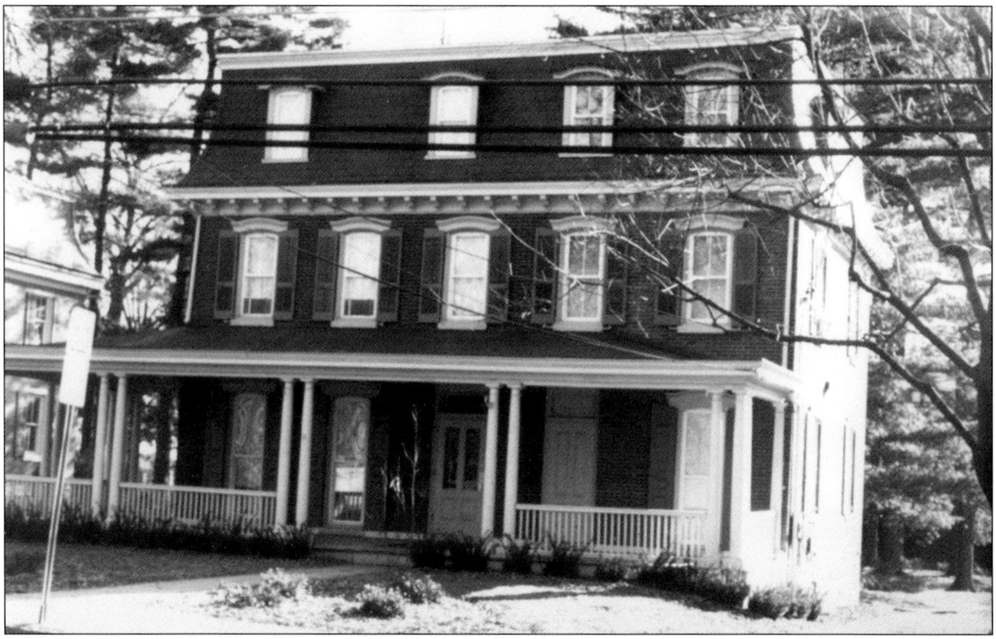

612 East Main Street, c. 1988. From 1889 to 1921, this building was the headquarters of the Perkiomen Valley Mutual Insurance Company. In 1937, the Ursinus Women's Club purchased it from Abraham D. Fetterolf. Ten years later, it was renamed Duryea Hall in honor of Rhea Duryea Johnson, who graduated from Ursinus in 1908 and in 1928 became the first woman to serve on the college's board of directors. (Courtesy of the Historical Society of Trappe, Collegeville, Perkiomen Valley.)

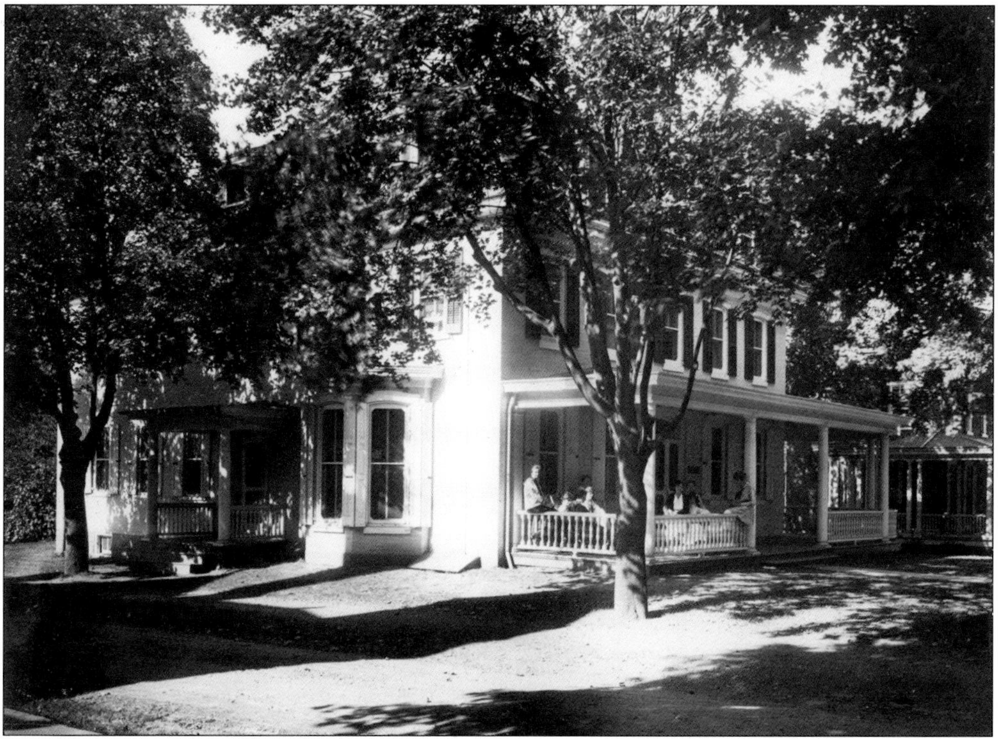

600 East Main Street. This structure was built in 1876 for Dr. John H.A. Bomberger, first president of Ursinus College. It was originally known as Zwinglihof after the Swiss theologian and Reformation leader Ulrich Zwingli. Dr. Bomberger lived here until his death in 1890, when it was bought by the college and became known as the President's House and later the College House. In 1908, Israel Shreiner donated $5,000 to enlarge it, and the following year, it became a women's dormitory, now known as Shreiner Hall. (Courtesy of the Ursinus College Archives.)

568 E. Main Street. Ursinus College acquired this house, known as Hobson Hall, from Edward and Mabel (Hobson) Fretz in 1944. Mabel's father, Freeland G. Hobson, and grandfather Frank M. Hobson both served as treasurers of the college. Built in the late 1800s, Hobson Hall's dramatic three-story tower, asymmetrical facade, and multiple porches exemplify the Queen Anne Revival style that was popular in America from about 1880 to 1910. (Photograph by Denae A. Zvarick.)

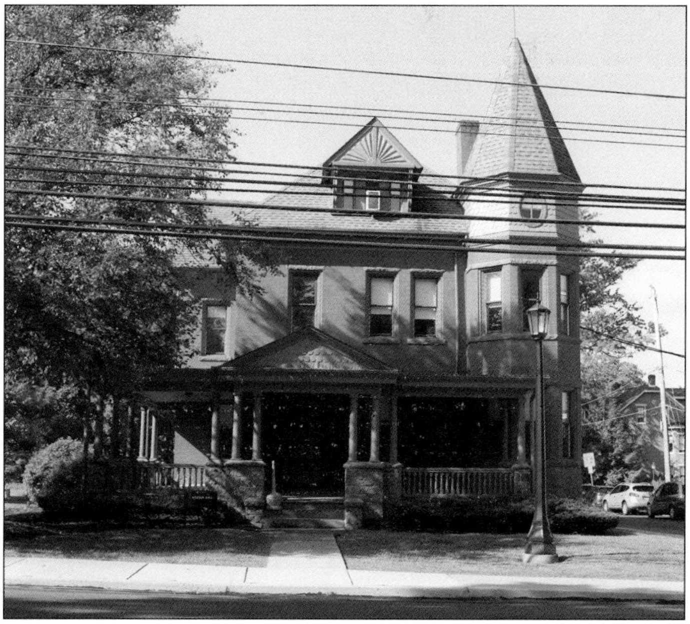

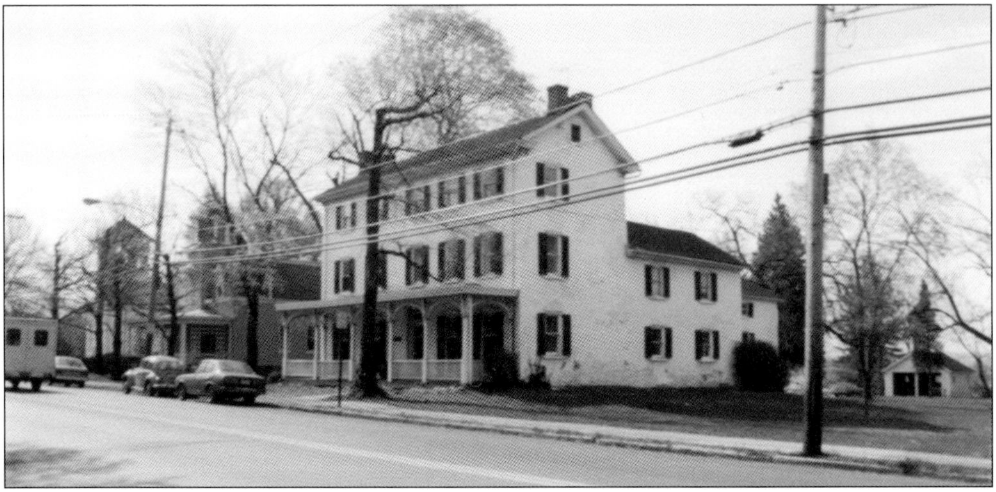

554 East Main Street, c. 1988. During the early 1800s, this three-story stone farmhouse was owned by William Tennent Todd, a spinning wheel maker. It was the first Collegeville residence of Rev. John H.A. Bomberger, founding president of Ursinus College. From 1867 to 1872, it was the home of Capt. Henry H. Fetterolf, who served in the Civil War. Fetterolf's daughter, Harriet "Hattie" Fetterolf, donated the house to Ursinus in 1948. (Courtesy of the Historical Society of Trappe, Collegeville, Perkiomen Valley.)

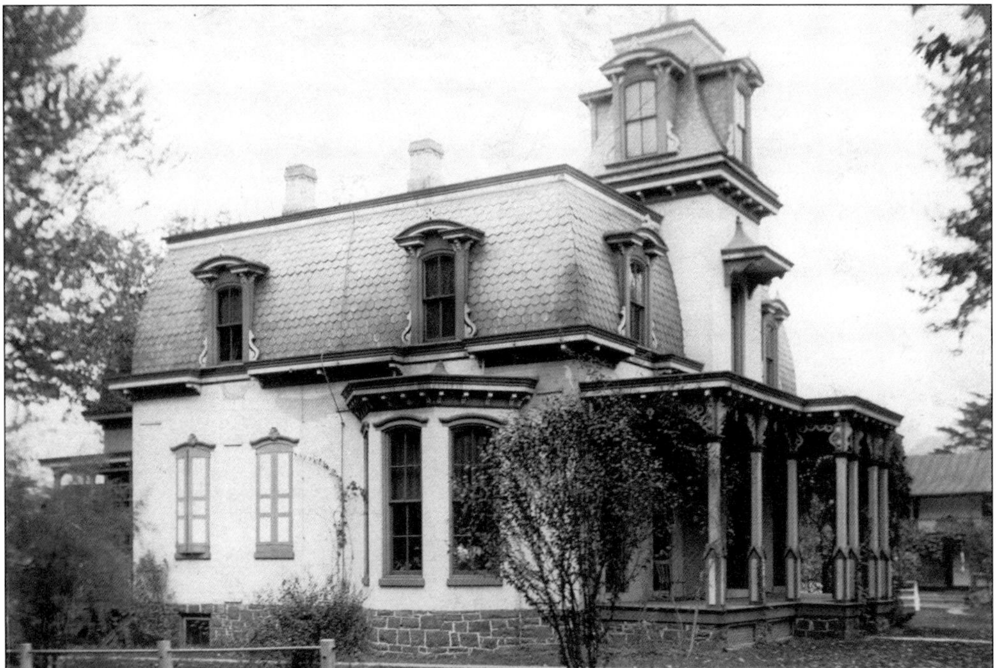

542 East Main Street, c. 1914. Known as the Super House, this building was constructed around 1878 for Henry William Super (1824–1897), vice president and "Professor of Mathematics, Mechanics, the Harmony of Science and Revealed Religion, etc." at Ursinus College. In 1890, he became the second president of Ursinus after Dr. Bomberger's death. Upon the death of Dr. Super's widow, Sarah Hobson, in 1914, the house became the college's property. It was occupied by Pres. George L. Omwake and his family beginning in 1916. (Courtesy of the Ursinus College Archives.)

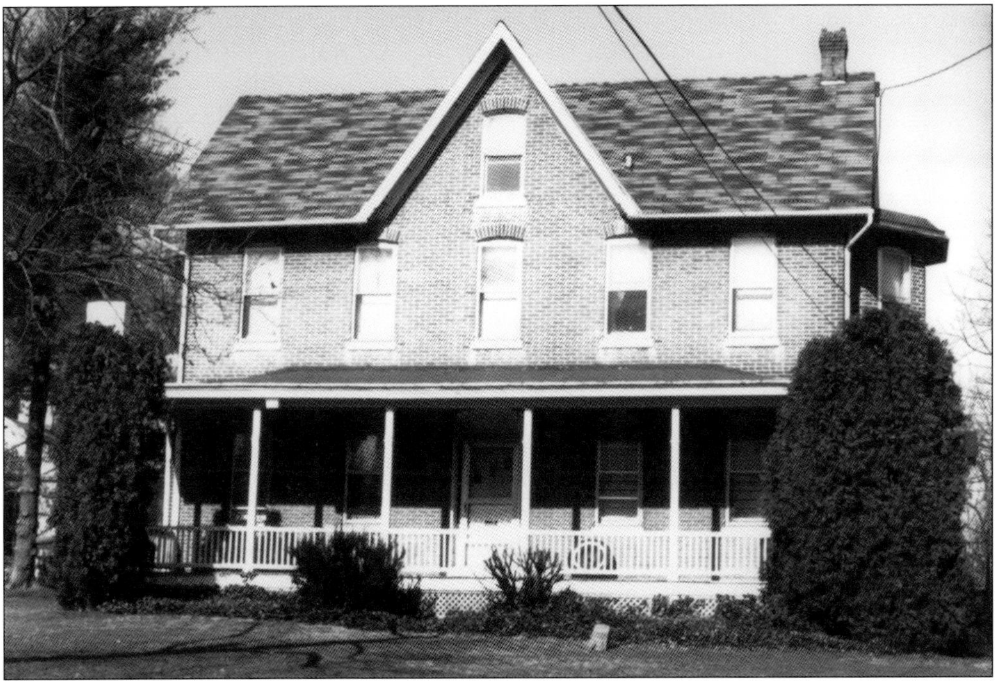

513 EAST MAIN STREET, C. 1988. Keigwin Hall was purchased by Ursinus in 1963 and named after Rev. Albert Edwin Keigwin (1869–1951), who served as president of the college from 1907 to 1912. It was initially used as a women's dormitory. (Courtesy of the Historical Society of Trappe, Collegeville, Perkiomen Valley.)

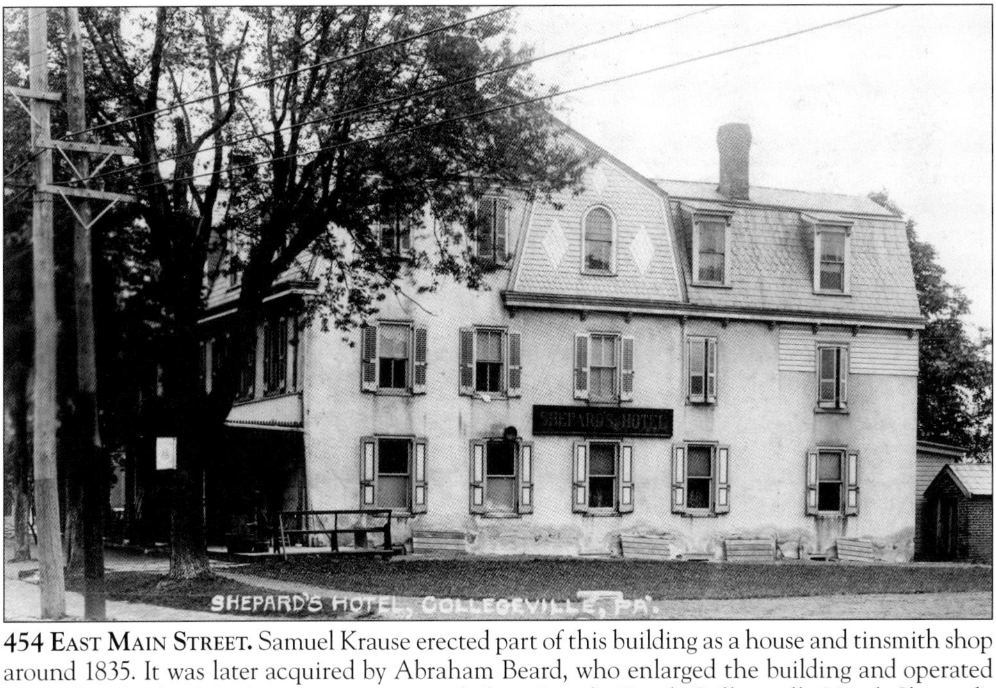

454 EAST MAIN STREET. Samuel Krause erected part of this building as a house and tinsmith shop around 1835. It was later acquired by Abraham Beard, who enlarged the building and operated it as a hotel, which had various names, including Beard's Hotel, Collegeville Hotel, Shepard's Hotel, and the Freeland House. (Courtesy of Jerry A. Chiccarine.)

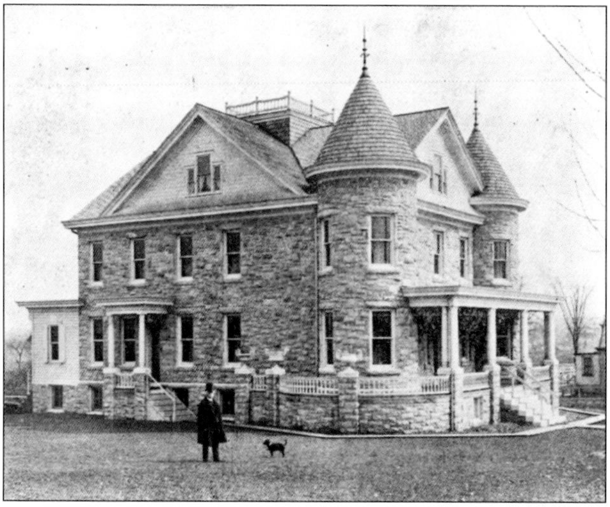

409 East Main Street, c. 1907. In 1903, Francis J. Clamer built a palatial new house at 409 East Main Street in Collegeville, equipped with the latest in modern conveniences. This photograph was taken during his second term as burgess (mayor) of Collegeville; he also served on the board of Ursinus College for many years. Ursinus leased the house, now known as Clamer Hall, for use as a girl's dormitory starting in 1936. Dr. Guilliam H. Clamer, son of Francis J. Clamer, donated it to the college in 1953. (Courtesy of Jerry A. Chiccarine.)

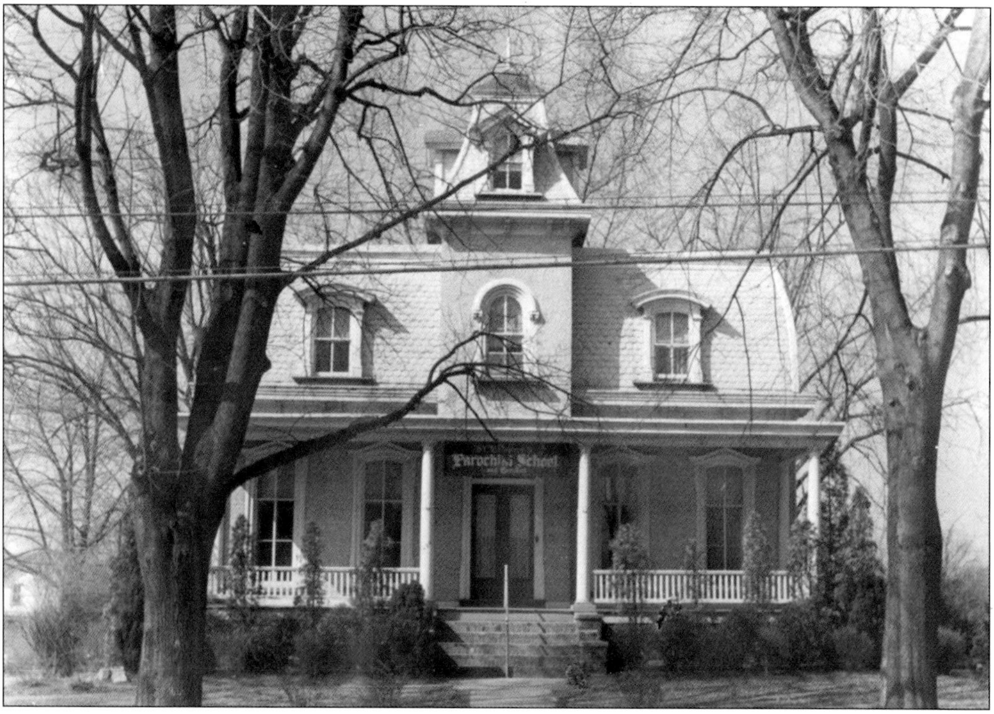

406 East Main Street, c. 1948. This ornate Victorian mansion was acquired by St. Eleanor Catholic Church in 1942 for use as a parochial school and convent. The previous owner, Elmer S. Poley, was a house carpenter and building contractor. It still stands and is currently used as an apartment building. (Courtesy of Jerry A. Chiccarine.)

Three

CHURCHES

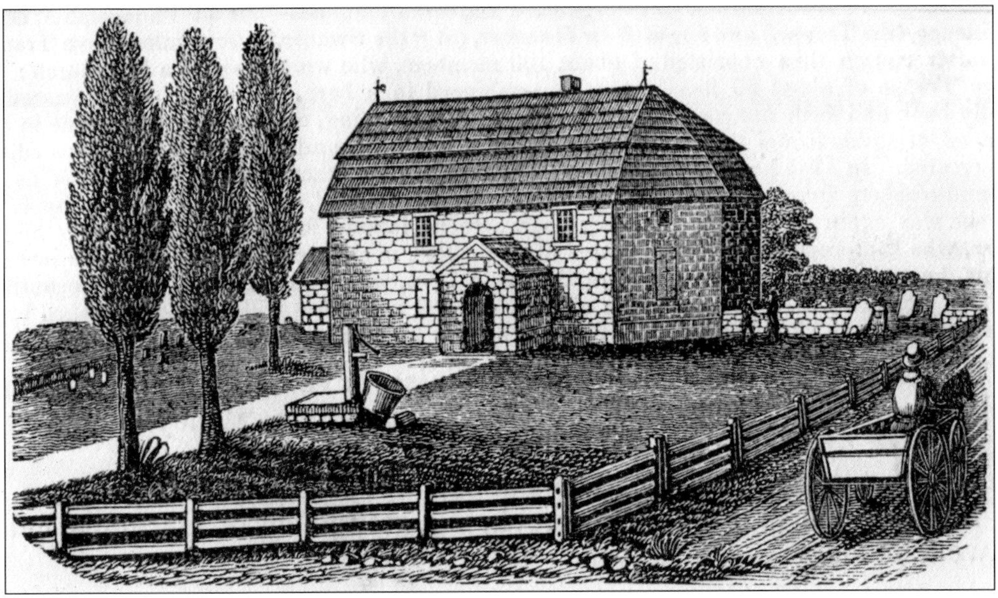

AUGUSTUS LUTHERAN CHURCH. Built between 1743 and 1745, Augustus Lutheran Church is one of the oldest buildings in Trappe and the oldest German Lutheran church still standing in Pennsylvania. Casper Stoever organized the congregation around 1730; Henry Melchior Muhlenberg served as its pastor from 1742 until his death in 1787. In September 1777, the church was taken over by the Continental Army. Many members of the Muhlenberg family and other prominent local residents are buried in the graveyard. In 1814, the building was updated with a new roof, new window sash, and board floor; the exterior was also stuccoed. This image is from Sherman Day's book *Historical Collections of the State of Pennsylvania*, published in 1843. (Author's collection.)

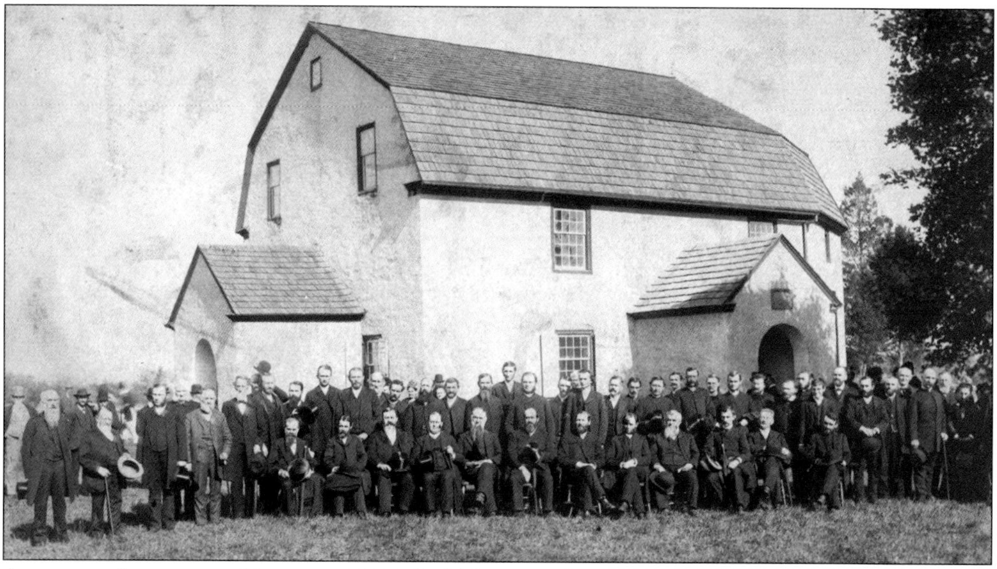

AUGUSTUS LUTHERAN CHURCH, 1887. On February 16, 1860, a severe windstorm destroyed part of the church roof and spurred talk of demolition, but Rev. William Augustus Muhlenberg, an Episcopal minister and great-grandson of the founder, helped raise funds to restore the building. In October 1887, the First District Conference of the Pennsylvania Ministerium was held at Augustus to commemorate the 100th anniversary of the death of Henry Melchior Muhlenberg (October 7, 1787). This photograph records that gathering. (Courtesy of Augustus Lutheran Church.)

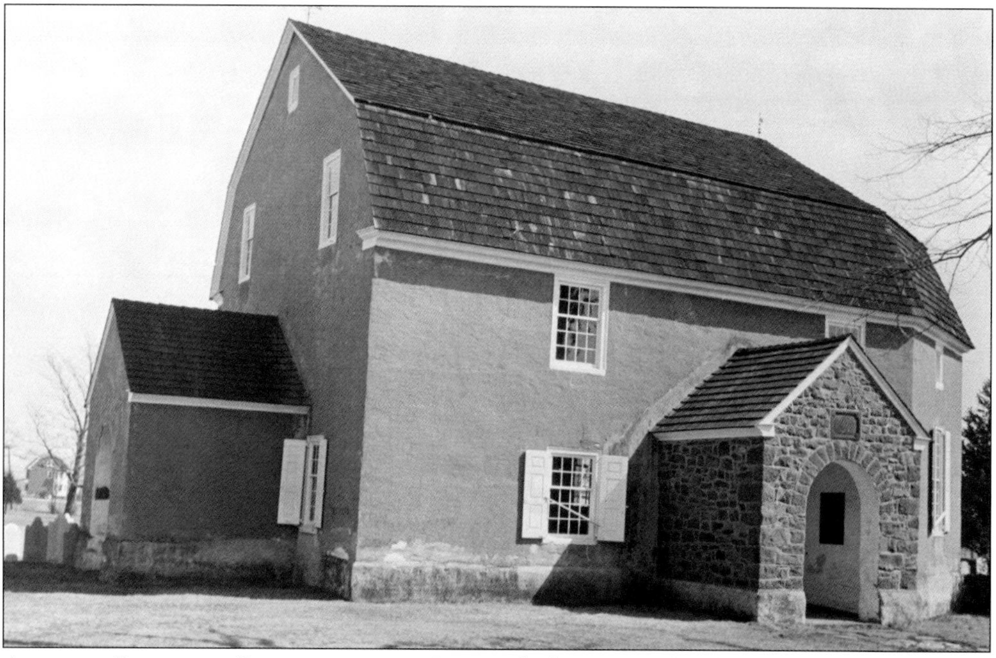

AUGUSTUS LUTHERAN CHURCH, C. 1940. During the late 1920s, the church was renovated under the direction of Dr. William O. Fegley to restore its Colonial appearance and Germanic details. The stove, chimney, and wooden floor were removed, and a concrete floor was installed. Much of the interior woodwork was also repainted. Located at 717 West Main Street in Trappe, the church was designated a National Historic Landmark in 1967. (Courtesy of Augustus Lutheran Church.)

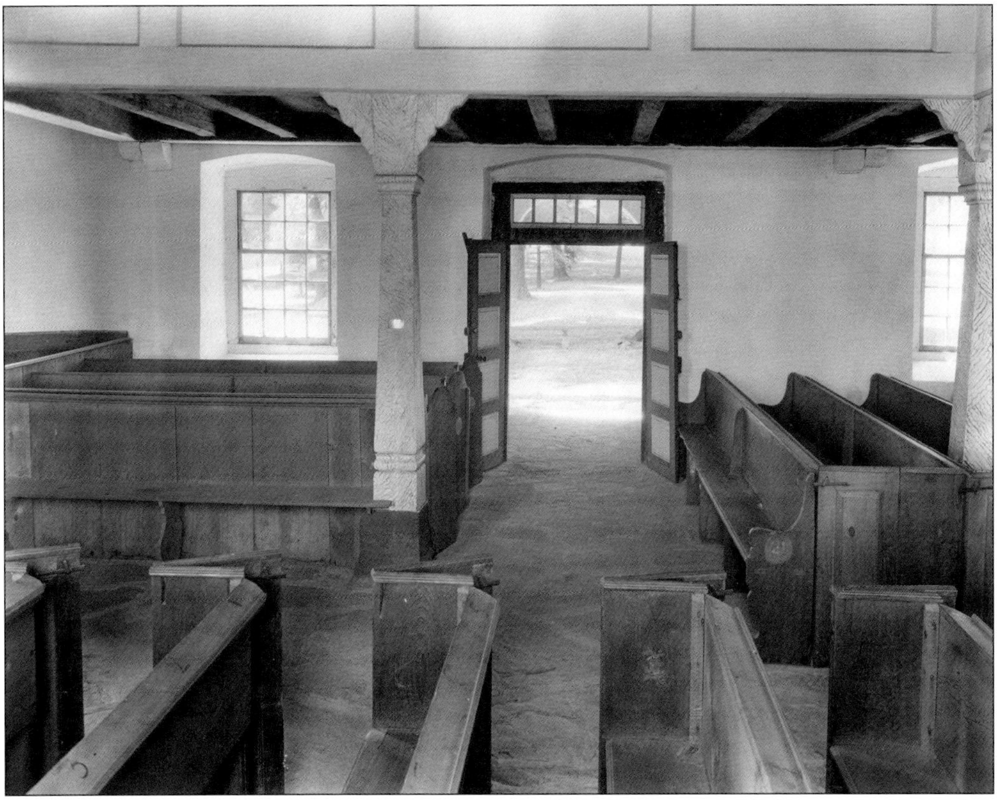

Interior of Augustus Lutheran Church. The church interior includes a wineglass pulpit and sounding board made of American black walnut, a native hardwood that grows plentifully in southeastern Pennsylvania. Above the pulpit is the organ loft, with a railing of flat vasiform balusters in the Germanic style. The original organ was built by Moravian instrument maker Johann Gottlieb Klemm of Philadelphia and installed at the church in 1751. (Both, courtesy of Augustus Lutheran Church.)

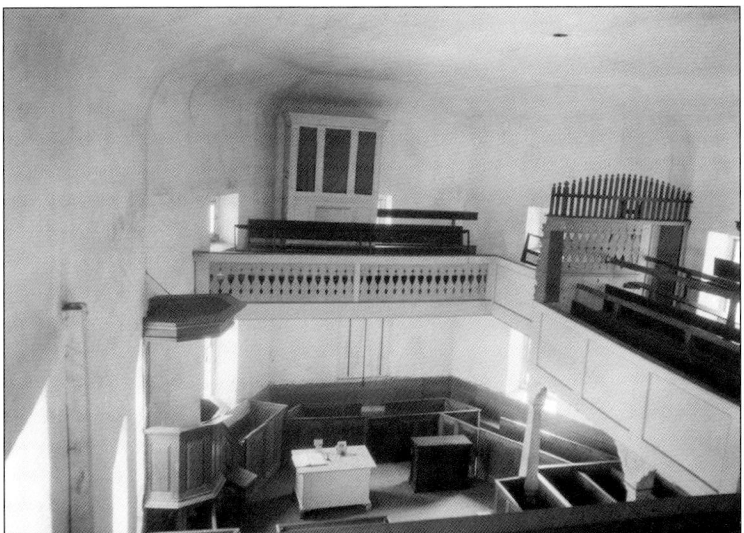

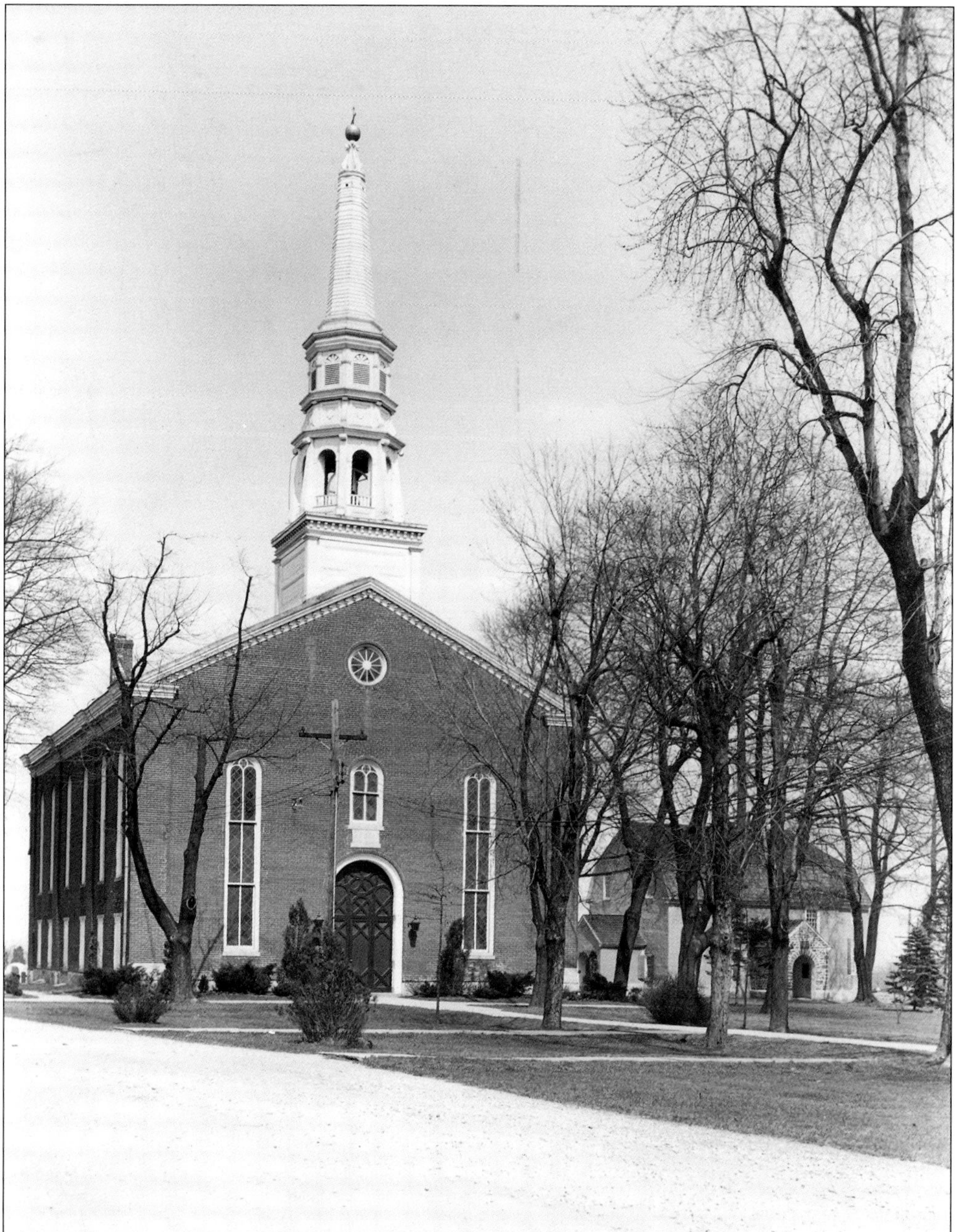

NEW CHURCH, 1937. In 1852, the Augustus Lutheran congregation finished the construction of a new brick church. As built, it had a large nave on the first floor, with enclosed pews and a rear gallery. The Sunday school, organized in 1836, met in the schoolhouse during the winter and the old church in the summer. In 1878, the congregation decided to remodel the brick church, moving the nave to the second floor and the Sunday school classes to the first floor. Stained-glass windows were also installed. The building was rededicated on January 14, 1879. This photograph shows the brick church in the foreground, with the older stone church in the background. (Courtesy of Augustus Lutheran Church.)

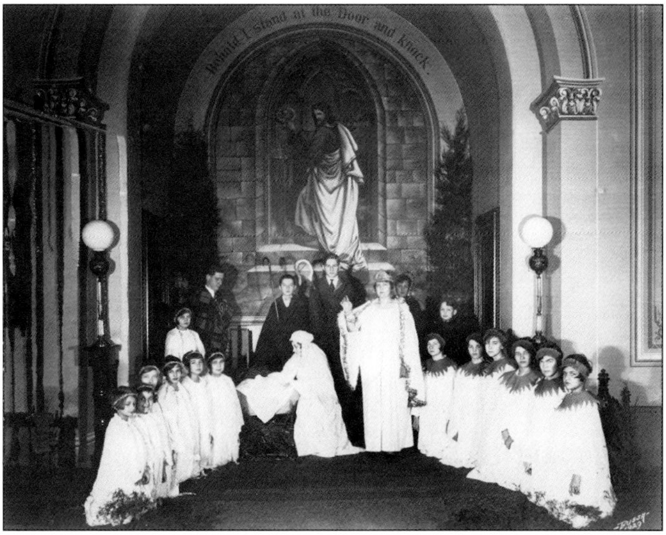

Mural, 1929. The brick church once had a large mural depicting Jesus standing at the threshold of a door, based on Revelations 3:20: "Behold I stand at the door and knock." The mural is clearly visible in this photograph of a living nativity from the Christmas pageant of 1929. (Courtesy of Augustus Lutheran Church.)

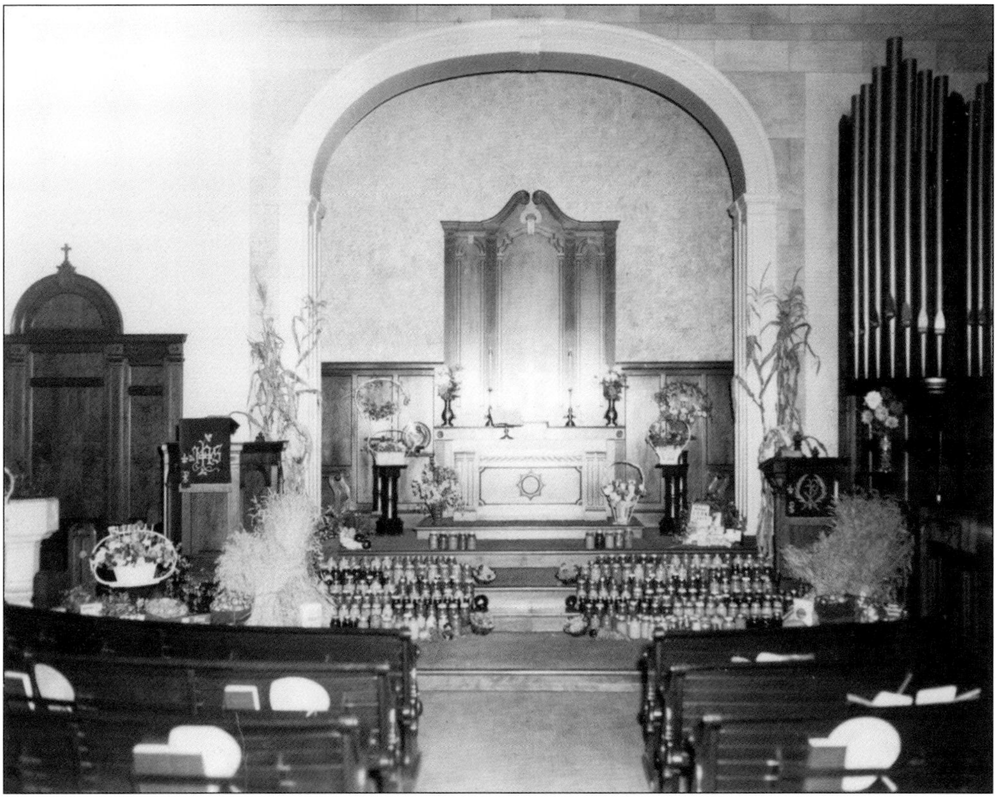

Harvest Home Display, 1944. By the time this photograph was taken in 1944, the mural had been painted over. The elaborate display of canned goods, flowers, cornstalks, and other homegrown produce was for a special Harvest Home service. This Pennsylvania German tradition was once observed by nearly all Lutheran and Reformed churches, as well as most Mennonite meetings, following the end of the grain harvest, typically in August or September. The produce was usually donated to the minister or a local charity. (Courtesy of the Historical Society of Trappe, Collegeville, Perkiomen Valley.)

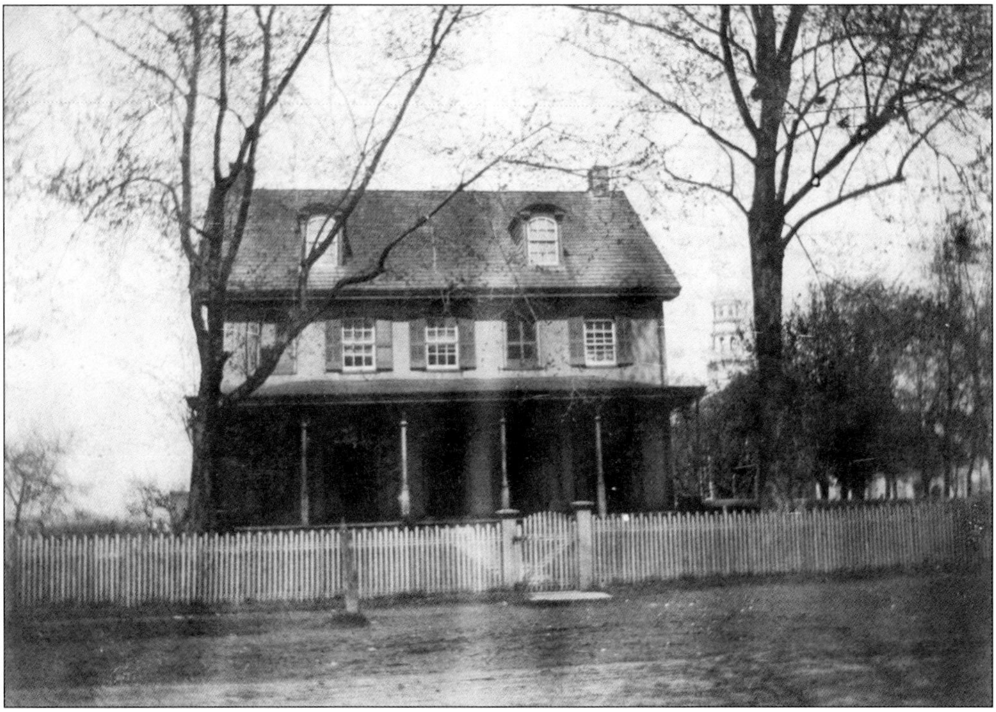

LUTHERAN PARSONAGE, C. 1890 AND 1906. In 1836, the Augustus Lutheran congregation built a permanent parsonage for its pastor, which remains in use today. The first minister to occupy the parsonage was Jacob Wampole, who served the congregation from 1837 to 1838. The parsonage was originally enclosed by a wooden picket fence, but by 1906, it had been replaced with a cast-iron fence and stone columns. (Both, courtesy of Augustus Lutheran Church.)

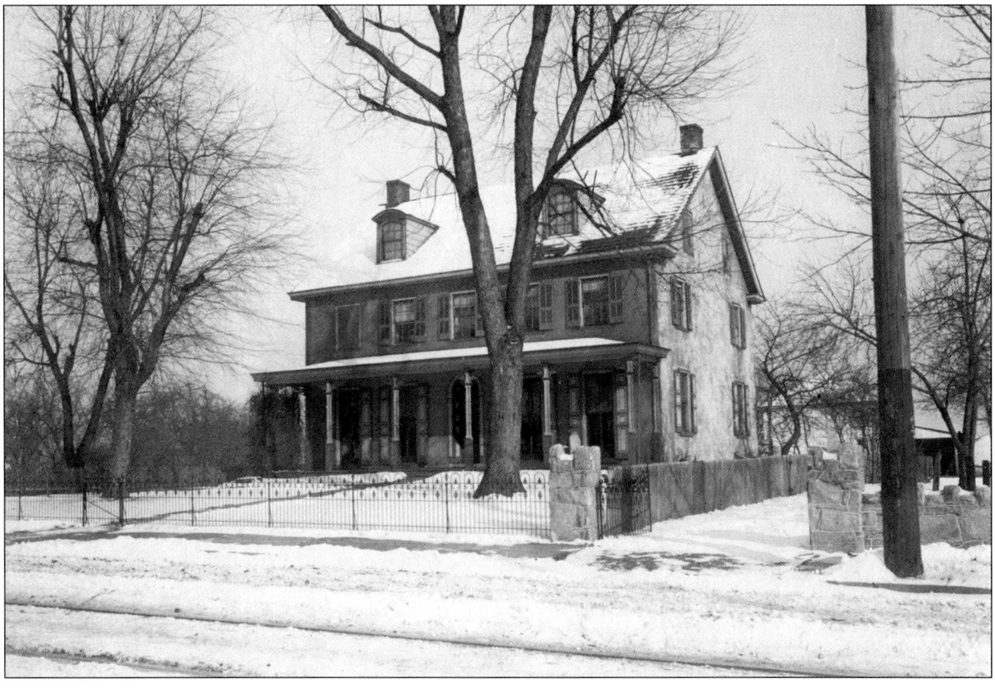

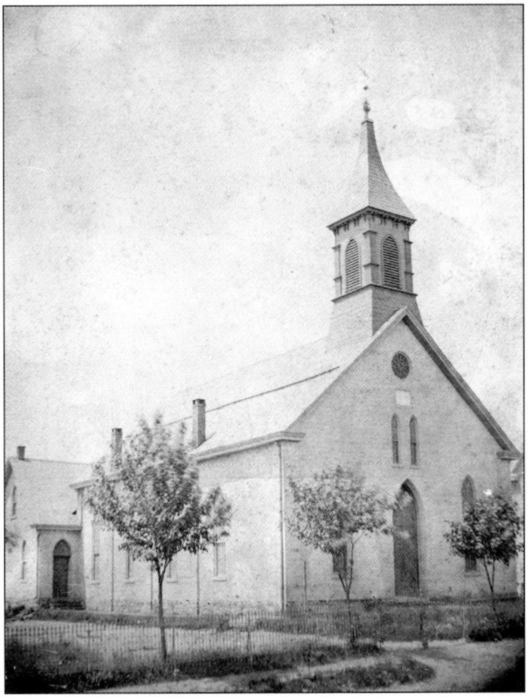

St. Luke Reformed Church, c. 1875. Founded in 1742, the St. Luke German Reformed congregation (now United Church of Christ) initially worshipped in a log church across the street in what is now the cemetery. A stone building replaced it on the same site in 1835. The present church at 200 West Main Street was erected in 1874 under the leadership of Rev. John H.A. Bomberger, founder of Ursinus College and a Reformed Church minister. This photograph was taken soon after its construction. In 1902, the iron fence was replaced by a stone wall, and the building was completely renovated two years later. (Courtesy of the Ursinus College Archives.)

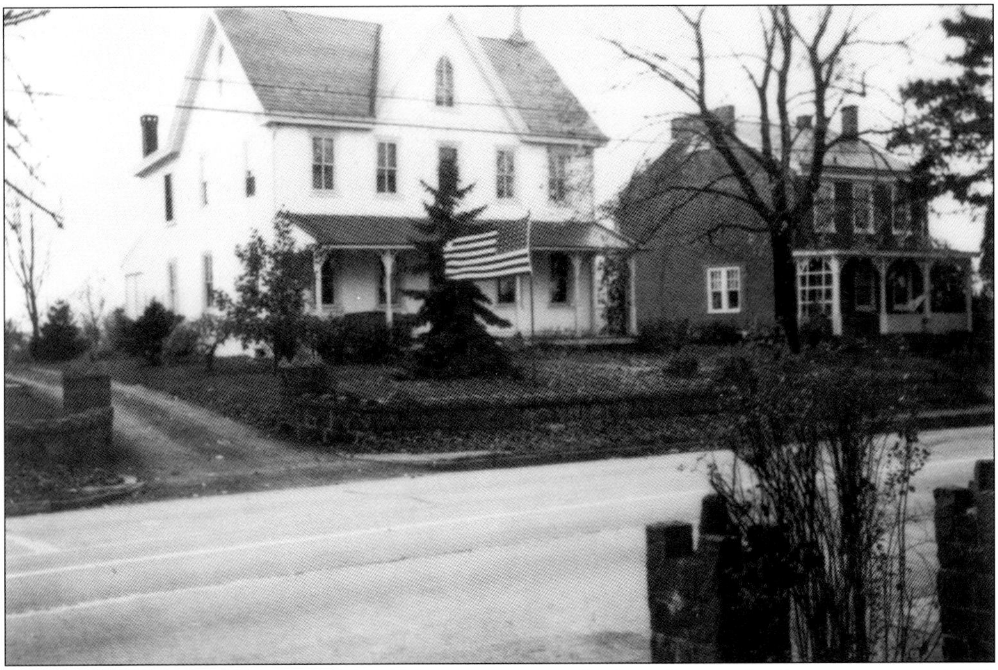

St. Luke Parsonage, 1942. The St. Luke congregation built its first and only parsonage in 1868. Rev. John H.A. Bomberger was the first minister to occupy it. The parsonage stood between the church at 200 West Main Street and the brick house at 212 West Main Street, which is visible at right and still stands. It was torn down about 1984 to make room for the construction of a new fellowship hall known as Moyer Hall. (Courtesy of the Historical Society of Trappe, Collegeville, Perkiomen Valley.)

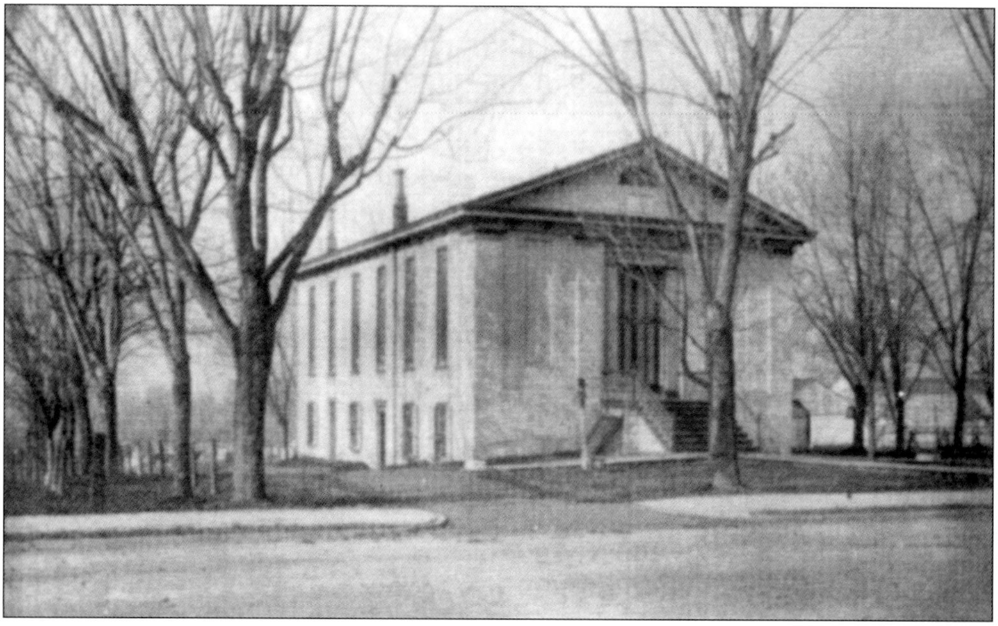

Trinity Reformed Church, c. 1874. Following a split within the Mennonite Church during the 1840s, former Mennonite bishop Abraham Hunsicker founded an independent church in 1854 that was initially called the Christian Meetinghouse at Freeland. In 1861, it became known as Trinity Christian Church. It was open to people of all Christian denominations, but in 1888, under the leadership of Rev. Joseph Hendricks, it merged with the Reformed Church, much to the dismay of Henry A. Hunsicker, son of Abraham Hunsicker and brother-in-law of Joseph Hendricks. The church played a prominent role in the abolition movement, and nearly three dozen Civil War veterans are buried in the cemetery. This c. 1874 photograph was taken after the building had been expanded 22 feet to the rear. (Courtesy of Kate Minardi.)

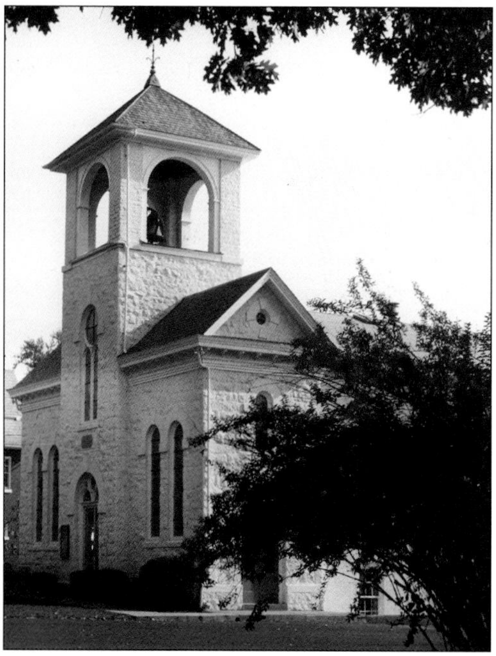

Trinity Reformed Church, c. 1965. The church was extensively remodeled in 1898, including a redesign of the facade and the construction of a bell tower; the bell itself was not installed until four years later. This photograph shows the church facade painted white, which Pastor Alfred L. Creager ordered in the 1960s to blend with the white walls of the Hendricks wing that was added to the rear in 1922. The paint was removed in 1991 to restore the original appearance of the church's stone facade. (Courtesy of the Ursinus College Archives.)

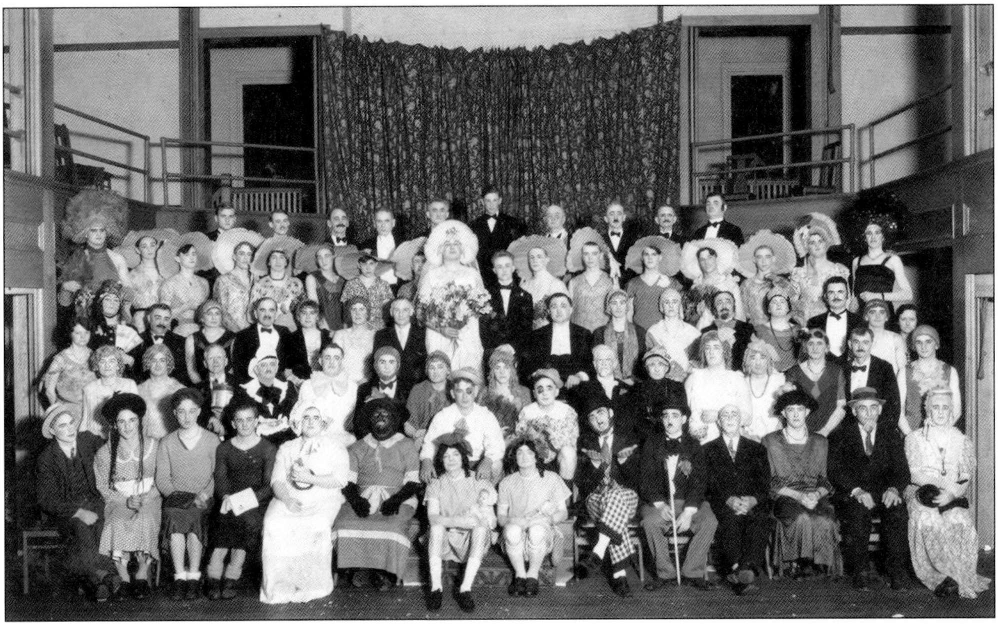

Trinity Reformed Church Theater, 1932. The Hendricks wing was designed for the use of the community and housed the first movie theater in Collegeville. The first film shown there was *Safety Last!*—a 1923 silent film comedy starring Harold Lloyd. This 1932 photograph shows the theater's interior with the cast of a so-called "Womanless Wedding," a comic performance in which male actors played all the traditional roles of a wedding party—male and female. Such plays often raised money for charitable causes or civic organizations. Dr. Samuel D. Cornish of Collegeville was the best man, and Edward Beckman of Trappe was the bride. (Courtesy of the Historical Society of Trappe, Collegeville, Perkiomen Valley.)

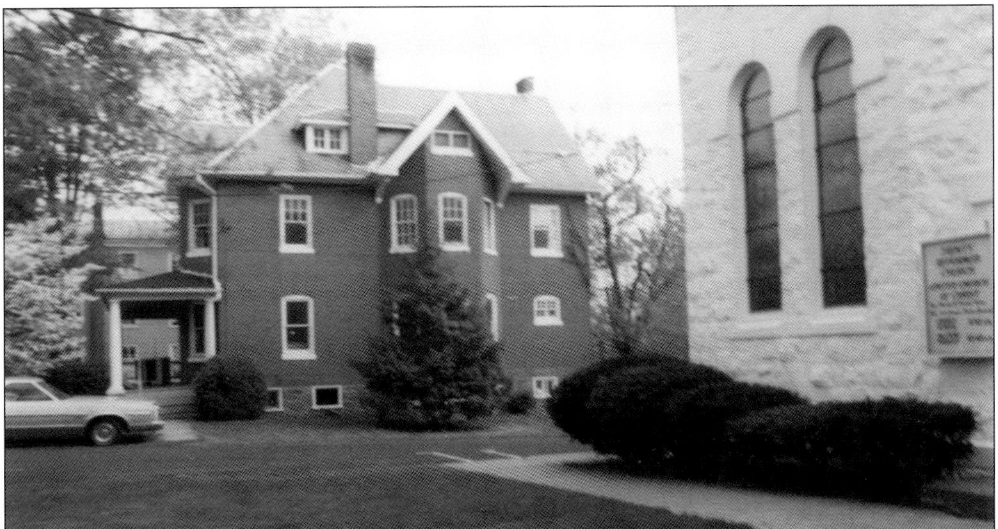

Trinity Parsonage, 1981. A brick parsonage was constructed in 1906 for Rev. Francis C. Yost, Trinity's second pastor. He served until 1911 and was succeeded by Rev. William S. Clapp. This photograph was taken in 1981, shortly before the parsonage was demolished to provide additional parking for the church. (Courtesy of the Historical Society of Trappe, Collegeville, Perkiomen Valley.)

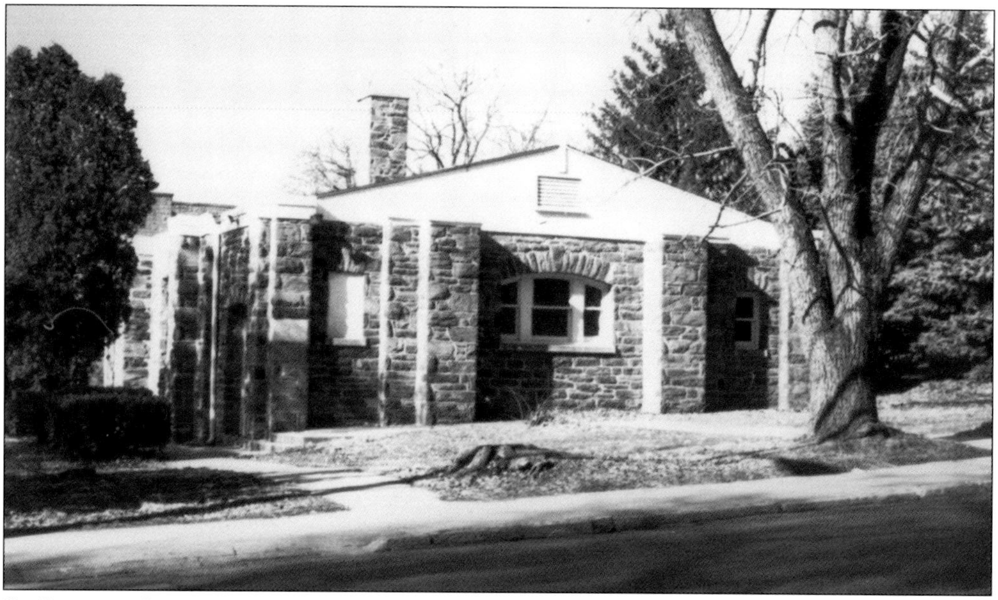

St. Eleanor Catholic Church, c. 1988. Originally known as St. Clare, this was the first Roman Catholic church in the Trappe and Collegeville area, founded by Rev. Thomas J. Sullivan in 1911. It was initially located at 416 East Main Street in Collegeville, where the house (previously owned by Dr. Edward A. Krusen) was used as a rectory and the barn behind it as its first church. The parish name was changed to St. Eleanor in 1921 after a new stone church was built; it was intended to be the basement of a larger structure, but the upper level was never built. In 1971, the congregation dedicated a much larger church at 647 Locust Street, which is still in use today. (Courtesy of the Historical Society of Trappe, Collegeville, Perkiomen Valley.)

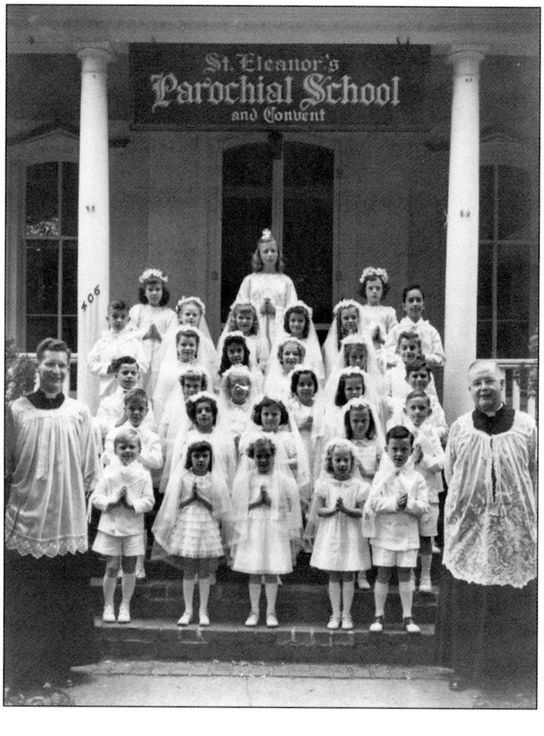

St. Eleanor's Parochial School and Convent, 1948. Under Rev. John O'Neill, the parish acquired the former Elmer Poley house at 406 East Main Street in 1942 to serve as a parochial school and convent. The school opened on February 15, 1943, with an initial enrollment of 61 students. This building was used for five years until a purpose-built school was constructed behind the church, at 416 East Main Street. The new school was dedicated on November 28, 1948. The First Holy Communion class of 1948 is pictured on the front steps of the convent school, with Rev. John Van Stone (left) and Rev. John O'Neill (right) standing to either side. (Courtesy of Jerry A. Chiccarine.)

Four

TRANSPORTATION

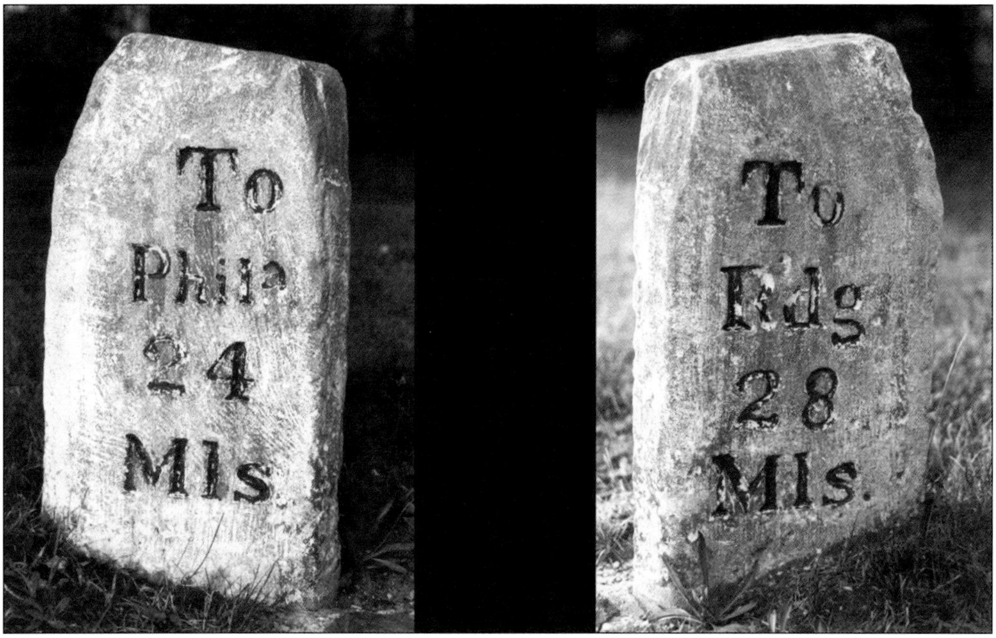

PHILADELPHIA–READING MILESTONE. This milestone, located near the Todd House (also known as Isenberg Hall) at 801 East Main Street in Collegeville notes the distance as 24 miles to Philadelphia on one side and 28 miles to Reading on the other. Trappe and Collegeville's location near the halfway point along the major thoroughfare between Philadelphia and Reading spurred the area's growth and necessitated the presence of multiple inns for travelers and teamsters. (Courtesy of the Ursinus College Archives.)

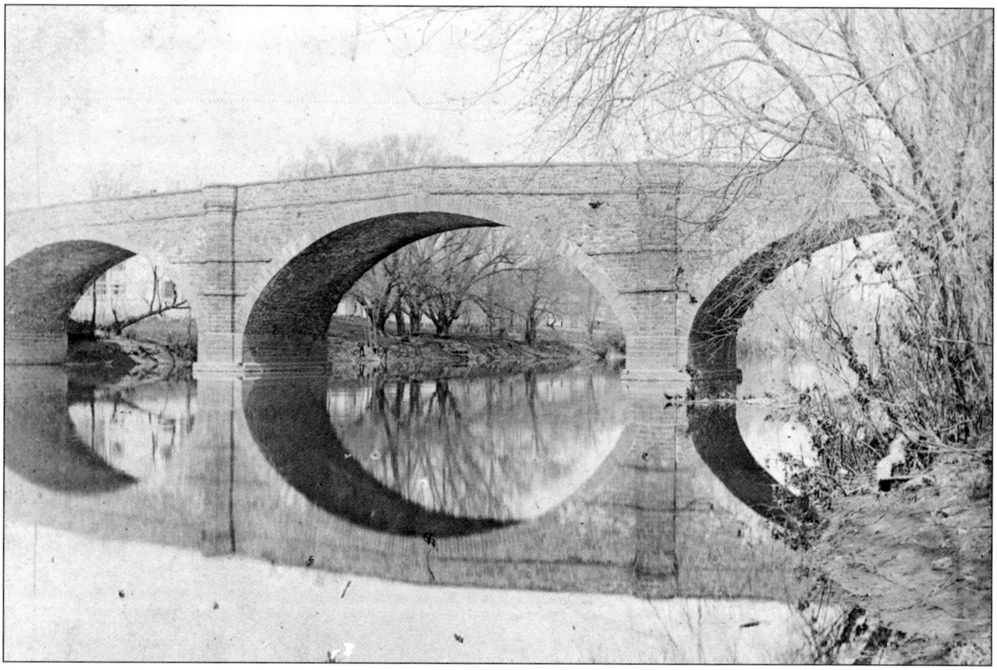

PERKIOMEN BRIDGE. Built in 1798–1799, the Perkiomen Bridge is one of the oldest stone-arch bridges still in use in the United States. Prior to its construction, people sometimes had to wait for days if the water was high or otherwise risk their lives crossing the creek. Designed and superintended by John Lewis, the bridge's masonry work was done by Samuel Beard, John Burk, Henry Priest, and John Pugh, together with carpenter George Boyer. Its six arches cover a total of 300 feet, with the center and largest arch spanning 76 feet. The north side of the bridge was widened by 15 feet in 1928 to add a third traffic lane and a sidewalk. (Courtesy of the Ursinus College Archives.)

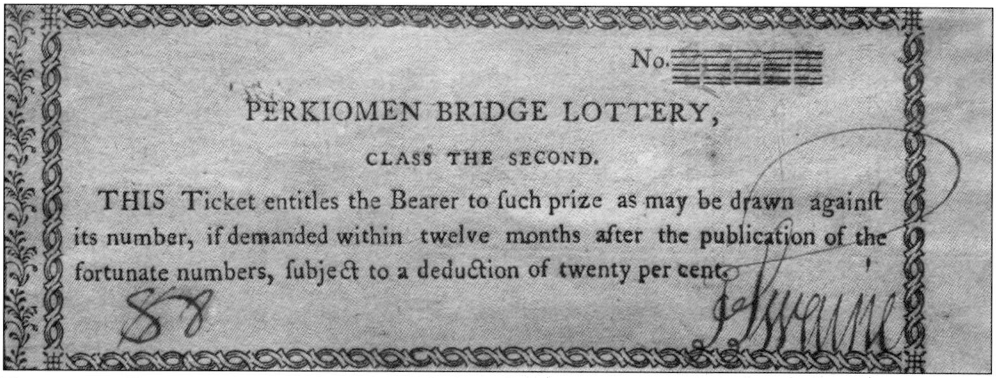

No.

PERKIOMEN BRIDGE LOTTERY,

CLASS THE SECOND.

THIS Ticket entitles the Bearer to ſuch prize as may be drawn againſt its number, if demanded within twelve months after the publication of the fortunate numbers, ſubject to a deduction of twenty per cent.

88

PERKIOMEN BRIDGE LOTTERY TICKET. To help raise funds for the bridge's construction, the state legislature approved a $20,000 lottery on February 21, 1797. Peter Muhlenberg of Trappe was appointed chairman of the finance committee; his brother-in-law, Francis Swaine, was a member of the committee and signed this lottery ticket as proof of its authenticity. The actual cost of the bridge was nearly $60,000, which was financed by the commissioners of Montgomery County, who then collected tolls to recover the expense. The toll was 2¢ each for foot passengers, 4¢ per horse or mule, 10¢ per score of hogs or sheep, and 20¢ for a score of cattle. Wheeled vehicles and sleighs were also assessed with rates from 6.25¢ for sleighs, up to 37.5¢ for four-horse vehicles. (Courtesy of Katharine and Chip Levengood.)

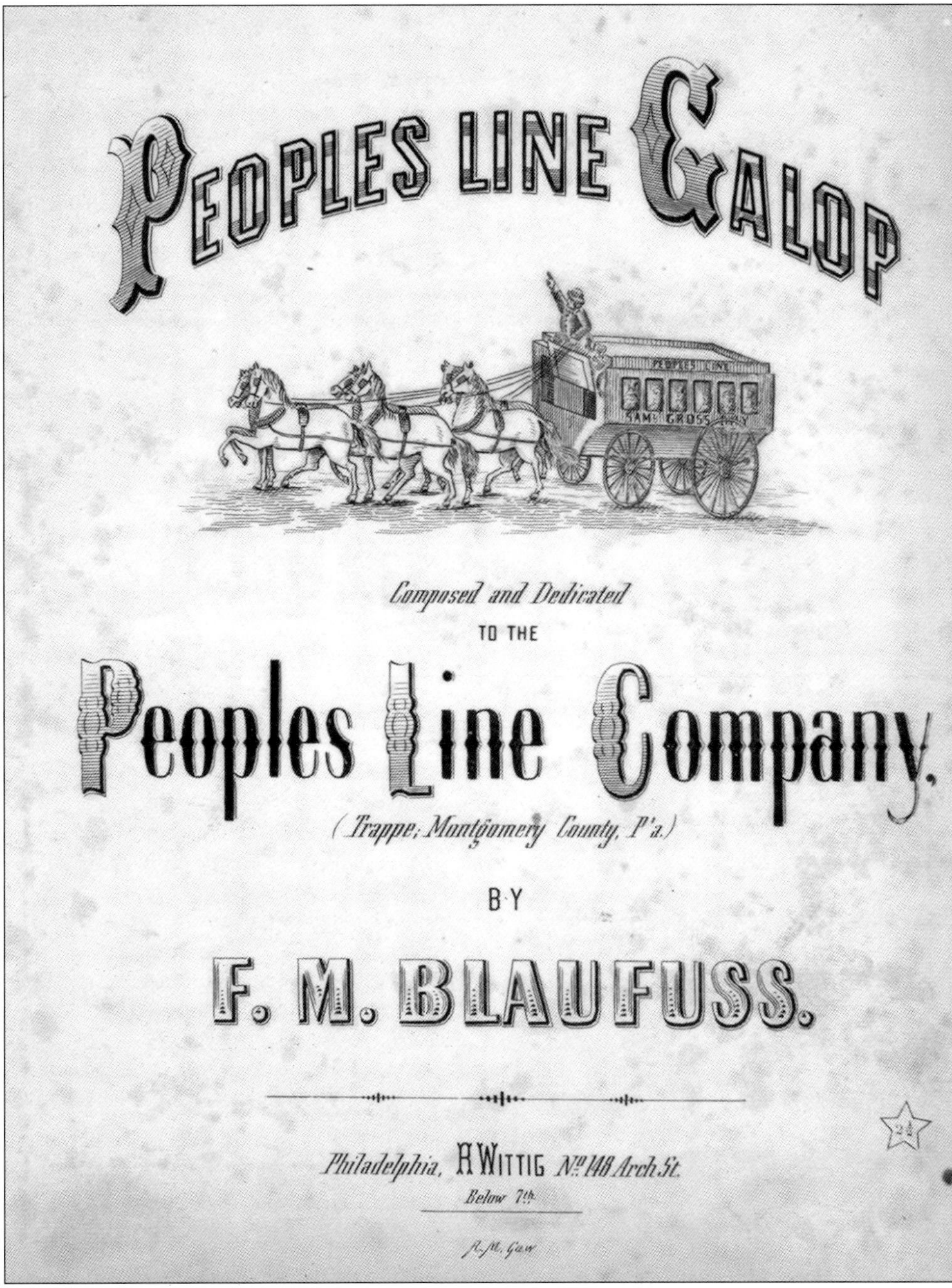

People's Line Company. Founded in July 1855, the People's Line Company was a stagecoach line that ran between Norristown and Trappe. In November 1855, it was acquired by Samuel Gross Fry, Samuel R. Shupe, and John Longstreth. The People's Line continued until 1857, when it was bought by a competing line owned by Samuel F. Hartranft of Norristown. Composer Frederick M. Blaufuss (1823–1872) wrote the "Peoples Line Galop" song and dedicated it to the company in 1856. A professor of instrumental music and music composition at the Pennsylvania Female College, Blaufuss also composed the "Glenwood Polka" in 1865. (Courtesy of the Lester S. Levy Collection of Sheet Music, Sheridan Libraries, Johns Hopkins University.)

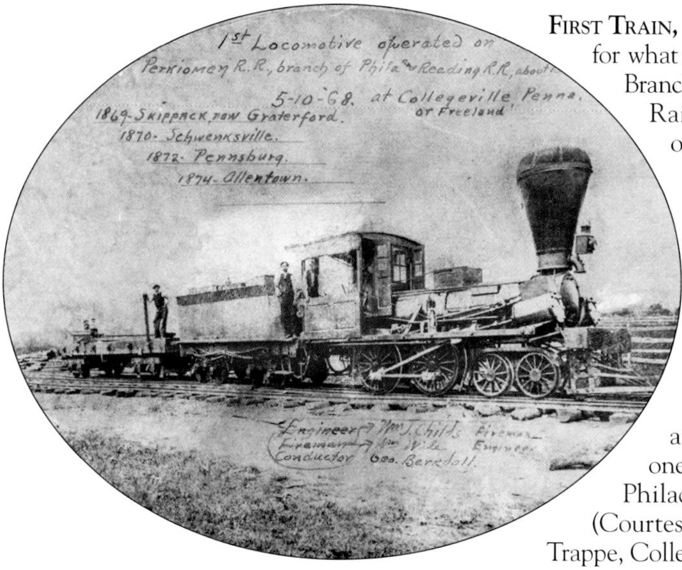

First Train, 1868. The first 10 miles of track for what would become the Perkiomen Branch of the Philadelphia & Reading Railroad were laid in 1868. The official opening of the line from Perkiomen Junction to Collegeville was on May 8, 1868. This photograph, dated May 10, 1868, shows the construction locomotive that hauled materials, such as ties and rails, to the end of the line each day as it was being built. This locomotive was built around 1842, and by 1868 was one of the oldest still in use on the Philadelphia & Reading Railroad. (Courtesy of the Historical Society of Trappe, Collegeville, Perkiomen Valley.)

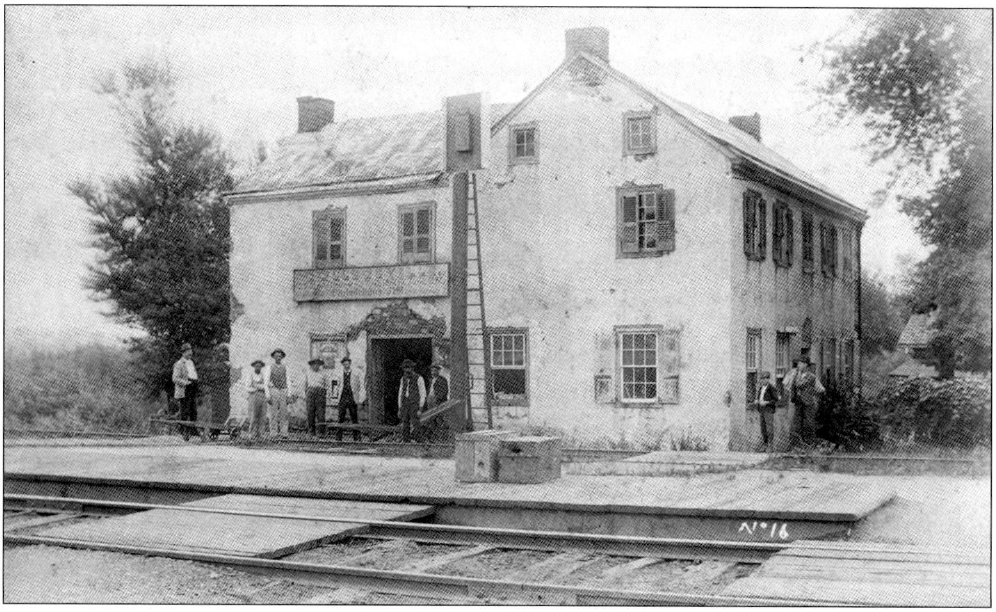

First Train Station, c. 1875. The first Collegeville train station was a c. 1840 stone house built for Adam Schrack on the site of the former mansion of Henry "Daddy" High, which burned in 1838. After the arrival of train service in 1868, the building was used as both a passenger station and freight depot. Locals complained about its poor condition, and Elwood S. Moser, editor of the *Independent*, denounced it as a "God-for-saken, ramshackle, torn-down place." Located on Main Street below the railroad tracks and next to the Railroad Hotel, the building was approved for demolition in 1892 following the completion of the new brick train station across the street in 1890. (Courtesy of the Historical Society of Trappe, Collegeville, Perkiomen Valley.)

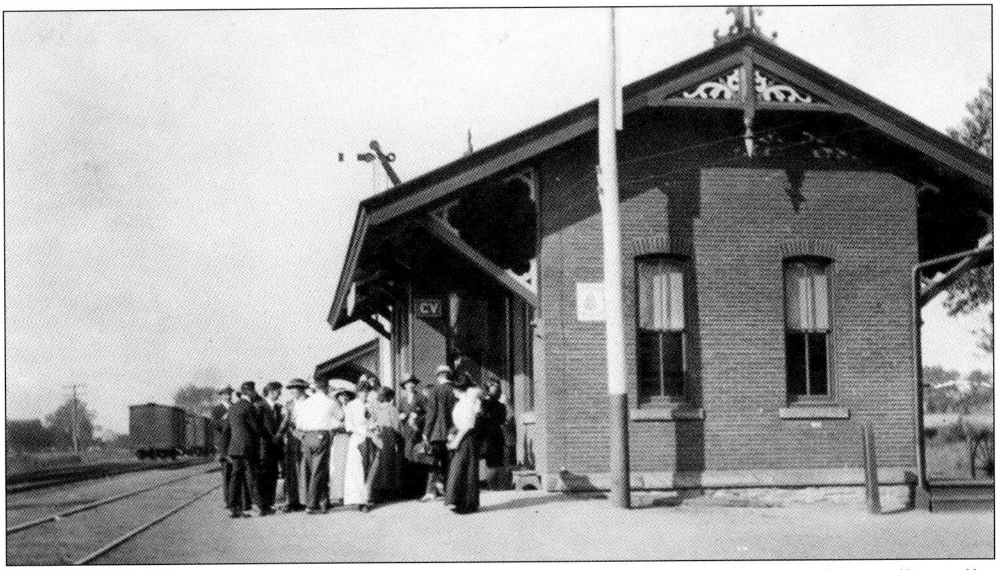

New Train Station, 1912. In 1890, a new brick train station was constructed in Collegeville. Summer tourists, local residents, and Ursinus College students were frequent passengers. Walking to the station to see a train come in was a popular college pastime. The station was used for passenger service until 1955 and housed a freight agent until 1967. The tracks above the station had been removed by 1980. After a brief period of use as a gift shop and then as an antiques store known as Freeland Studio, the station was demolished on June 22, 1984, and replaced by a Pizza Hut. The Collegeville Diner now occupies the site. (Courtesy of the Ursinus College Archives.)

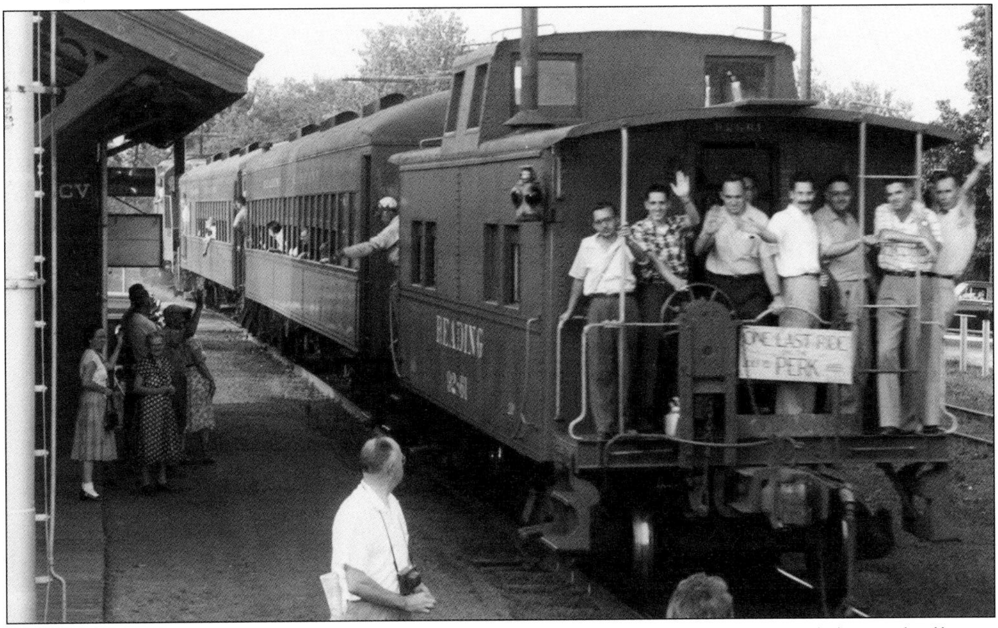

Last Train, 1955. Alternate modes of transportation, particularly the automobile, gradually put the railroad out of business. By 1947, only one passenger train ran each way daily. The last passenger train to depart from the Collegeville station was on July 15, 1955. In this photograph, which shows the final train just before its departure, the men on board hold a sign denoting the occasion as "One Last Ride on the Perk" above the date. (Courtesy of the Ursinus College Archives.)

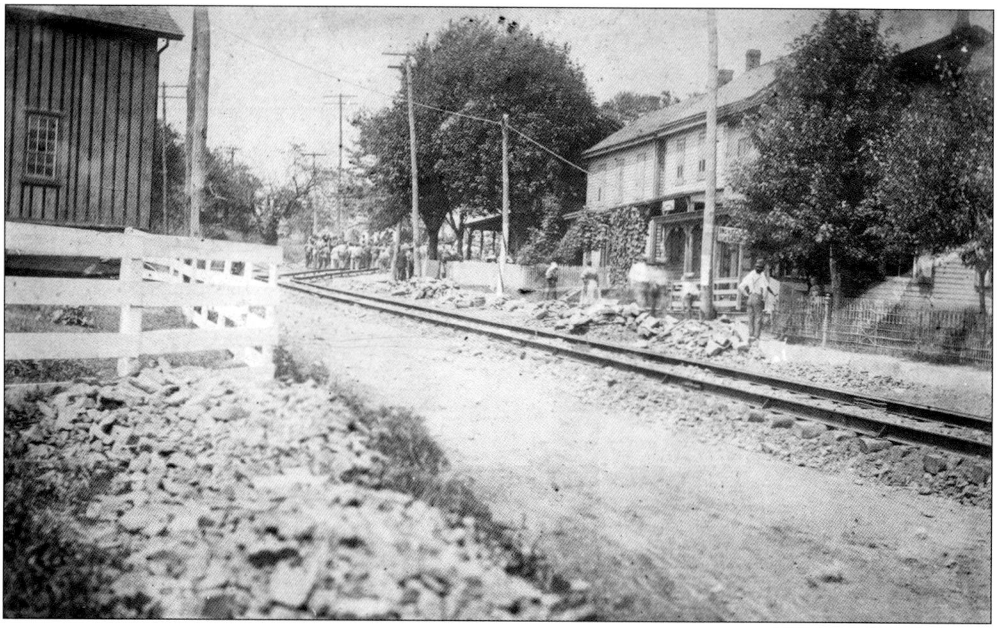

Trolley Tracks, 1897. In 1893, workers for the Schuylkill Valley Traction Company started laying tracks to extend the trolley line from Norristown to Collegeville. Four years later, the company paid $2,500 to the Borough of Collegeville for a right-of-way along Main Street to extend the line through the borough. The funds were used to straighten, widen, grade, and macadamize the street. On August 14, 1897, workers began to lay tracks through Collegeville. This required crossing the Perkiomen Railroad, to which the railroad company strongly objected. After carloads of railroad workers arrived and began pulling up the new trolley tracks, a physical brawl ensued with pick handles and shovels used as weapons. A court decision later that year ruled that the trolley tracks were permitted to cross the railroad but required the traction company to pay for a watchman. This photograph shows the tracks in Collegeville, with a glimpse of Gristock's lumberyard at left. (Courtesy of the Ursinus College Archives.)

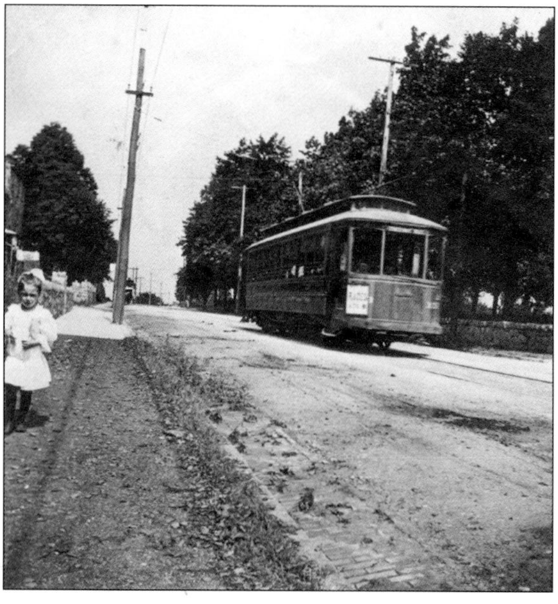

Trolley in Trappe, c. 1910. The trolley tracks were soon extended up Main Street through Trappe, with the first trolley car traveling the new line on July 18, 1901. During the process of installing the tracks, the grade of Main Street was lowered significantly in some areas, leading many property owners to build stone retaining walls to prevent erosion of their front yards. Many of these walls remain standing today and are a distinctive feature of the local streetscape. (Courtesy of the Historical Society of Trappe, Collegeville, Perkiomen Valley.)

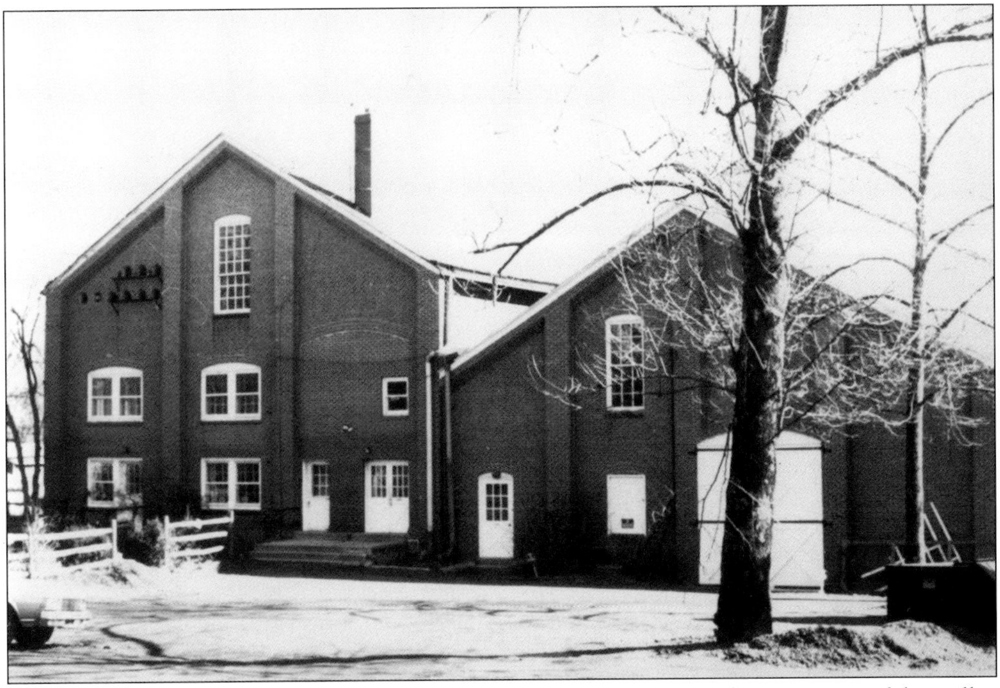

Powerhouse, c. 1988. To supply the additional electricity required by the expansion of the trolley line through Collegeville and Trappe, the Schuylkill Valley Traction Company erected a large brick powerhouse in 1901. Located at 45 First Avenue, the powerhouse had coal-fired generators that were used to supply electricity until 1918. It was then used by W.H. Gristock & Sons to store lumber, until it was purchased by Jacob Ervin "Erv" Shainline in 1970 and became a Sunday market for selling antiques and collectibles. Shainline's daughters now operate the business. (Courtesy of the Historical Society of Trappe, Collegeville, Perkiomen Valley.)

Trolley Ticket. This one-way ticket was issued by the Schuylkill Valley Traction Company between 1895 and 1910, when the company came under the control of Reading Transit & Light Company. The ticket was found in a monogrammed travel trunk given to Anna Weikel (b. 1890) by her parents prior to her departure to study at the West Chester Normal School. She later married Charles E. Wismer Sr. and moved to Trappe in 1927. (Courtesy of Matthew G. Wismer.)

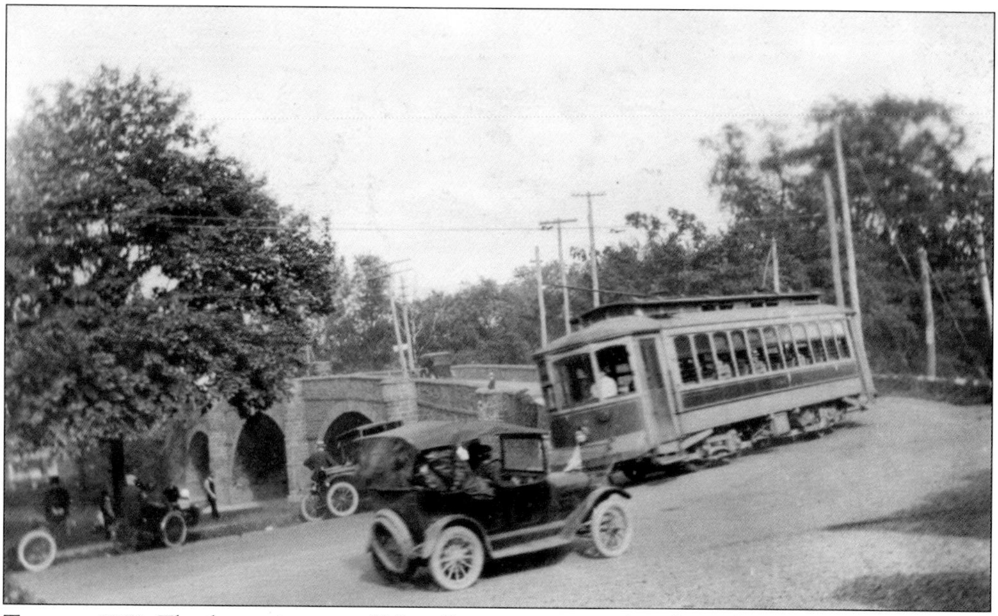

Trolley, 1921. The dramatic curve of Main Street as it approaches the Perkiomen Bridge is captured in this photograph of a trolley car crossing the bridge toward Collegeville while an automobile passes it on the right. For many years, Collegeville had an ordinance that required motorists to blow their horns when approaching the bridge. In August 1918, the *Independent* noted, "No less than 450 autos passed over the bridge between 9 a.m. and 3 p.m. and a number of drivers failed to blow their horns." (Copyright Bruce Clark; used with permission.)

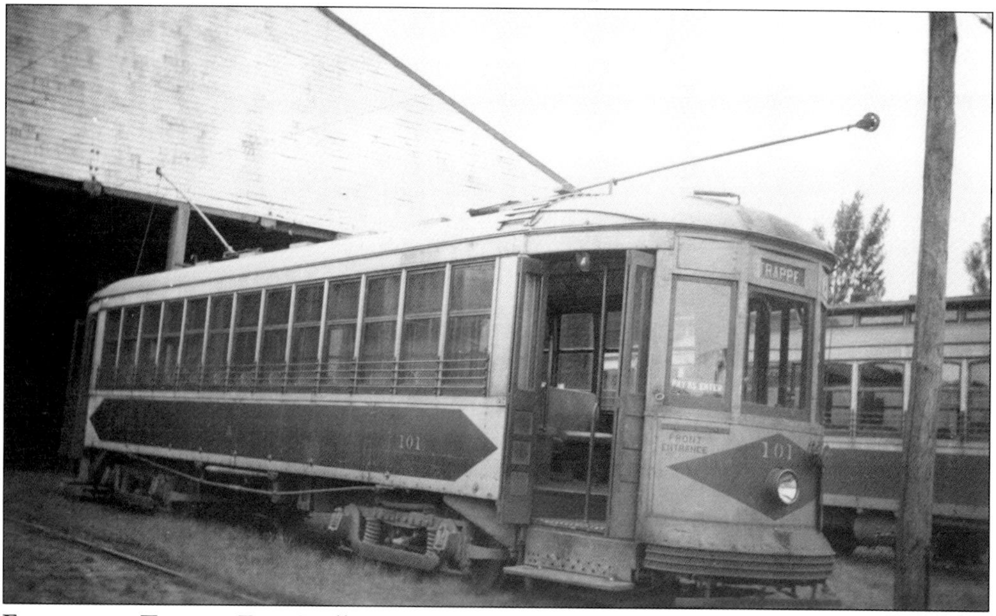

End of the Trolley Era. Trolley service was discontinued on September 9, 1933, and the trolley tracks were soon abandoned. Some of the cars were parked at the Riverside carbarn in West Norriton Township, including this one with "Trappe" still showing as its destination. The carbarn was later converted to a potato chip factory; it burned to the ground in 1944. (Courtesy of Kate Minardi.)

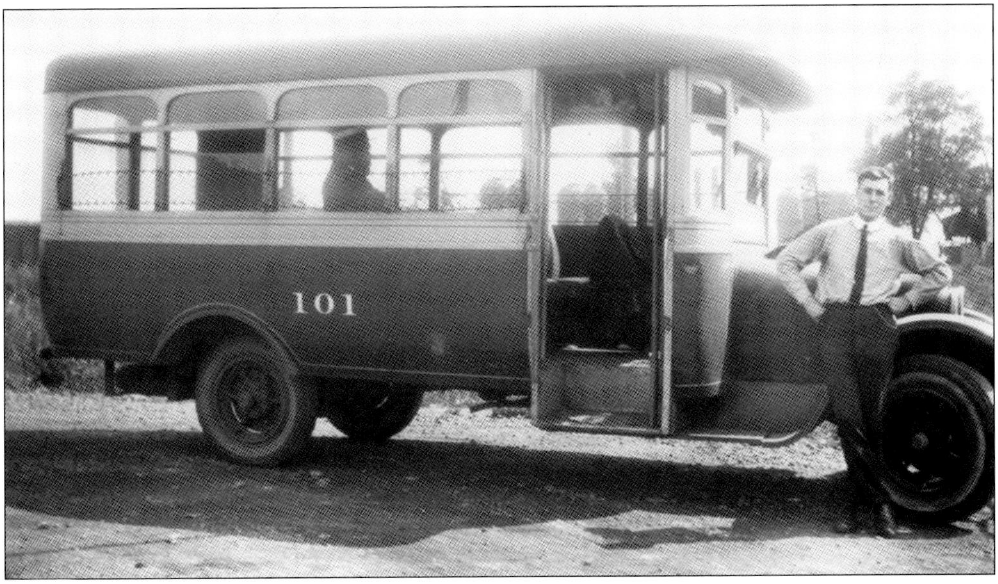

Schuylkill Valley Bus Line. The trolley was immediately replaced with a bus service known as Schuylkill Valley Lines. This photograph of Pearl P. Schrack was taken in the late 1940s at the bus stop located at the intersection of Collegeville Road and Germantown Pike. The Collegeville Inn is in the background. The Schuylkill Valley Lines bus service ended in 1975 and was replaced by buses from the Southeastern Pennsylvania Transportation Authority, or SEPTA. (Above, courtesy of the Historical Society of Trappe, Collegeville, Perkiomen Valley; below, courtesy of a private collection.)

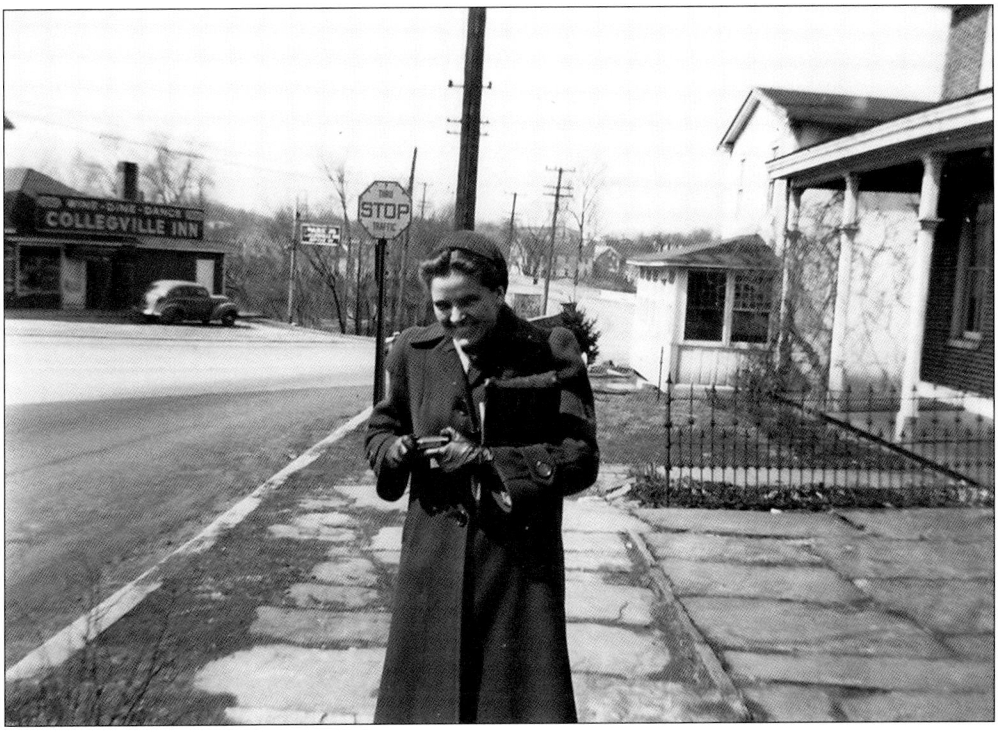

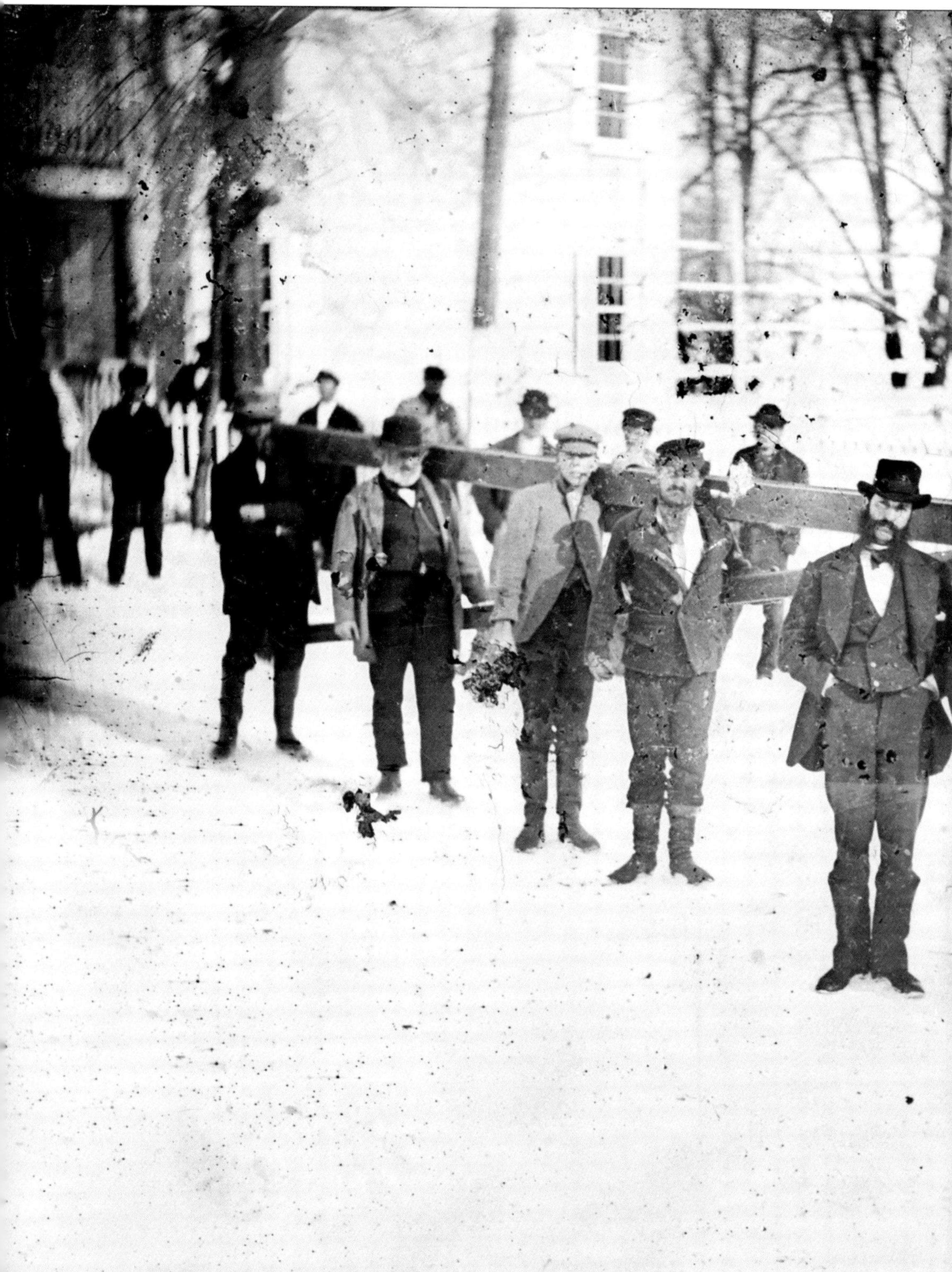

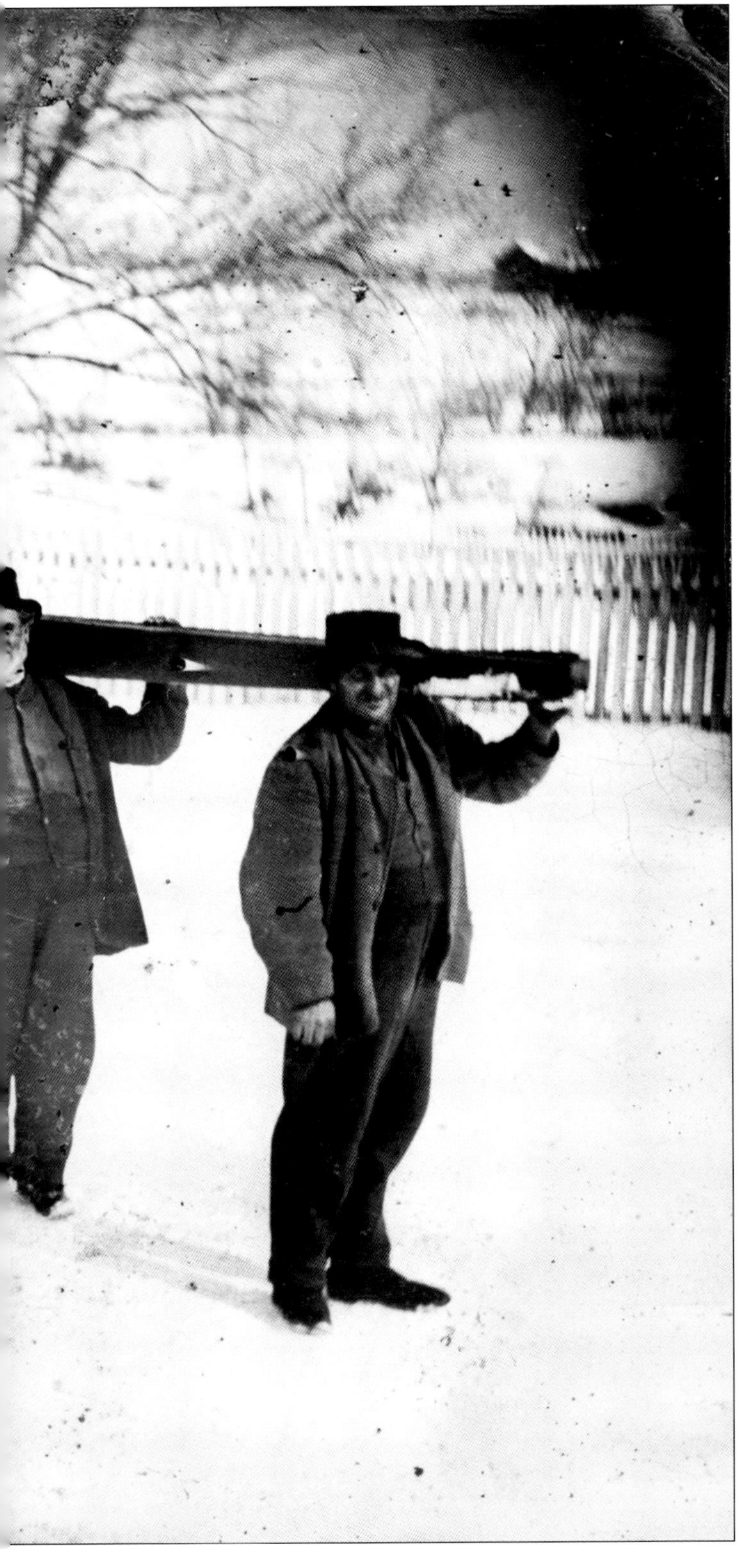

Toll Gate Removal, 1873. In 1810, the Perkiomen & Reading Turnpike Company was authorized to erect a turnpike with tollgates permitted every five miles, but specifically prohibited from erecting a tollgate within a mile of the Perkiomen Bridge. Much to the anger of local residents, the company did so anyway. In 1867, the tollhouse was burned down, and the gate was thrown into the creek. A new structure was soon erected, but on January 30, 1873, the Pennsylvania Supreme Court ruled that it was illegal. On learning of the verdict, a group of men removed the tollgate and once again threw it into the Perkiomen Creek. They are identified in an accompanying note as William Roberts, farmer; Jack Robinson, liquor dealer; Harry Schenk, storekeeper; L. Ingram, auctioneer; Jackson Shambough, farmer; "Colonel" Johnson, farmer; Abel Fox, paperhanger; Willard Brinton, farmer; Jacob Brunner, blacksmith; and David Longaker, hotelkeeper. (Courtesy of the Historical Society of Trappe, Collegeville, Perkiomen Valley.)

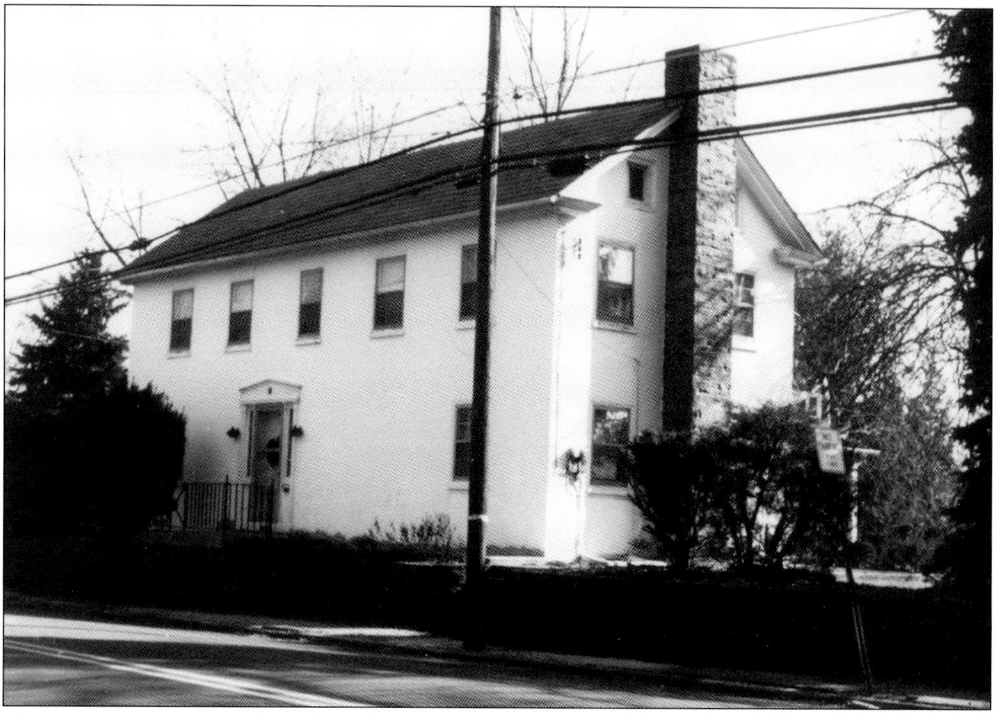

TOLLHOUSE, c. 1988. Built in the early 1800s, this stone dwelling was the first tollhouse in Trappe. The building still stands at 12 West Main Street. In the 1820s, John Todd was the gatekeeper. (Courtesy of the Historical Society of Trappe, Collegeville, Perkiomen Valley.)

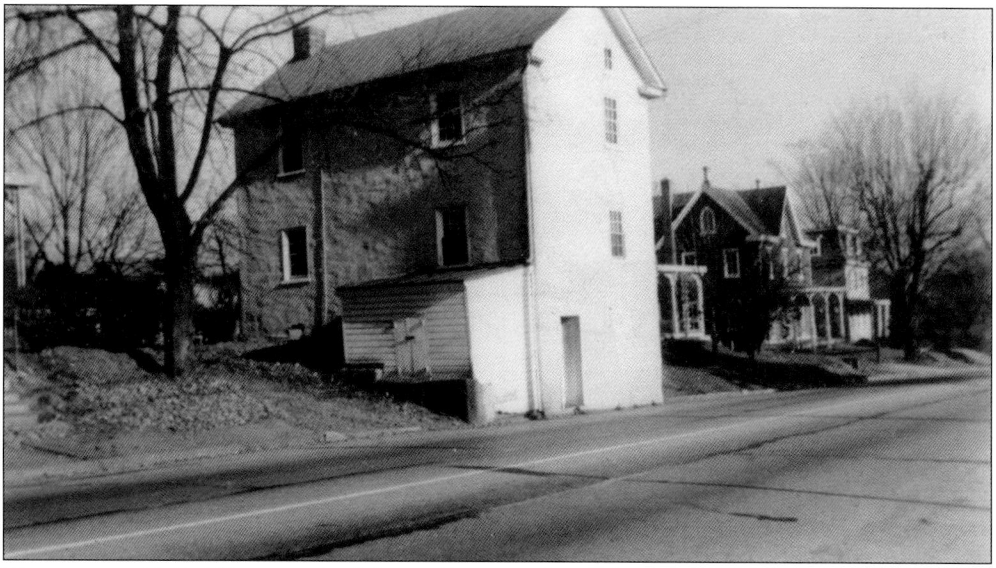

TOLLHOUSE, 1941. The arrival of the trolley was the end of the toll road era in Trappe and Collegeville. To prepare for the trolley line's extension from Collegeville, Trappe abolished the designation of Main Street as a toll road in 1900. This tollhouse remained standing until 1941, when the borough acquired it in order to demolish the building and widen Main Street. It was located on the borough line between what is now 955 East Main Street in Collegeville and 1 West Main Street in Trappe. (Courtesy of Richard A. Holcombe.)

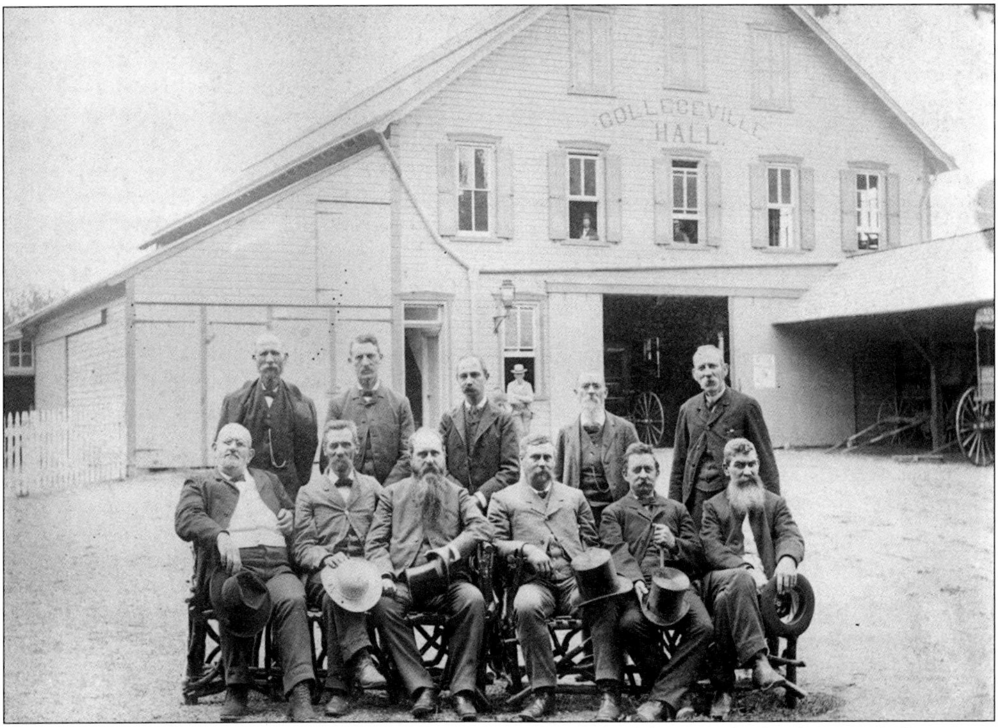

From Carriages to Automobiles. The two-story frame building in the background above was a carriage works, probably located near the Collegeville train station. Note the large sliding door on the lower level through which a carriage can be seen inside the building; two more carriages are parked under the shed-roof structure at right. The upper level of the building is painted with the words "Collegeville Hall," suggesting it was also used as a meeting place. It may be the "Agricultural Hall" indicated on the 1877 Montgomery County atlas as located in Collegeville between the post office and train station. By the time the photograph below was taken in the 1930s, the building had been converted to an automobile repair shop and gas station. (Above, courtesy of Robert L. Brant; below, courtesy of the J. Howard Fenstermacher Collection.)

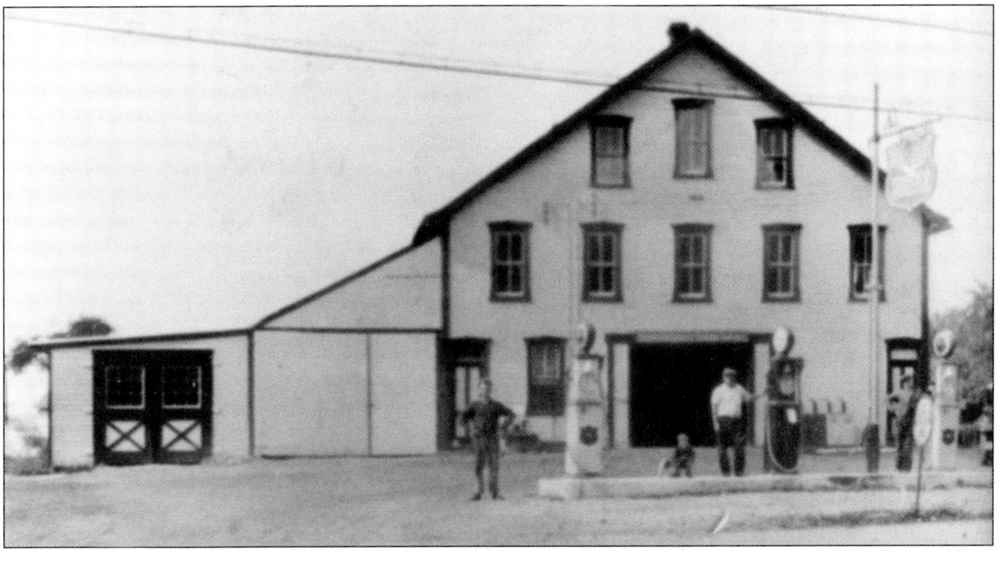

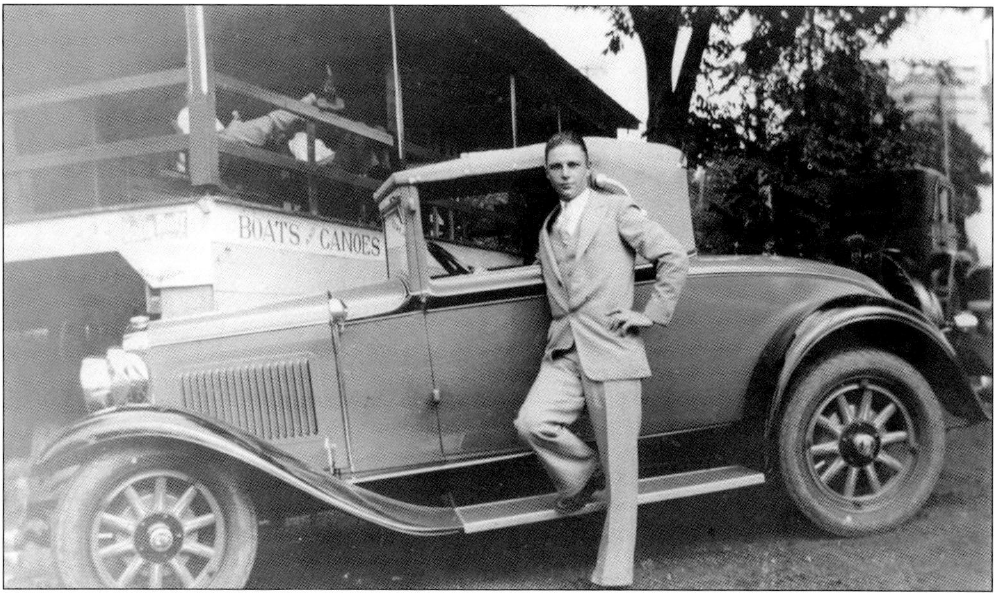

CARL ESPENSHIP, C. 1930. Better known by his nickname "Caddie," Carl Espenship is listed as a 29-year-old resident of Trappe Borough in the 1940 census. His parents were Abram and Mary (Alderfer) Espenship. The sporty automobile he is standing beside in this photograph is a c. 1929 Nash Coupe Cabriolet. (Courtesy of the Historical Society of Trappe, Collegeville, Perkiomen Valley.)

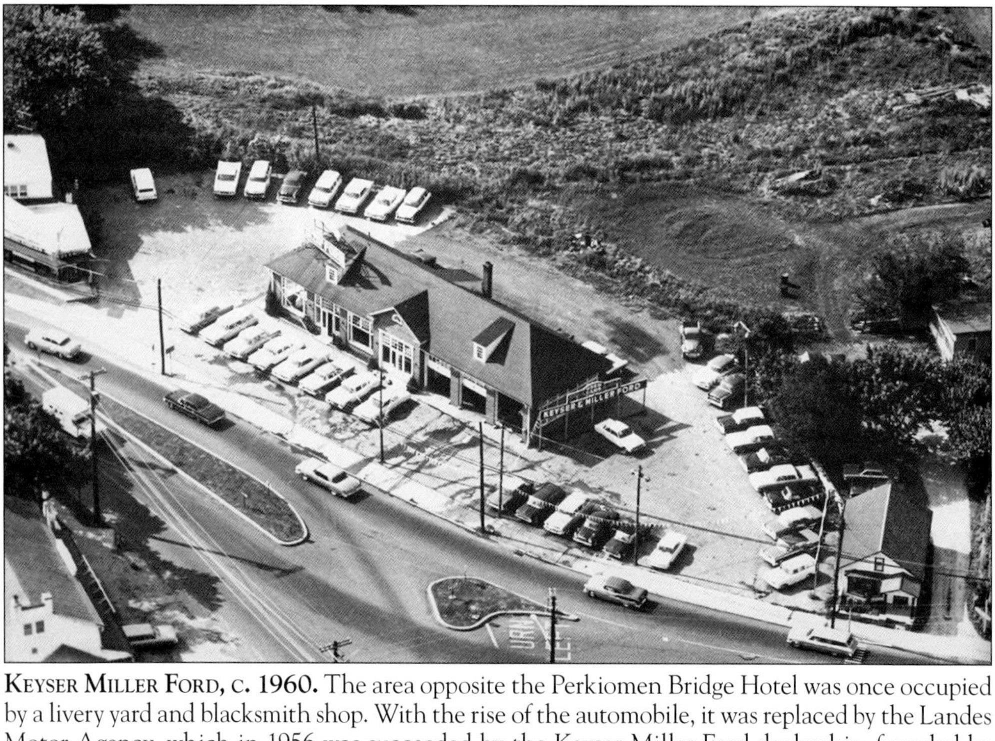

KEYSER MILLER FORD, C. 1960. The area opposite the Perkiomen Bridge Hotel was once occupied by a livery yard and blacksmith shop. With the rise of the automobile, it was replaced by the Landes Motor Agency, which in 1956 was succeeded by the Keyser Miller Ford dealership, founded by Howard Keyser and still in operation today. (Courtesy of a private collection.)

Five

Business and Industry

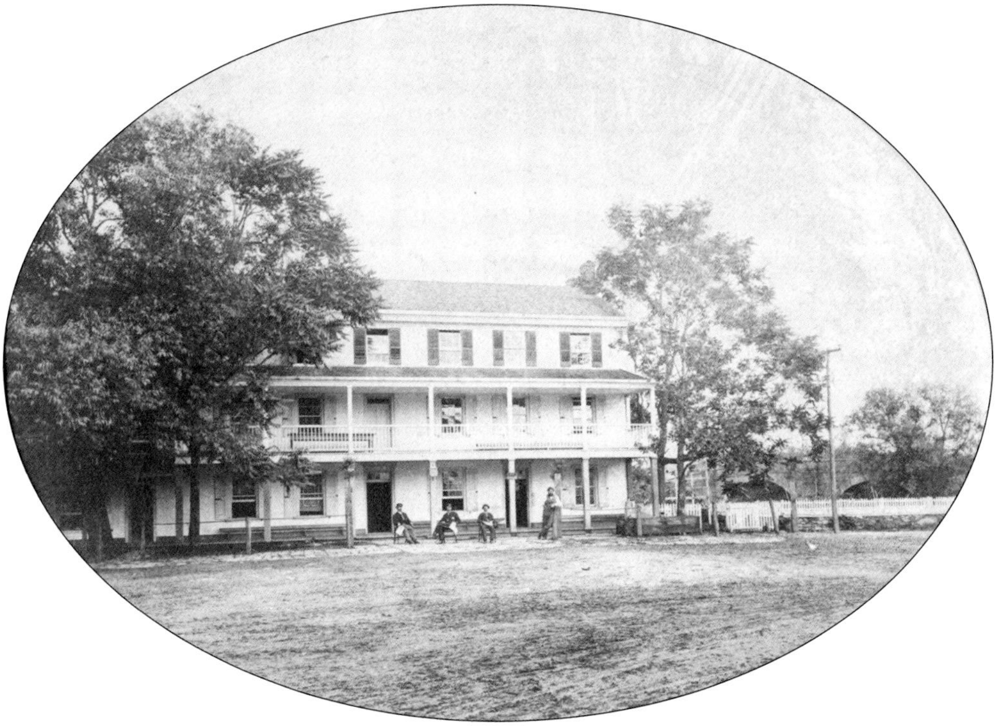

Perkiomen Bridge Hotel, c. 1900. The Perkiomen Bridge Hotel has greeted travelers for more than three centuries. According to local tradition, it is the oldest extant hotel in the country, and the oldest portion was built for Edward Lane around 1701. The building is located on the west bank of the Perkiomen Creek where Germantown and Ridge Pikes converge at a shallow crossing once known as Philip's Ford; not until the completion of the Perkiomen Bridge in 1799 did the hotel get its present name. By 1798, the tavern consisted of a two-story stone building measuring 33 by 25 feet, with a one-story stone kitchen of 30 by 20 feet. It was further expanded in the 1800s, and because of its location along the Perkiomen Creek, it became a fashionable hotel and summer resort for boating, swimming, and fishing. (Courtesy of Robert L. Brant.)

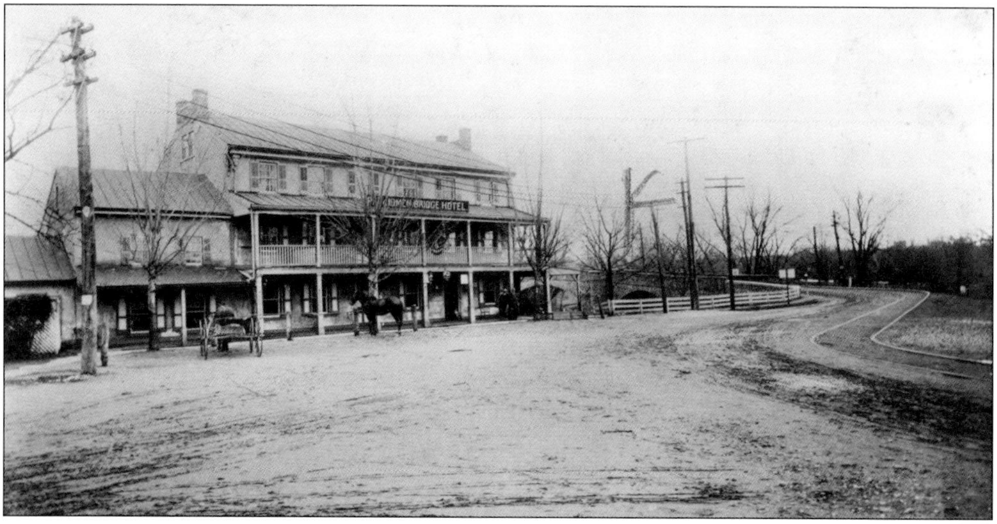

Perkiomen Bridge Hotel, c. 1910. Tensions between local residents and the hotel's clientele waxed and waned over the years. In 1899, the Collegeville Borough Council threatened to revoke its license, complaining that the hotel had become a "public nuisance" whose patrons were "disreputable parties who indulge in shouting, whooping, pounding of drums, using profane and improper language and drunkenness to an extent that it has become a source of annoyance to the citizens of the town." (Courtesy of the Historical Society of Trappe, Collegeville, Perkiomen Valley.)

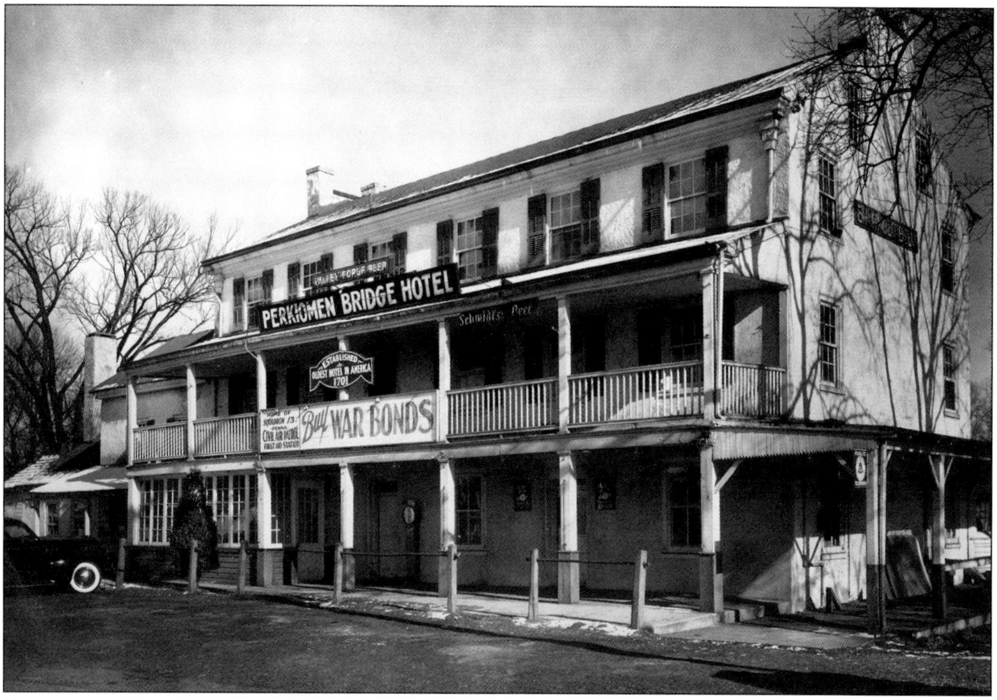

Perkiomen Bridge Hotel, c. 1942. Over the years, proprietors of the Perkiomen Bridge Hotel have included Jack Sheppard, William F.A. Titus, John E. Martin, and Charlie Bender; Linwood Yost after 1937; and brothers Samuel and Anthony Chiccarine in 1945. In this photograph, a banner urging people to "Buy War Bonds" hangs from the hotel's front porch during World War II. (Courtesy of Jerry A. Chiccarine.)

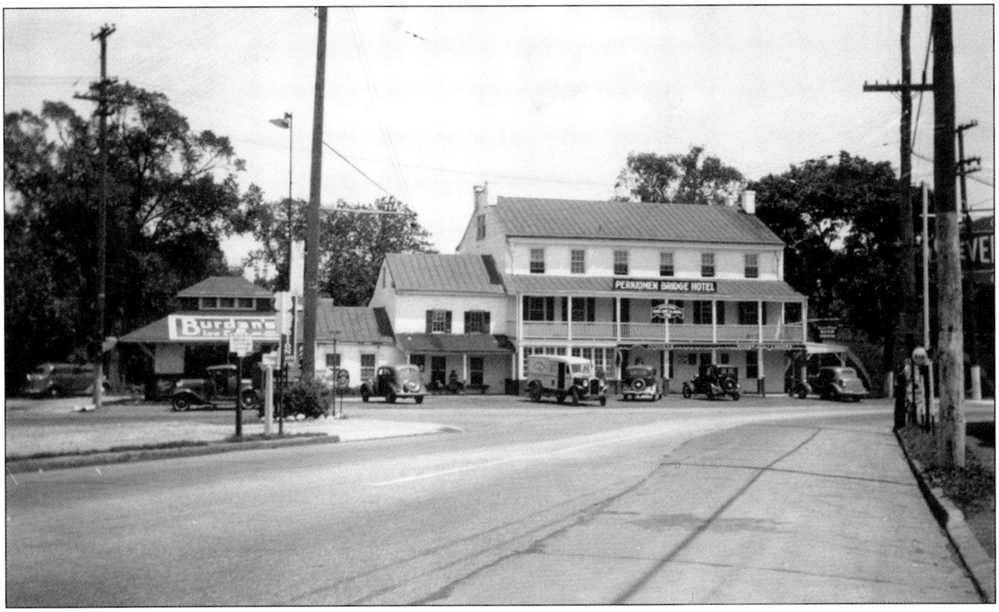

Perkiomen Bridge Hotel Snack Bar, c. 1935. By the early 1930s, the Perkiomen Bridge Hotel had opened an ice cream stand and snack bar adjacent to the main building. In this photograph, a sign on the snack bar's roof advertises Burdan's ice cream. A local favorite, Burdan's was founded in nearby Pottstown in 1899. Another photograph taken in 1933 shows the building with a sign reading "Perkiomen Bridge Hotel Snack Bar / Flavorite Ice Cream." (Courtesy of Jerry A. Chiccarine.)

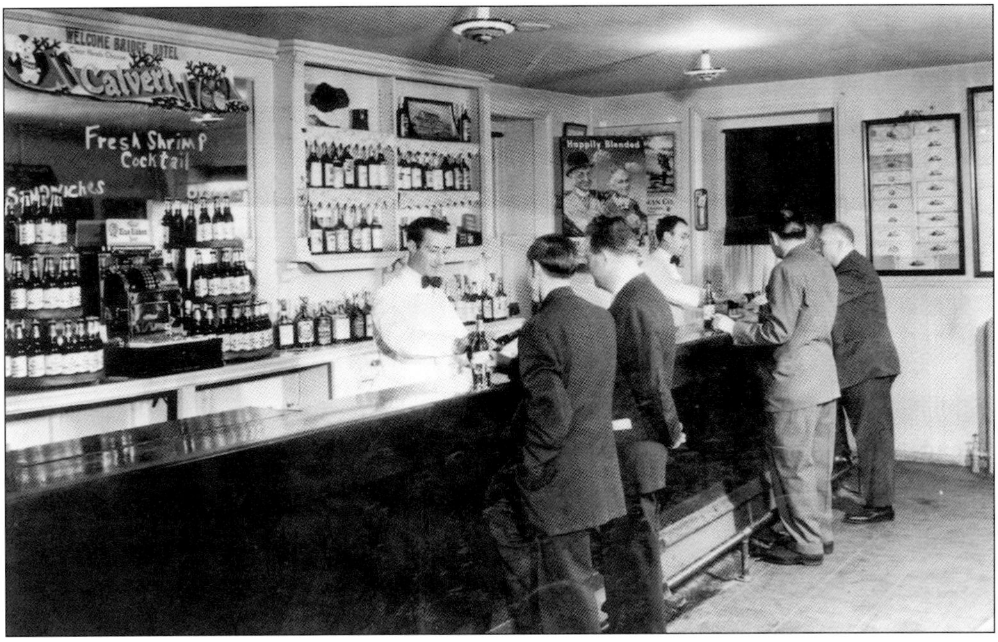

Perkiomen Bridge Hotel Barroom, c. 1950. The bartender at left is Anthony Chiccarine, who acquired the hotel in 1945, together with his brother Samuel Chiccarine at right behind the bar. Anthony left the partnership in 1956, and Samuel operated the hotel until 1974, when his sons Samuel Jr. and Louis took over the establishment. They owned it until the early 1980s, when the hotel was sold out of the Chiccarine family. (Courtesy of Jerry A. Chiccarine.)

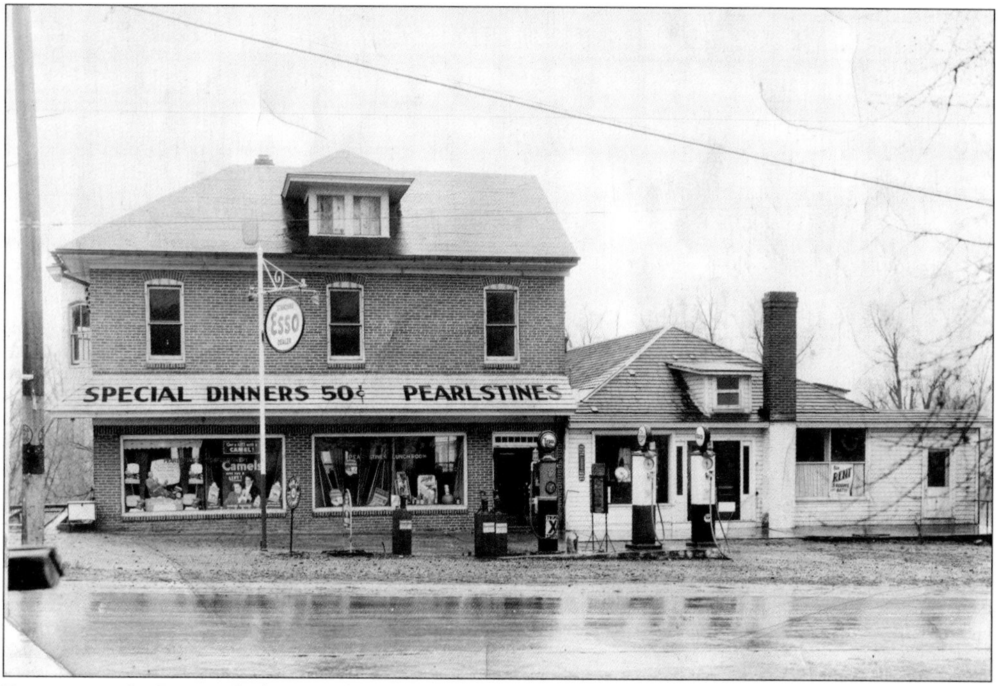

PEARLSTINE'S. Located along Ridge Pike and the Perkiomen Creek, just over the Collegeville border with Lower Providence Township, Pearlstine's was a popular attraction for locals and tourists alike. It boasted an amusement hall, theater, and refreshments, as well as a boat landing and rental cottages. (Courtesy of Jerry A. Chiccarine.)

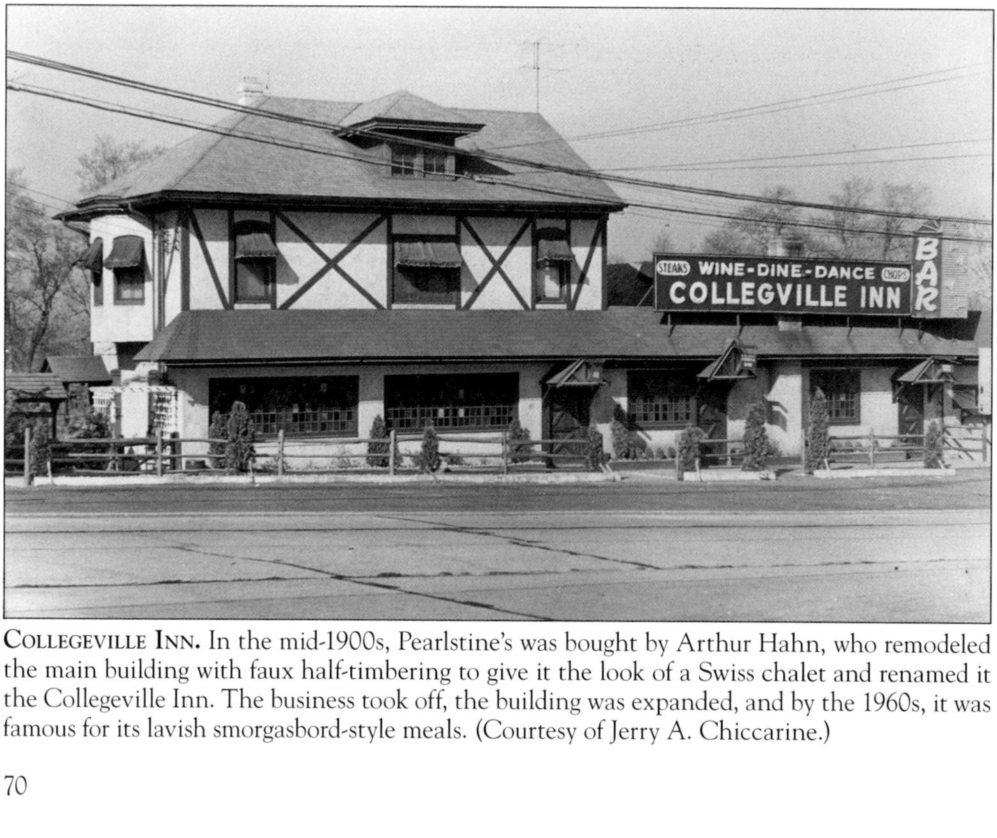

COLLEGEVILLE INN. In the mid-1900s, Pearlstine's was bought by Arthur Hahn, who remodeled the main building with faux half-timbering to give it the look of a Swiss chalet and renamed it the Collegeville Inn. The business took off, the building was expanded, and by the 1960s, it was famous for its lavish smorgasbord-style meals. (Courtesy of Jerry A. Chiccarine.)

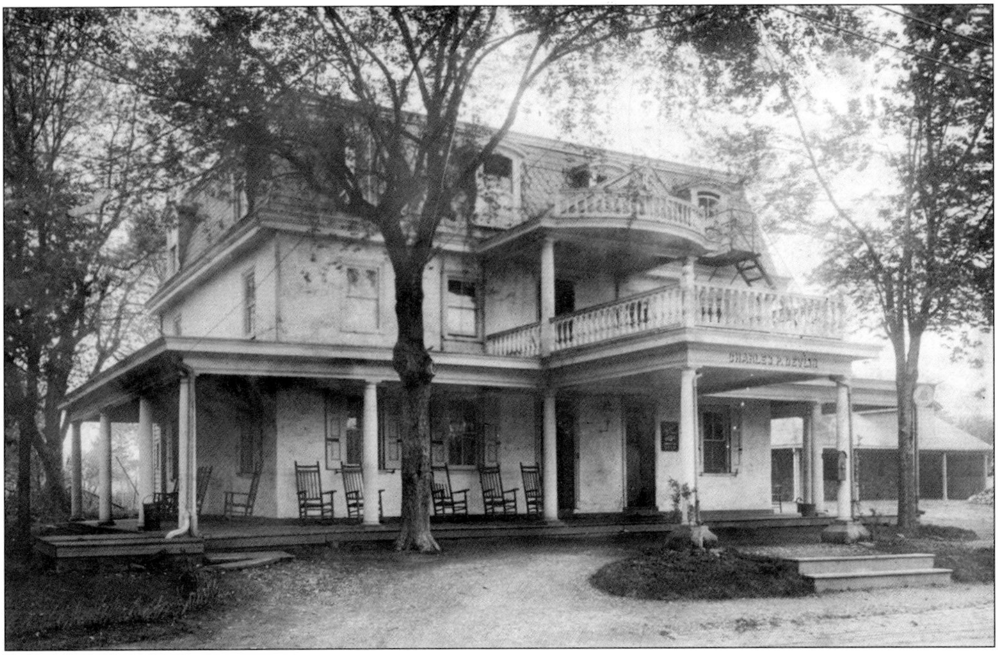

LAMB HOTEL, 724 WEST MAIN STREET. Located across from Augustus Lutheran Church, the Lamb Hotel was built around 1800. One of the first proprietors was Cornelius Tyson Sr. In 1836, it was bought by schoolmaster and future US congressman Jacob Fry Jr. (or "Honest Jacob") and described in the deed as a "certain Tavern stand, Sign of the Golden Lamb." A multitiered front porch was added during the Victorian era and remained through the tenure of Charles P. Devlin, an Irish innkeeper who moved from Philadelphia to Trappe around 1910. The porch was long gone by the time the photograph below was taken in 1976. (Above, courtesy of Jerry A. Chiccarine; below, courtesy of the Historical Society of Trappe, Collegeville, Perkiomen Valley.)

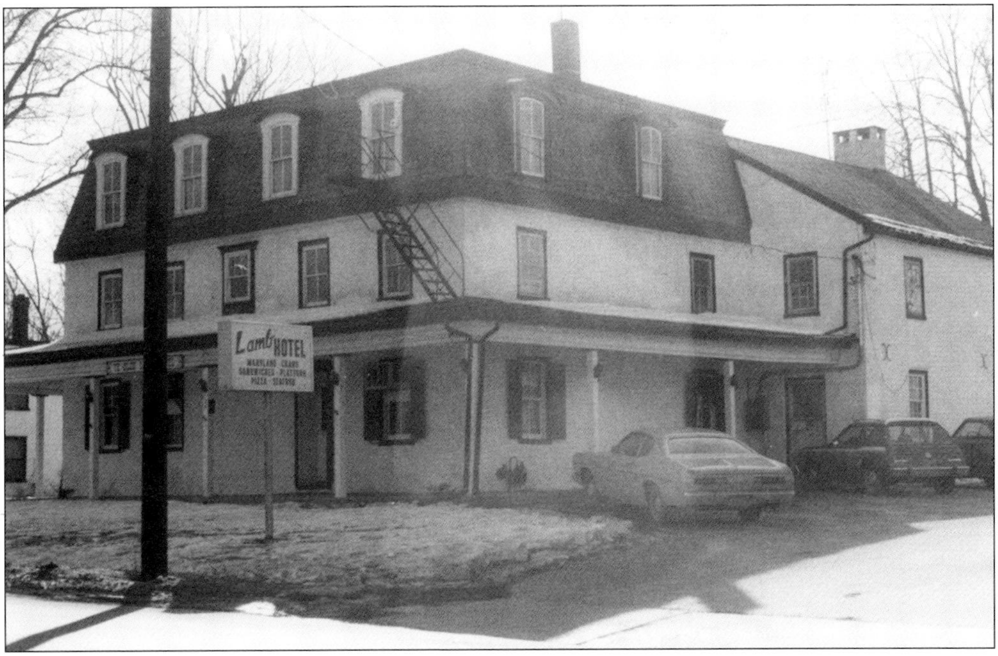

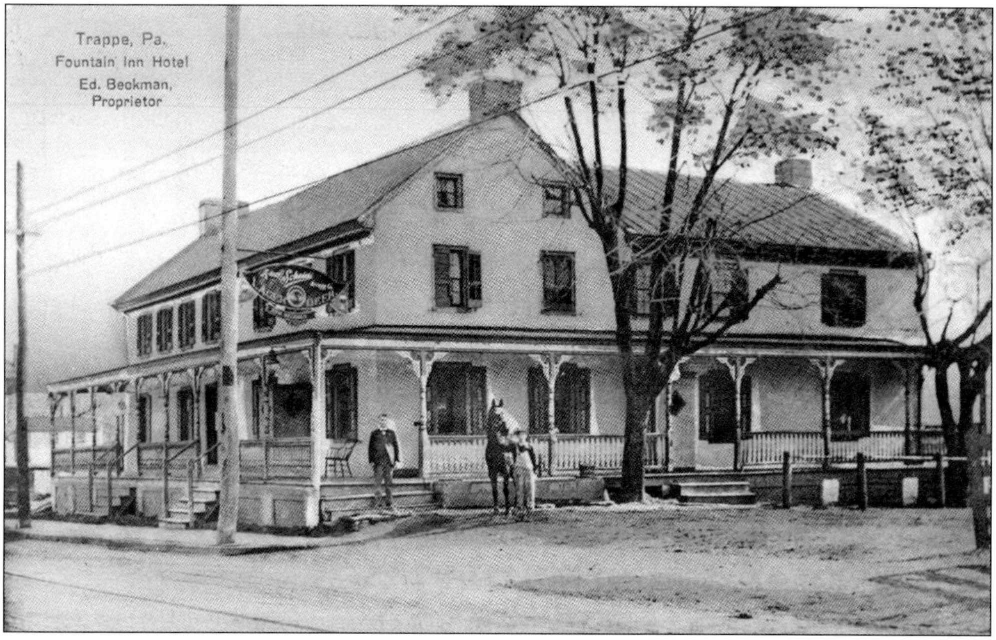

TRAPPE TAVERN, C. 1910. Originally known as the Fountain Inn, this building has served as a tavern since it was established in the late 1700s. By 1823, the inn's barn, sheds, and stables could accommodate up to 75 wagons and 150 horses. A nearby spring (described as the "Big Spring" in an 1821 deed) provided water via underground wooden pipes to a distillery and the inn, which had three fountain pumps in the yard for watering thirsty horses. Traces of the spring remain in the pond located at nearby Rambo Park. During the tenure of Edward Beckman, from 1897 to 1930, the tavern was advertised as a "drover's headquarters" with "first-class accommodations." (Both, courtesy of Jerry A. Chiccarine.)

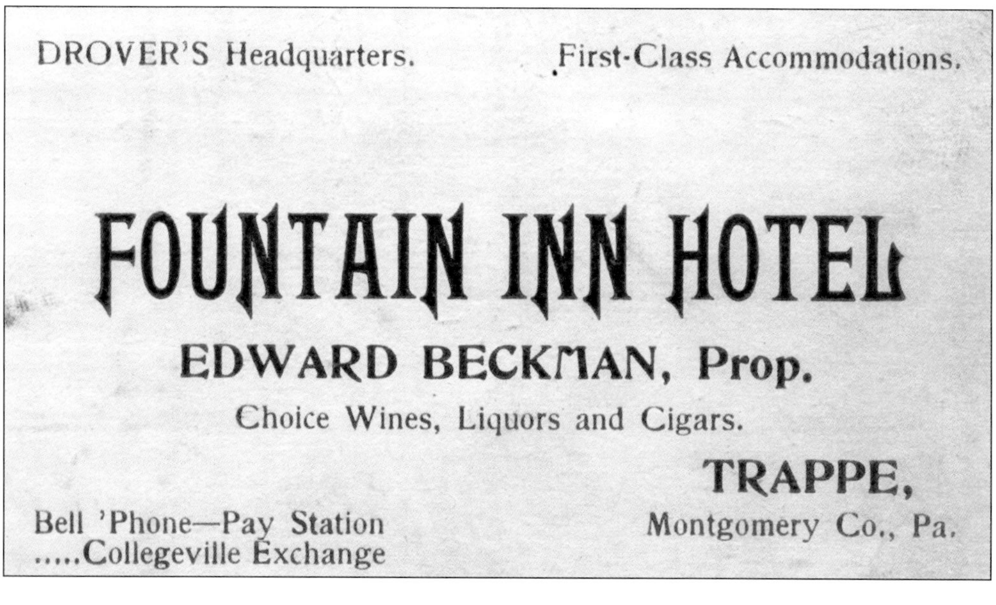

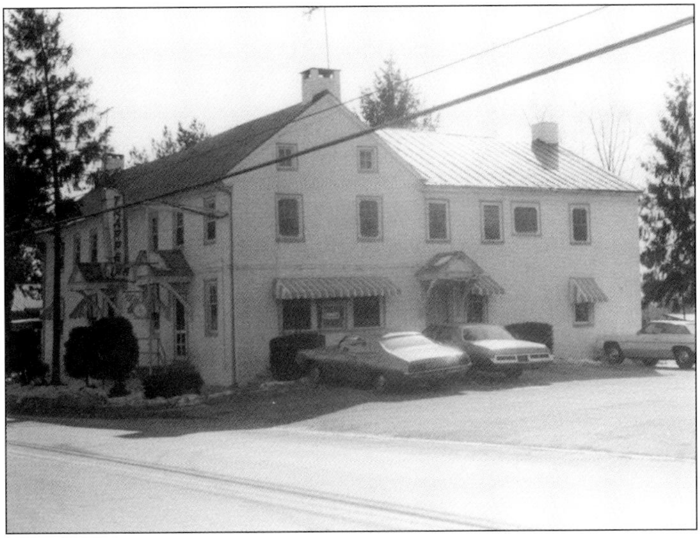

TRAPPE TAVERN, 418 WEST MAIN STREET, 1976. Long after the wraparound porch was removed from the Trappe Tavern, patrons continued to enter the building via one of two front doors. Later, the entrance was moved to the west side, where it remains today. The tavern is still a favorite haunt of local residents. (Courtesy of the Historical Society of Trappe, Collegeville, Perkiomen Valley.)

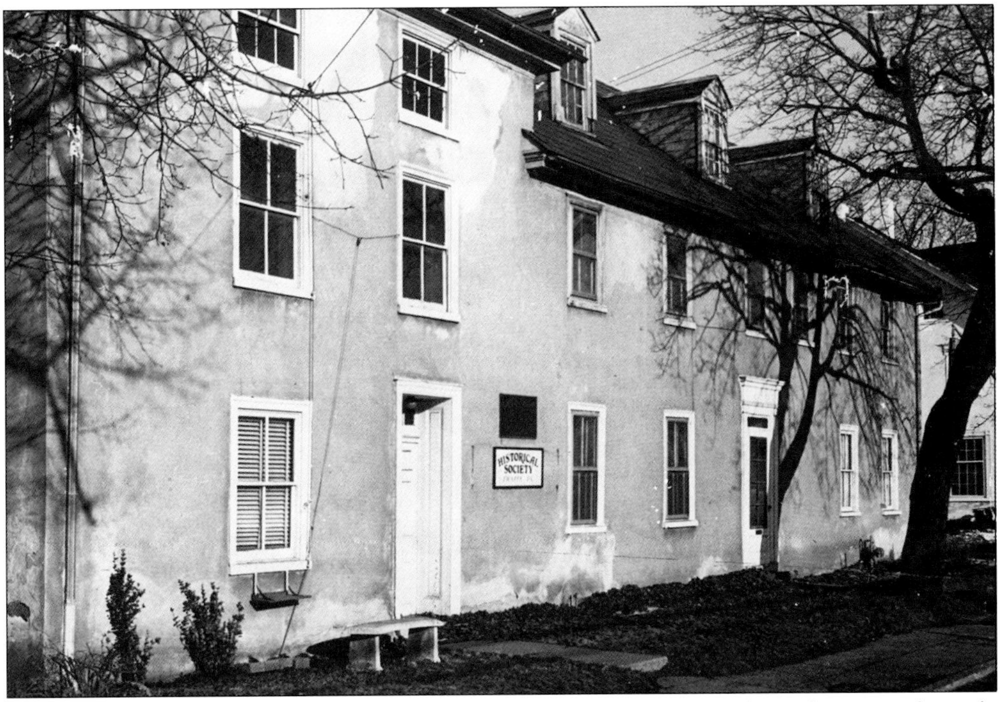

DEWEES TAVERN, 301 WEST MAIN STREET. Built in several stages from the mid-1700s to the early 1800s, the oldest section of this building (right) was the home of Andrew Miller, a joiner and bellows maker, and his wife, Anna Maria Ewald. In 1827, it was acquired by Dr. Jacob Dewees but sold just five years later in a sheriff's sale, at which time it was described as the Sign of the Brig Holker. Enos and Margaret Lewis bought the property, and in 1838, they conveyed it to Mary Catharine "Mother" Dewees, who operated it as a popular boardinghouse until 1855. The building also served as a polling place and stagecoach stop. (Courtesy of the Historical Society of Trappe, Collegeville, Perkiomen Valley.)

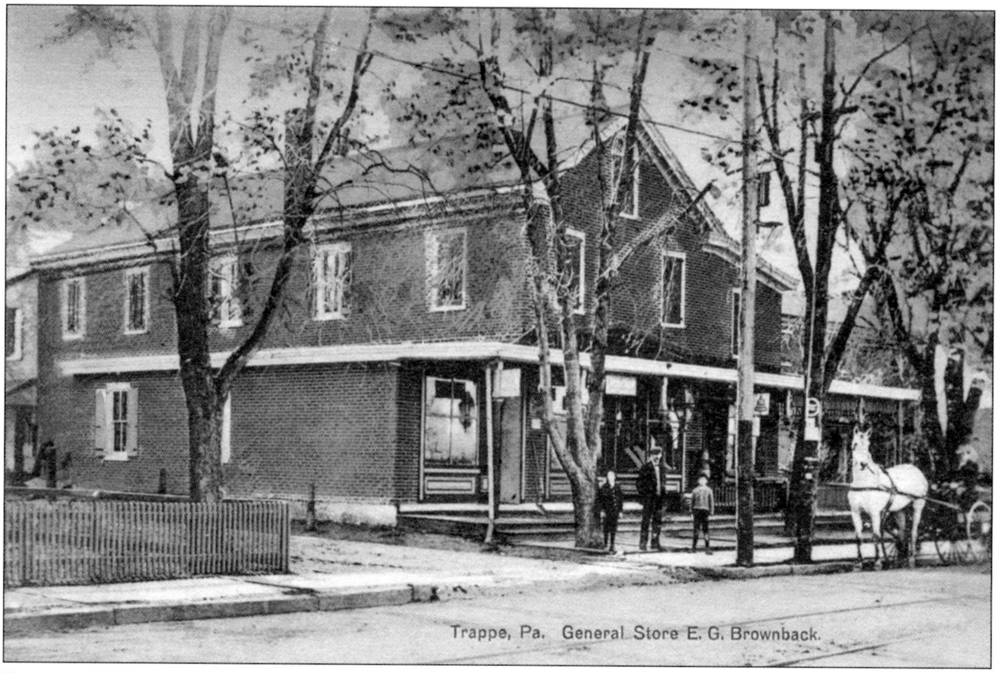

BROWNBACK STORE, 538 WEST MAIN STREET. Built as a blacksmith shop for Joseph Heneks around 1835, this building was sold to Abram Treichler, also a blacksmith and Heneks's brother-in-law, in 1852. It changed hands again in 1856 when it was bought by John K. Beaver (1824–1906), who used it as a general store. A tailor by trade, Beaver first worked in Skippack before moving to Trappe, where he founded a mercantile firm known as Beaver & Shellenberger. He operated a general store at 538 West Main Street for 20 years before turning it over to his son-in-law Edwin G. Brownback and retiring in 1895. (Above, courtesy of Jerry A. Chiccarine; below, courtesy of the Historical Society of Trappe, Collegeville, Perkiomen Valley.)

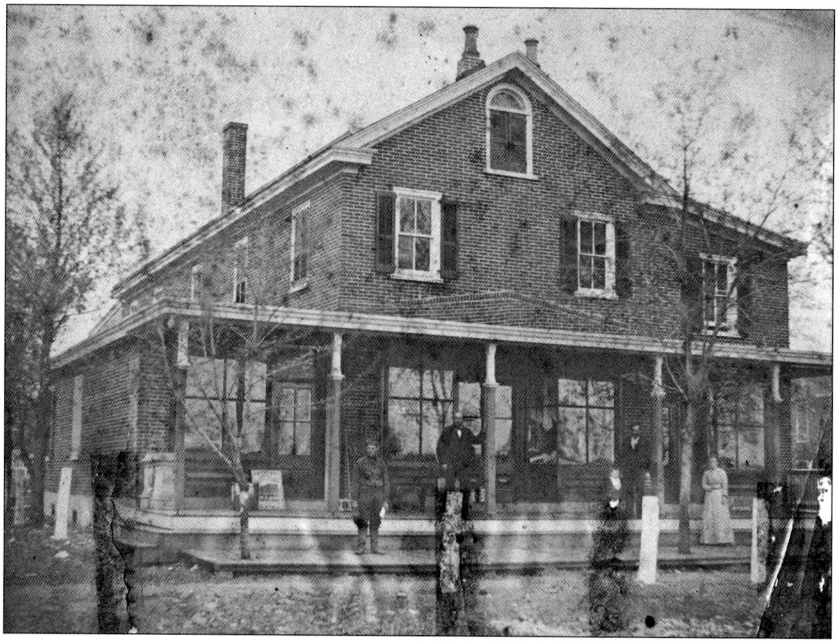

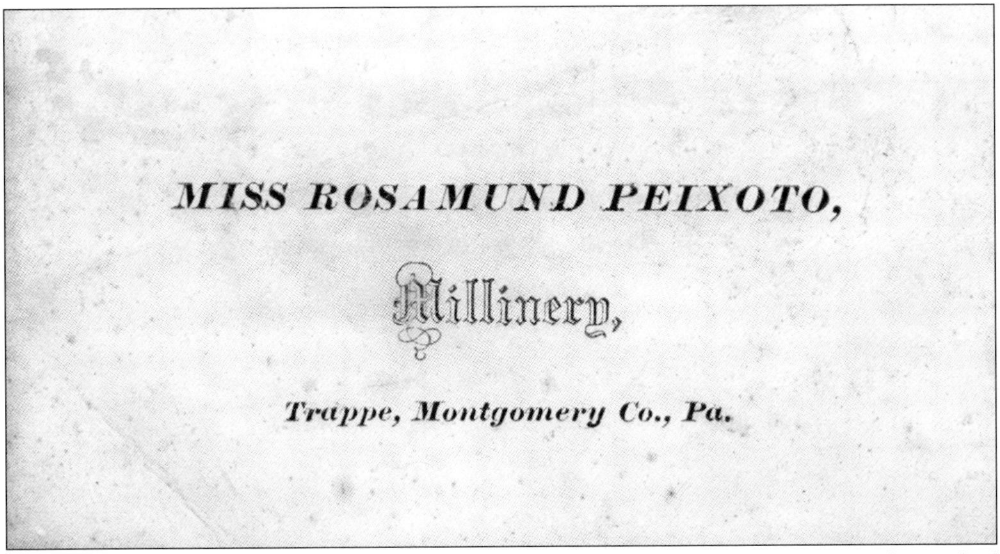

Rosamund Peixoto, Milliner. This trade card was used by Rosamund Peixoto, who worked in Trappe as a milliner prior to her marriage to William A. Fry in 1868. Her father, Engelbert Peixoto, was a German Reformed minister who served numerous congregations in southeastern Pennsylvania. (Courtesy of the Historical Society of Trappe, Collegeville, Perkiomen Valley.)

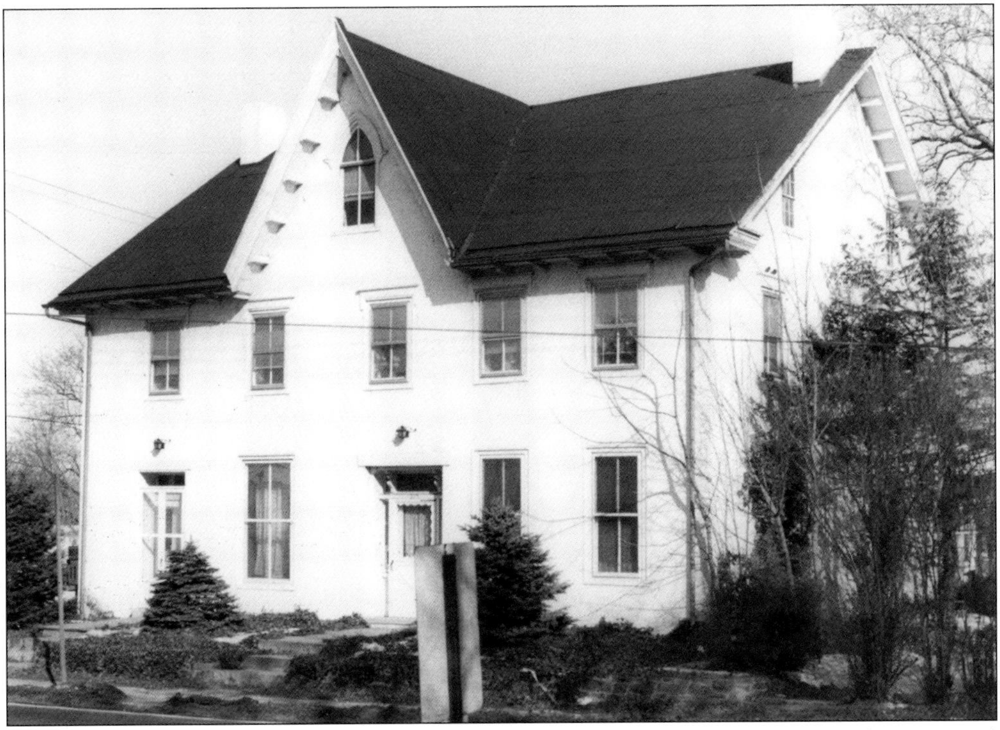

219 West Main Street, c. 1988. Built in 1845 for Daniel Fry, this structure served as a general store and dwelling house. The inscription "Dry Goods" is still faintly visible on the stone threshold at the entrance to the store. On January 6, 1881, the *Independent* announced that Franklin Boyer Rushong was opening a general store in the old Fry storeroom on April 1 of that year. (Courtesy of the Historical Society of Trappe, Collegeville, Perkiomen Valley.)

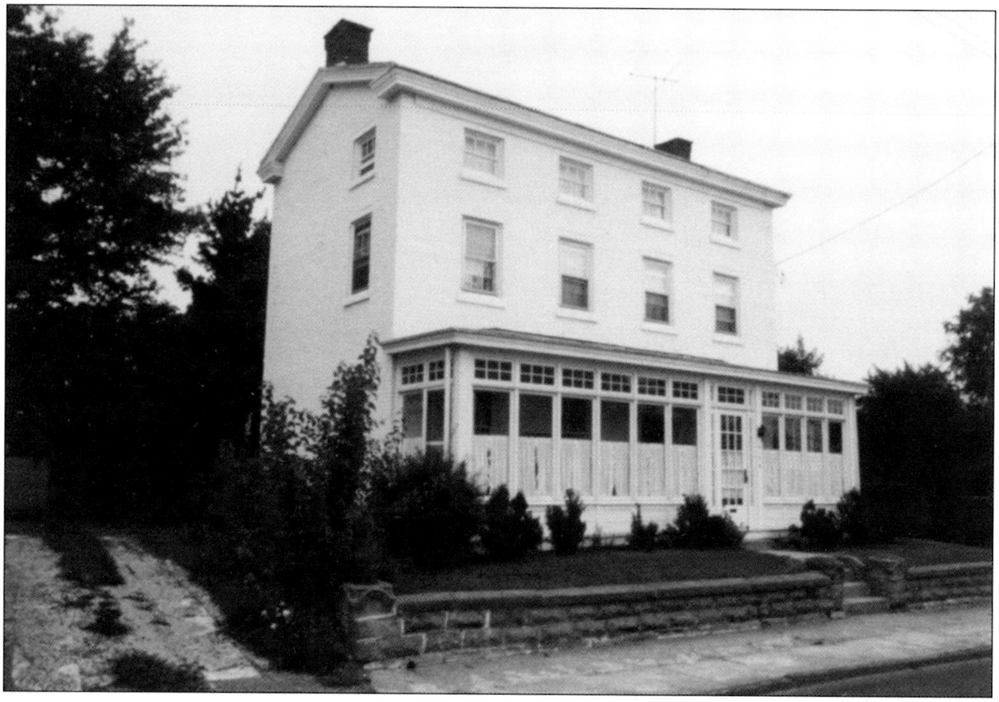

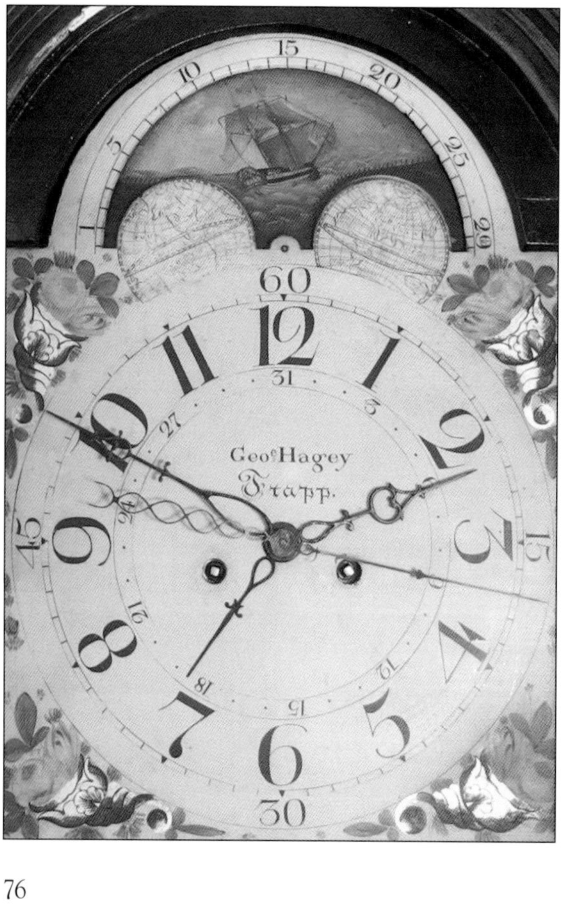

417 West Main Street. Built around 1830, this house was the residence of George Hagey, a renowned clockmaker, from 1832 to 1844. Born in nearby Lower Salford Township, Hagey was the second generation of his family to make clocks. He made both 30-hour and eight-day movements. The example at left includes a moon phase dial and sweep second hand. (Both, courtesy of the Historical Society of Trappe, Collegeville, Perkiomen Valley.)

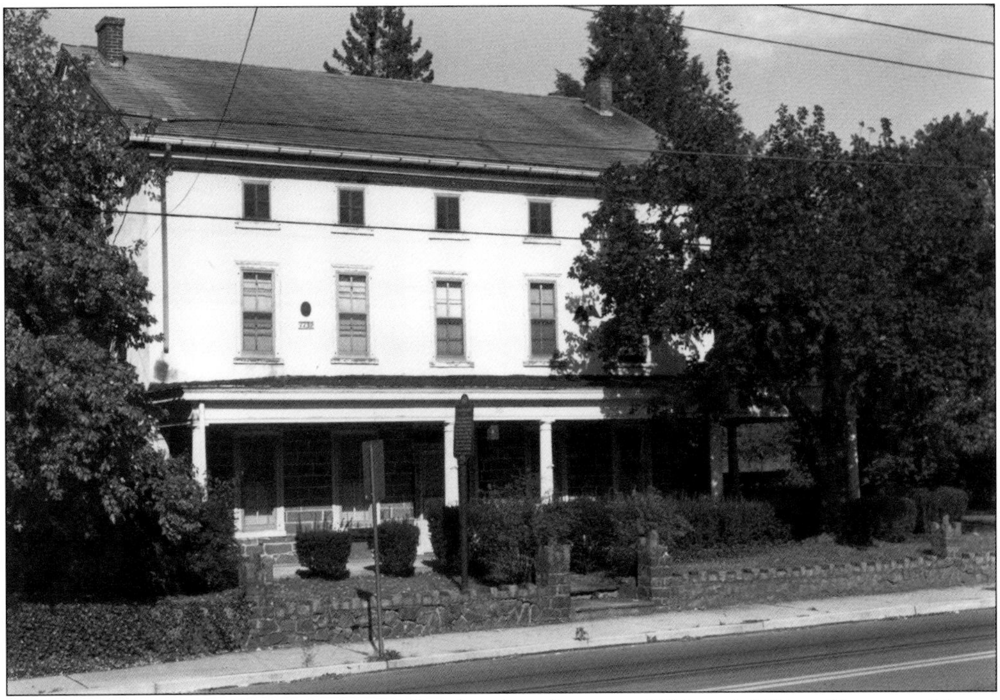

201 WEST MAIN STREET. Built for Jacob Schrack Jr. between 1750 and 1755 and home to Henry and Mary Muhlenberg from 1776 to 1787, this house was purchased by Frederick and Violet Grimison in 1954. There, Frederick operated a business known as Muhlenberg House Antiques until his death in 1971. The house was acquired by the local historical society in 1989 and was subsequently restored to its c. 1776 appearance and opened to the public as a museum. (Both, courtesy of the Historical Society of Trappe, Collegeville, Perkiomen Valley.)

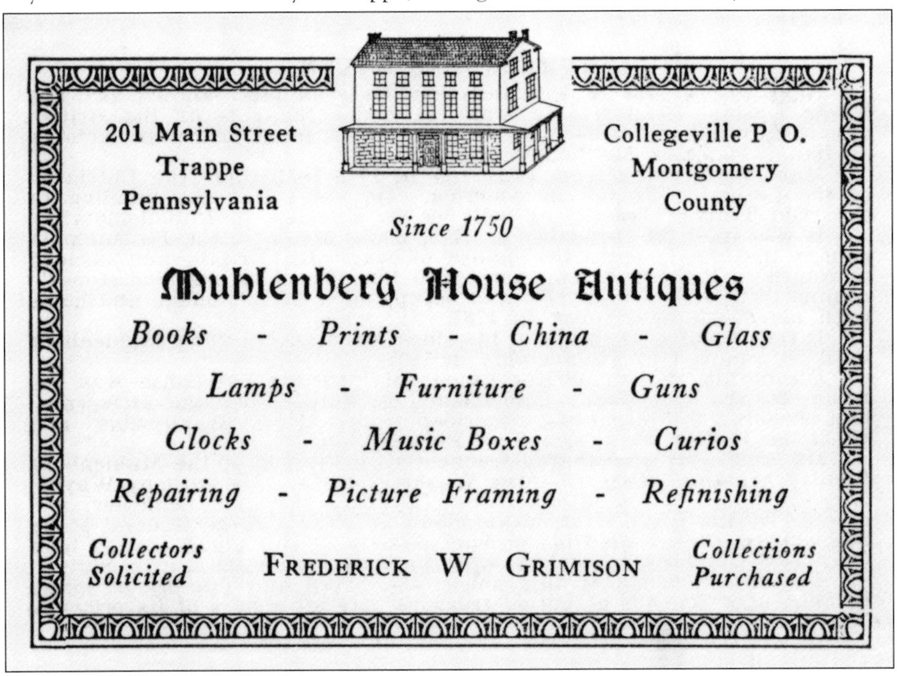

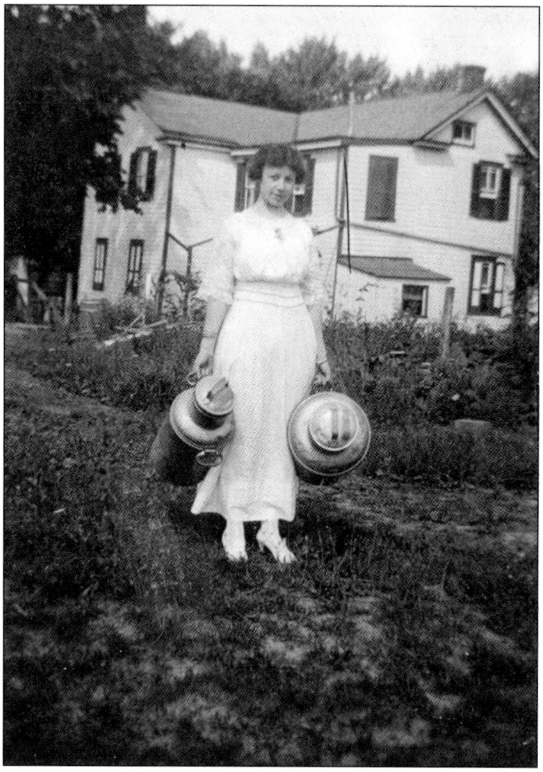

DAIRYING, 1915. Raising dairy cattle has been a major part of the local agricultural community for generations. In this photograph, dated July 1915, an unidentified young woman from Collegeville holds a pair of empty milk cans. Her spotless white dress and heeled shoes suggest that she was not prepared to do farm work, however. (Courtesy of Kate Minardi.)

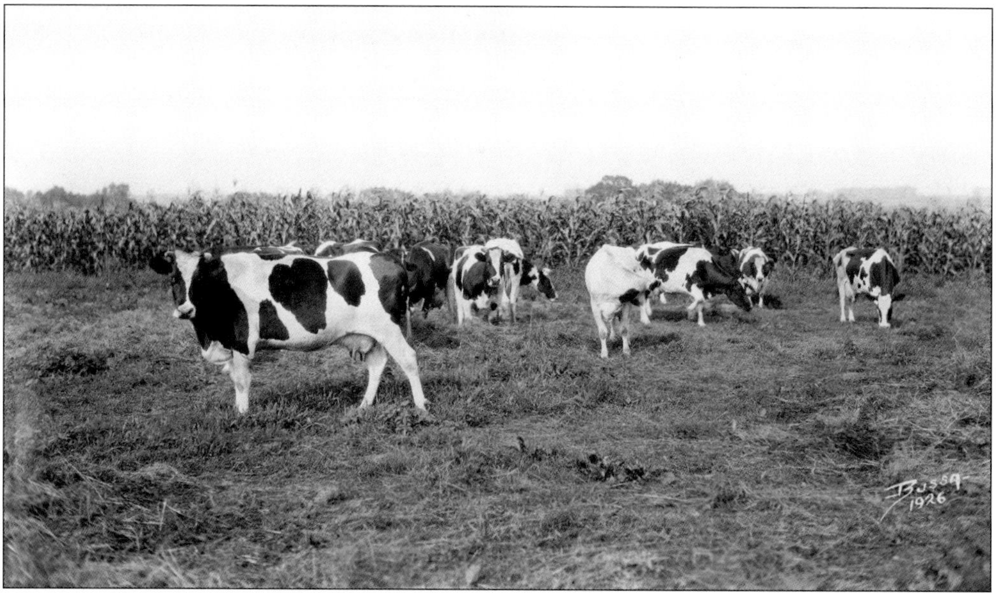

DAIRY CATTLE, 1926. In 1909, Ursinus College purchased a 22-acre tract of land in Collegeville, including a stone barn, from the Spangler family. The college renovated the barn, added a modern dairy stable and silo, and hired Clarence E. McCormick as the farm manager. A herd of 10 Holstein-Friesian cows were purchased in 1921, seen here grazing beside a cornfield in 1926. The herd was sold in February 1936, and the barn was torn down in 1963 to make way for the college's new heating plant. (Courtesy of the Ursinus College Archives.)

ROYER BARN, C. 1930. Dr. Lewis Royer built this large dairy barn on what is now Northern Star Farm, located at 97 East Third Avenue in Trappe. It burned to the ground on December 18, 1931, as a result of a threshing accident. More than 100 head of cattle survived the fire, creating an urgent need for temporary shelter until a new barn could be built. A vacant barn was found across the Perkiomen Bridge in Collegeville, and with the help of friends and neighbors, the cows were driven down Main Street and over the bridge, where they stayed for the next six months. (Courtesy of Matthew G. Wismer.)

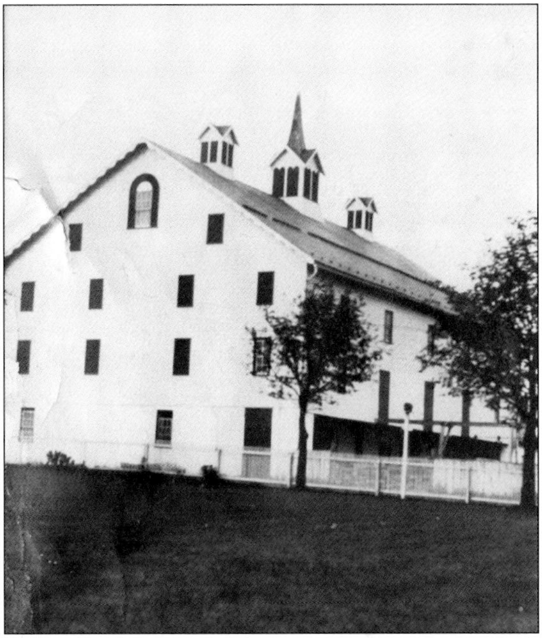

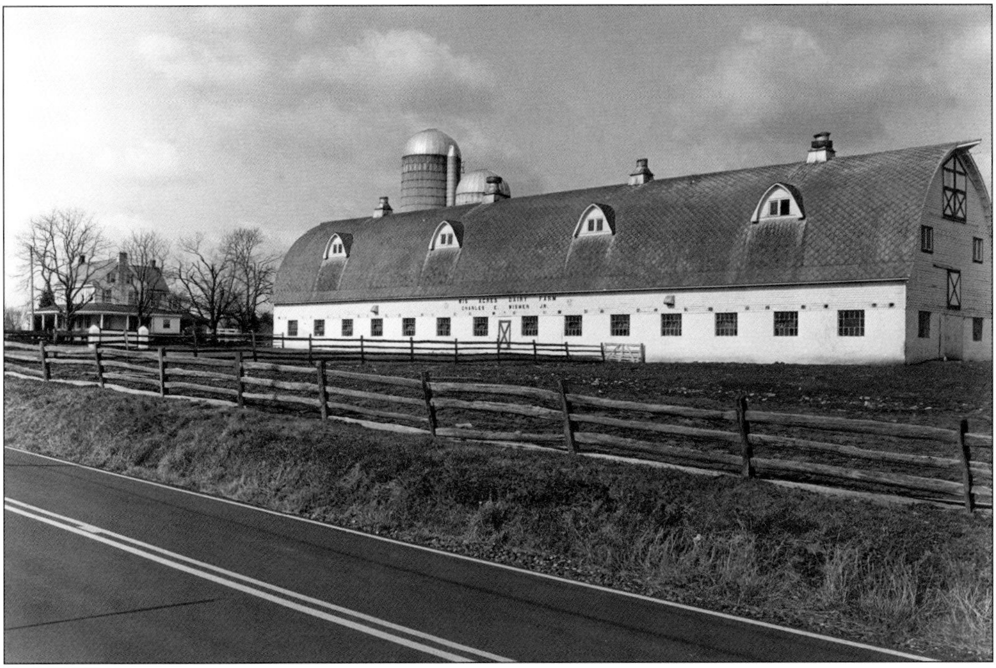

WISMER BARN, 1992. Construction began on the Wismers' new barn in early 1932, with a plan based on a Midwestern design. Measuring 196 feet long and 38 feet deep, the new barn had stanchions for 100 cows, complete with automatic waterers, and could store up to 400 tons of hay in the upper level. With pointed arches rising 45 feet above the ground, the new barn was a technologically advanced agricultural superstructure. Like its predecessor, it too was lost in a fire, this time due to a spark from a hay-mowing operation on June 10, 1997. The 150-head herd of cattle was moved 20 miles away to East Greenville while a new barn was built in just over three months. (Courtesy of Matthew G. Wismer.)

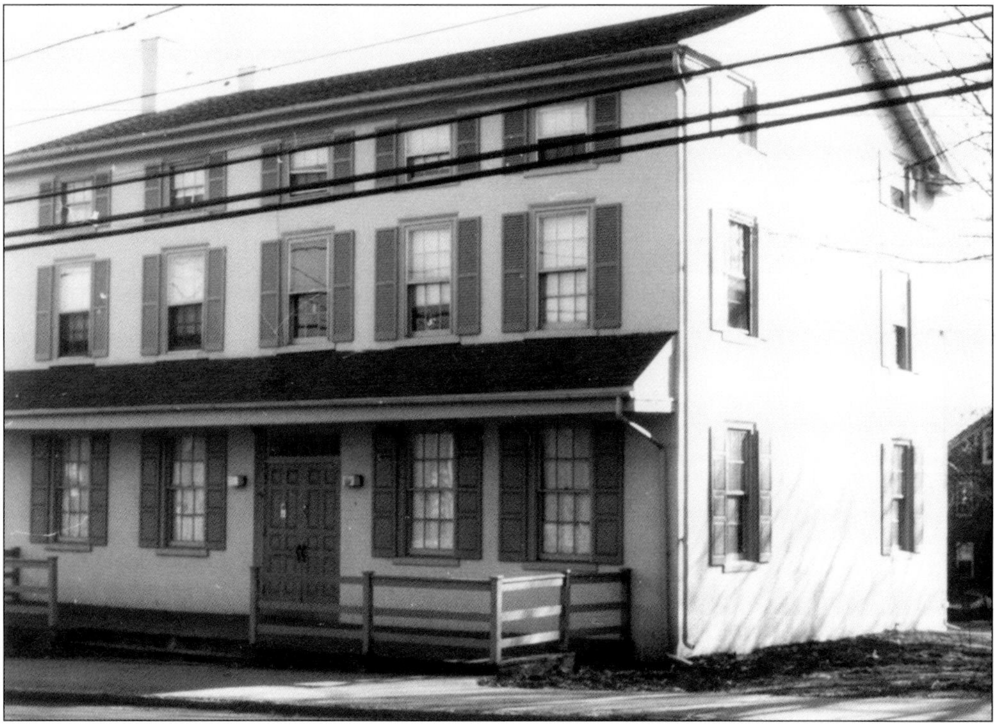

HOBSON'S STORE, 500 EAST MAIN STREET, C. 1988. Frank M. Hobson ran a general store at the corner of Fifth Avenue and East Main Street in Collegeville from 1856 until his retirement in 1880. A century later, it became a men's dormitory at Ursinus College and is now known as Commonwealth Hall. (Courtesy of the Historical Society of Trappe, Collegeville, Perkiomen Valley.)

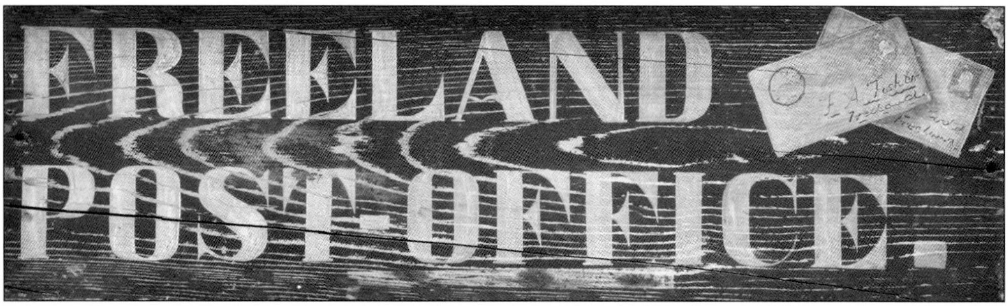

FREELAND POST OFFICE. This painted wooden sign is from the Freeland Post Office, established on December 10, 1862, and located in Frank Hobson's store at 500 East Main Street. The post office only lasted six years before the name was changed back to Perkiomen Bridge on August 27, 1868. The name was finally changed to Collegeville on January 18, 1870, after the new railroad station that was created in 1868. (Courtesy of the Ursinus College Archives.)

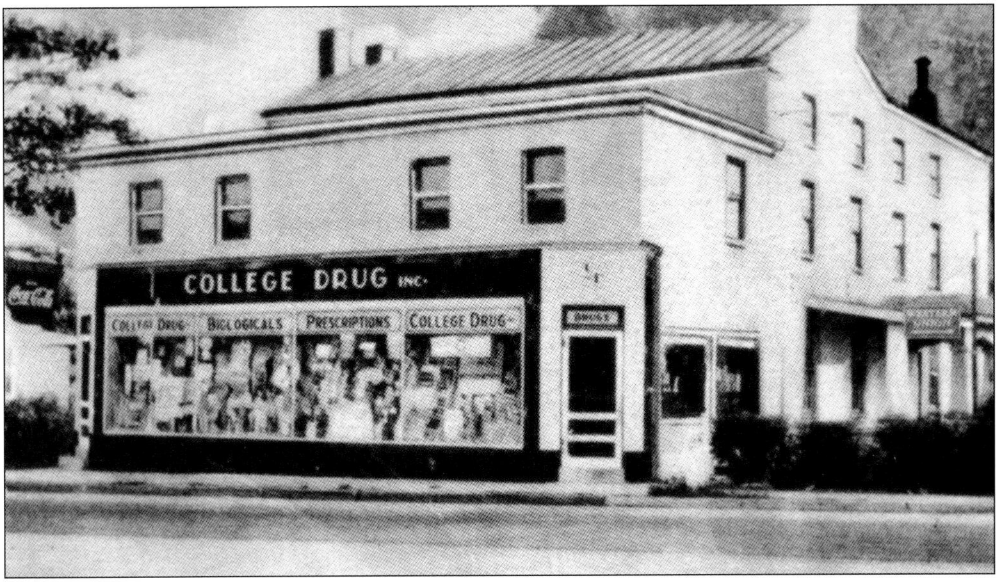

College Drugstore, 488 East Main Street, c. 1938. Operated by the Winkler family during the early to mid-1900s, the College Drugstore carried "biologicals," as well as prescription medications and household supplies. A soda fountain was added in the 1950s and quickly became a popular local hangout. The building is now home to Marzella's Pizzeria. (Courtesy of Jerry A. Chiccarine.)

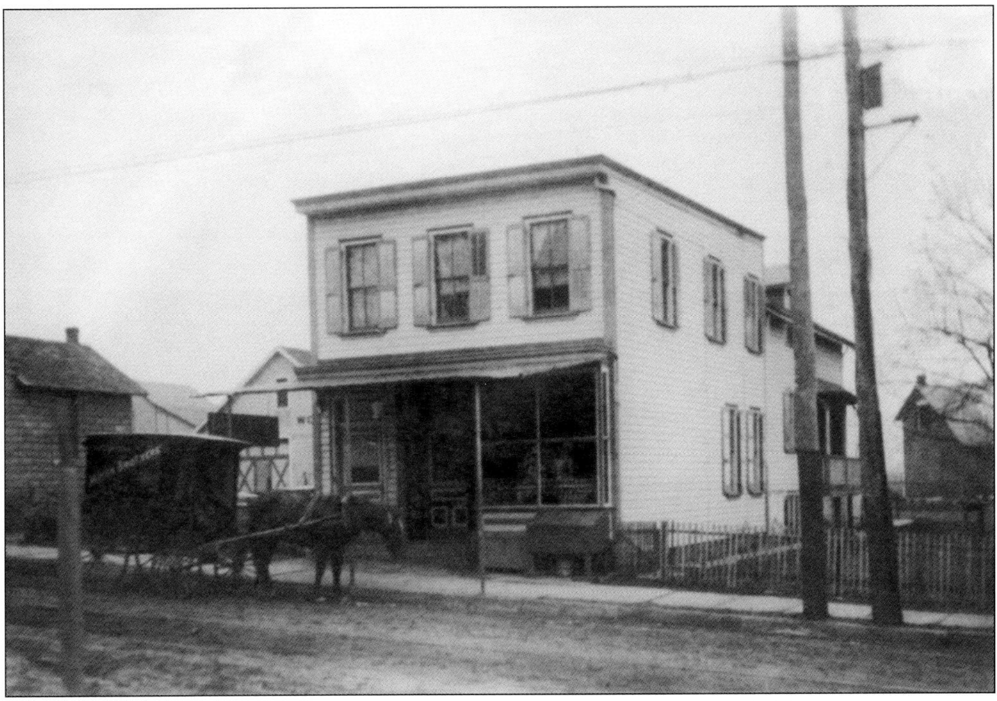

Moyer Brothers Store, 331 East Main Street, c. 1906. In the early 1900s, Arlington and Otto Moyer co-owned the Moyer Brothers general store in Collegeville. Their name appears on the horse-drawn wagon parked in front of the store. Arlington later established a specialty linen store, and Otto ran an insurance agency in the nearby town of Royersford. (Courtesy of Richard K. Allebach.)

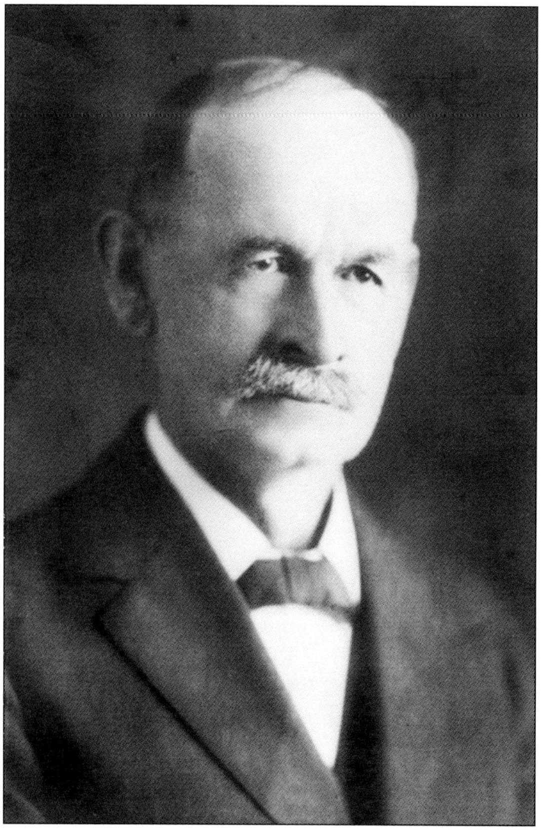

Elwood S. Moser. In 1875, Elwood Smith "Daddy" Moser founded the *Independent* weekly newspaper, initially known as the *Providence Independent*. Vol. 1, No. 1, as seen below, was issued on June 3, 1875. Known as an independent thinker, Moser was a Democrat in a heavily Republican county who strove to ensure that his newspaper appealed to people of all classes and political persuasions. The newspaper's original motto was "Independent in all things—Neutral in Nothing." (Both, courtesy of the Historical Society of Trappe, Collegeville, Perkiomen Valley.)

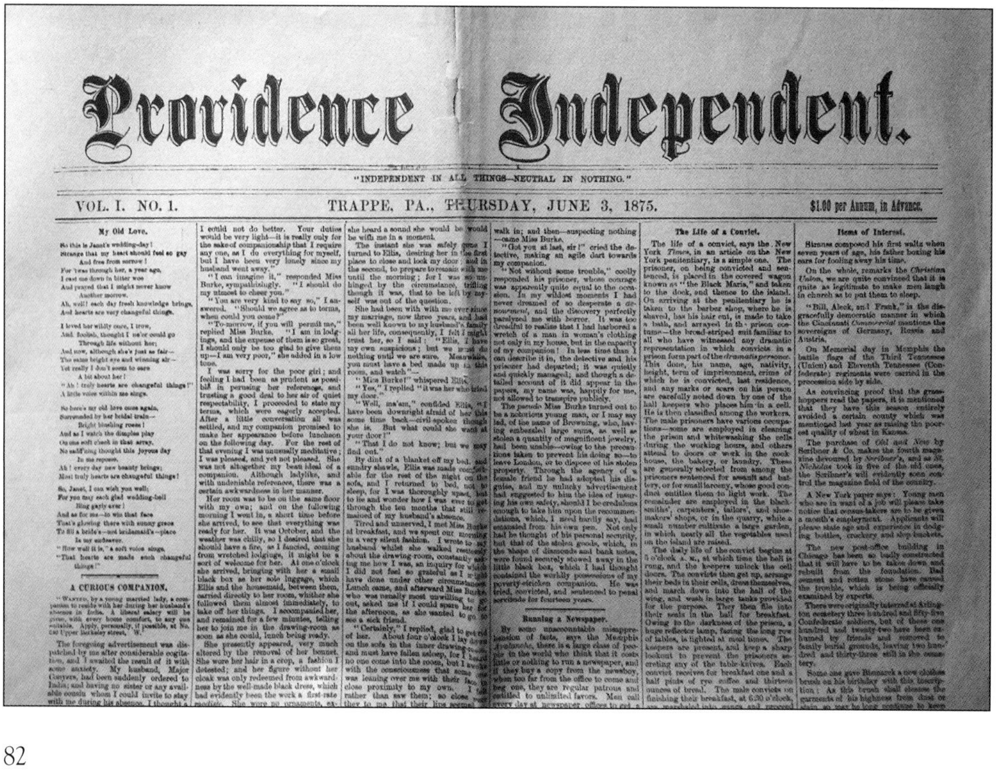

Providence Independent.

"INDEPENDENT IN ALL THINGS—NEUTRAL IN NOTHING."

VOL. I. NO. 1. TRAPPE, PA., THURSDAY, JUNE 3, 1875. $1.00 per Annum, in Advance.

My Old Love.

A CURIOUS COMPANION.

The Life of a Convict.

Running a Newspaper.

Items of Interest.

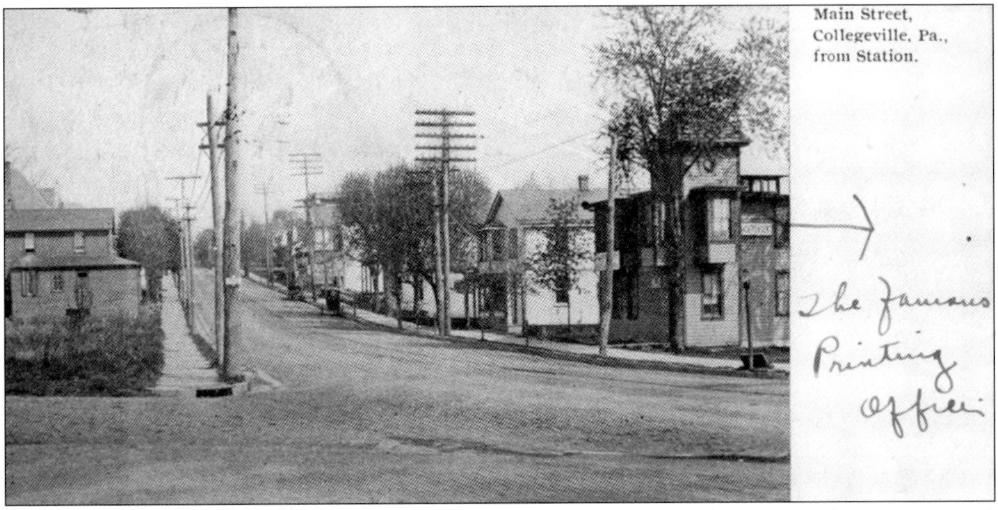

THE *INDEPENDENT* PRINTSHOP, C. 1907. For the first eight years, the *Independent* was printed in Trappe, just a few doors east of the Fountain Inn (now the Trappe Tavern), but in 1883, the printshop was moved to the corner of East Main Street and Third Avenue in Collegeville—literally. On April 9, 1883, the building was lifted from its foundation and pulled down Main Street by a six-horse team, much to the astonishment of local residents. It still stands at 307 East Main Street and is currently a dental office. (Courtesy of Jerry A. Chiccarine.)

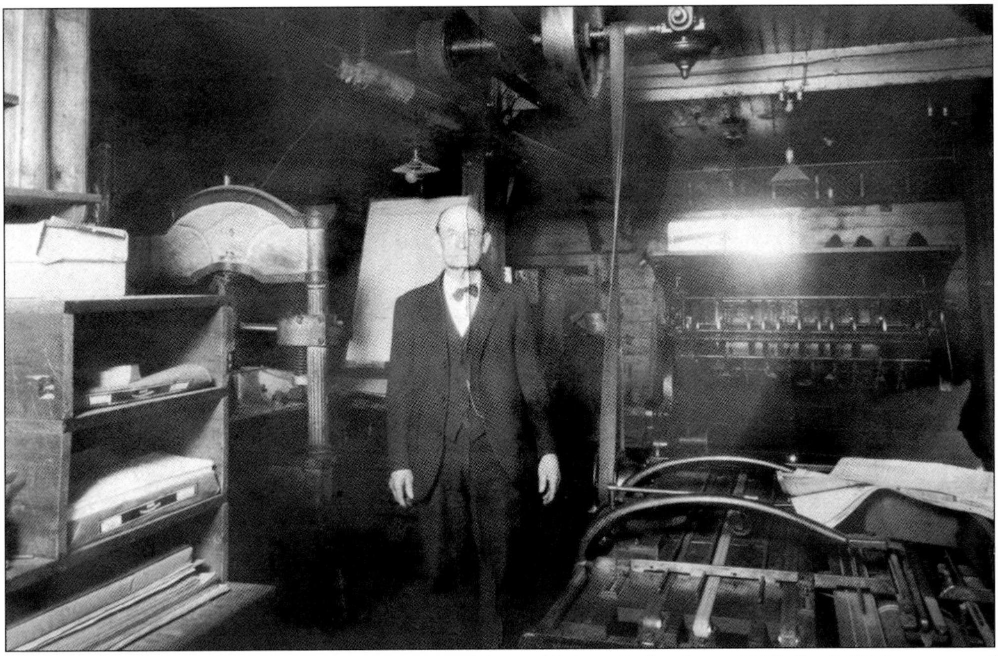

THE *INDEPENDENT* PRESSROOM, 1925. After Elwood Moser's death in 1935, Paul W. Levengood acquired the paper from Moser's estate with financing from Collegeville National Bank. In 1971, John Stewart bought the newspaper, by then called the *Independent and Montgomery Transcript*, and ran it until his death in 1997. Another major figure in the newspaper's history was J. Howard Fenstermacher, who worked for the *Independent* from 1917 until his retirement in 1990 at age 86. He started the popular "Rambling at Random" column in 1924 and continued it for many years. (Courtesy of the Historical Society of Trappe, Collegeville, Perkiomen Valley.)

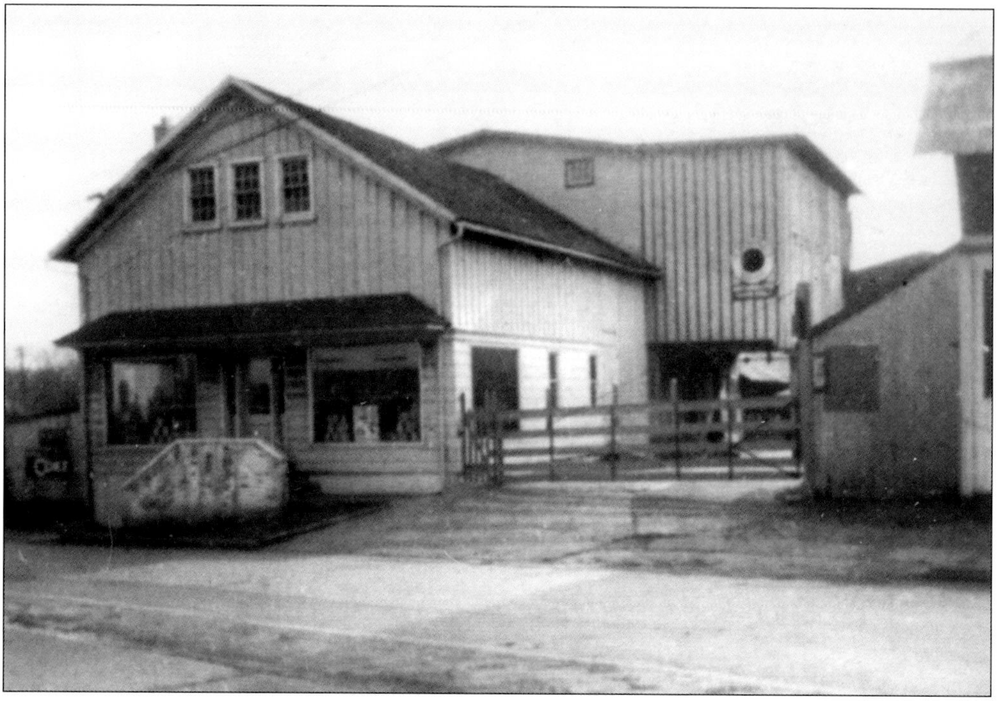

GRISTOCK'S FEED AND LUMBER YARD, 1955. The county atlas of 1871 shows Zimmerman, Gristock, and Bean's lumber, coal, and feed yard at the south corner of Second Avenue and East Main Street, near the Collegeville train station. During the 1880s, it was run by partners William H. Gristock and George Vanderslice. The receipt below records the purchase of oats, corn, and bran by Abel Rambo and is dated April 23, 1883. After 1894, the business was known as W.H. Gristock & Sons. Frank W. Gristock died in 1942, but his son-in-law D. Sterling Light and grandson Frank W. Light ran the business until 1969. (Above, courtesy of Kate Minardi; below, courtesy of the Historical Society of Trappe, Collegeville, Perkiomen Valley.)

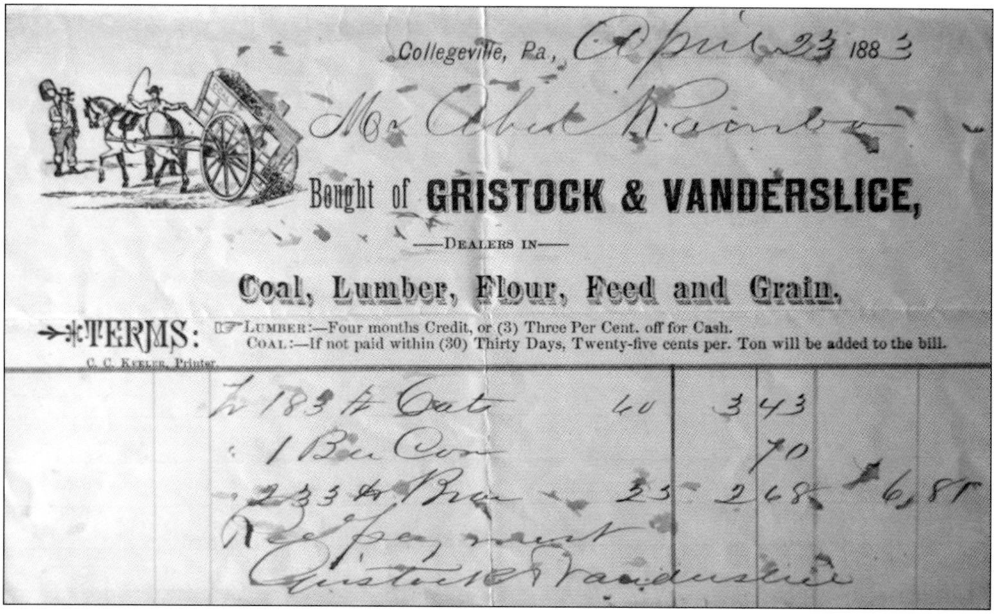

Collegeville, Pa., April 23 1883

Mr Abel Rambo

Bought of **GRISTOCK & VANDERSLICE,**

—DEALERS IN—

Coal, Lumber, Flour, Feed and Grain.

TERMS: LUMBER:—Four months Credit, or (3) Three Per Cent. off for Cash.
COAL:—If not paid within (30) Thirty Days, Twenty-five cents per. Ton will be added to the bill.

C. C. KEELER, Printer.

To 183 # Oat	40	3 43		
1 Bu Corn		70		
233 # Bran	25	2 68		6 81

Rec'd payment
Gristock & Vanderslice

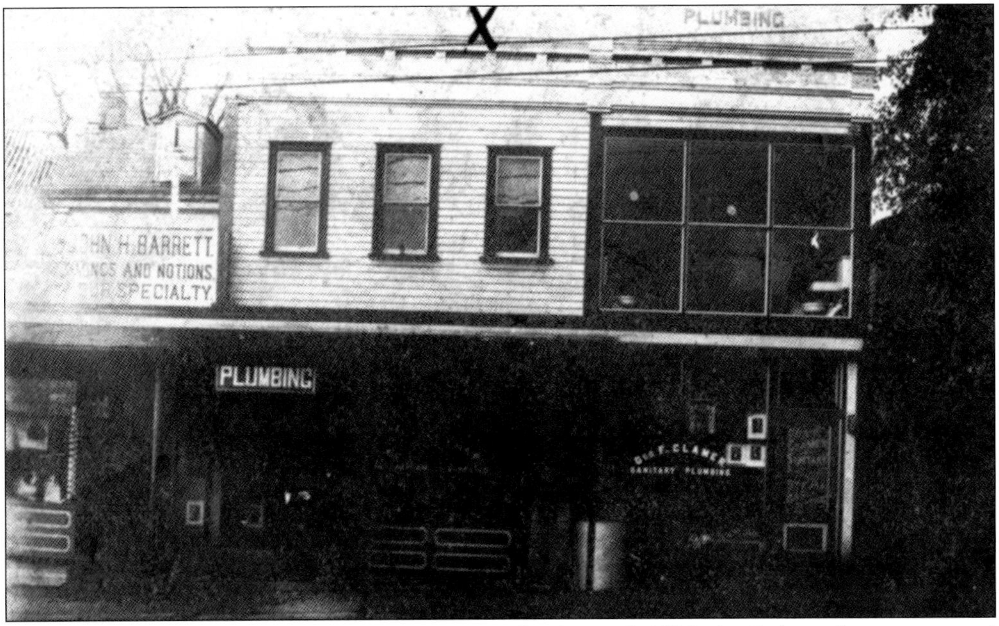

Clamer's Hardware and Plumbing, c. 1900. On June 16, 1898, the *Independent* announced the opening of a hardware store and bicycle repair shop run by George F. Clamer, nephew of Francis J. Clamer. George was also a trained plumber. His sister Frances Clamer Barrett sold sewing notions and trim in the adjacent room. The store still stands at 342 East Main Street in Collegeville. (Courtesy of Jerry A. Chiccarine.)

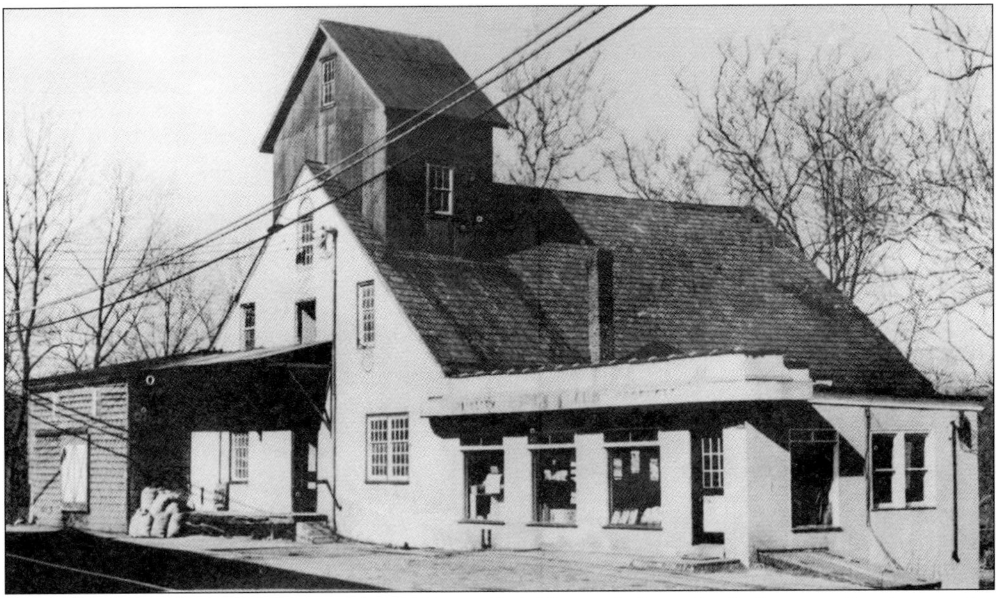

Collegeville Mill. Built in 1874, the Collegeville Mill stood along the Perkiomen Creek, near the intersection of Ninth Avenue and Gravel Pike. It was bought by Francis J. Clamer in 1898 and became known as Clamer's Mill. In the early 1900s, the side of the mill was painted with the inscription "F.J. Clamer / Grain, Flour / And All Kinds of Mill Feed." The Borough of Collegeville bought the building in 1969 to convert it into a community center, but it was destroyed in a fire on August 12, 1972. (Courtesy of the Historical Society of Trappe, Collegeville, Perkiomen Valley.)

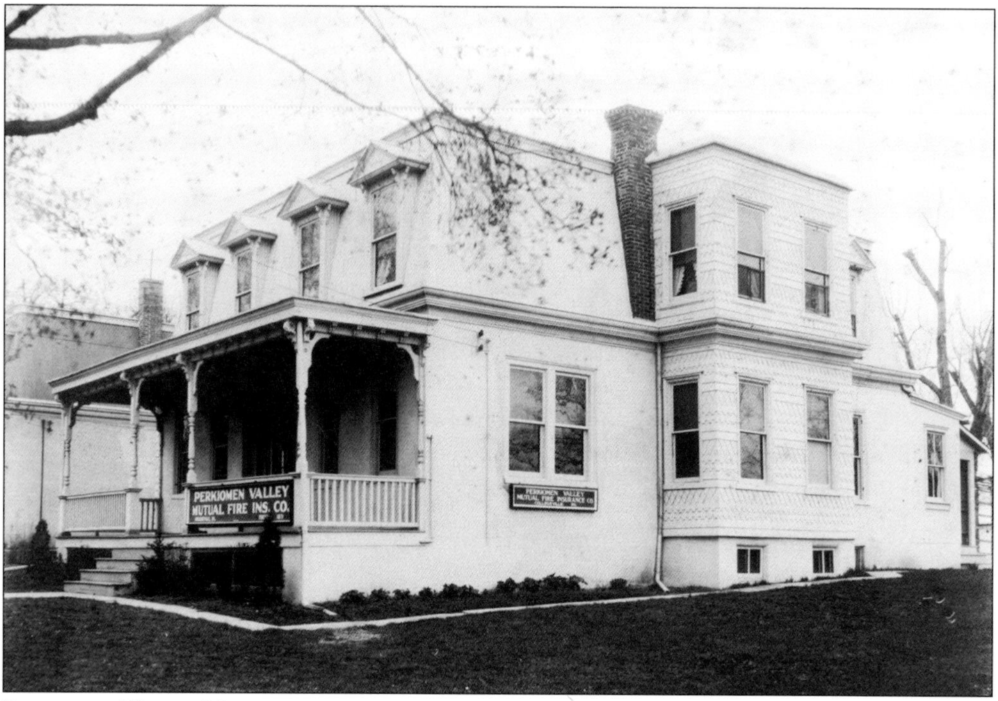

PERKIOMEN VALLEY MUTUAL FIRE INSURANCE COMPANY. From 1872 to 1889, the Perkiomen Valley Mutual Fire Insurance Company, incorporated in 1871, operated out of a small frame building in Trappe, still standing at 378 West Main Street. From 1889 to 1921, its headquarters were the former home of Abraham D. Fetterolf at 612 East Main Street (now Duryea Hall). It then moved to a mansard-roofed building at 379 East Main Street. In 1938, the company built a two-story brick structure at 373 East Main Street and occupied the first floor; the upper floor was rented as apartments. The company was acquired by the Pennsylvania National Insurance Company in 1964 and relocated to Harrisburg four years later. (Both, courtesy of the Historical Society of Trappe, Collegeville, Perkiomen Valley.)

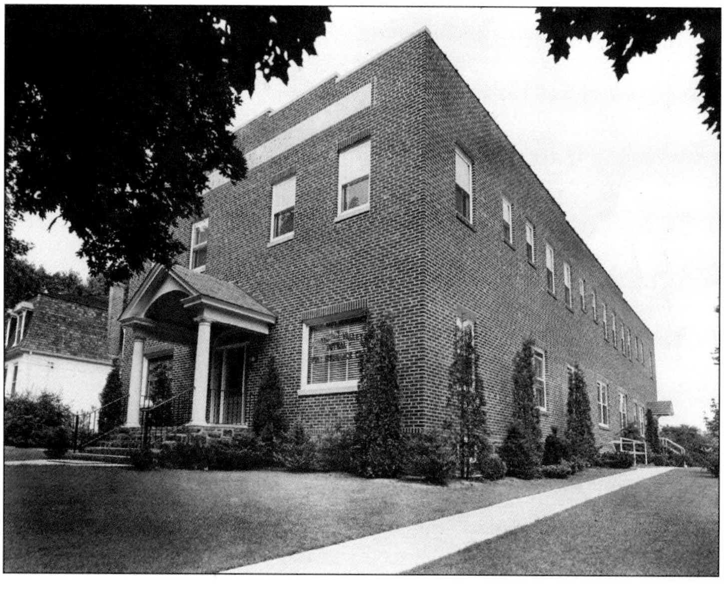

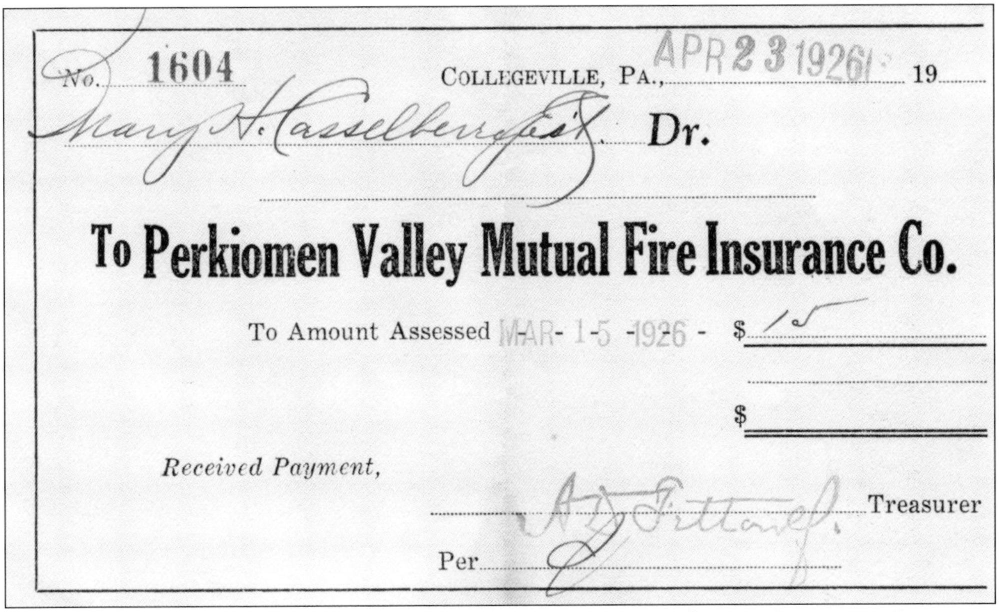

No. 1604 COLLEGEVILLE, PA., APR 23 1926 19

Mary H. Casselberry Est. Dr.

To Perkiomen Valley Mutual Fire Insurance Co.

To Amount Assessed MAR 15 1926 $15

$

Received Payment,

A. D. Fetterolf Treasurer

Per

INSURANCE RECEIPT, 1926. This receipt notes the payment of $15 by the estate of Mary H. Casselberry to the Perkiomen Valley Mutual Fire Insurance Company. It is dated April 23, 1926, and is signed by treasurer Abraham D. Fetterolf. Casselberry was the daughter of Rev. Joseph Hendricks of Trinity Reformed Church in Collegeville. (Courtesy of Jerry A. Chiccarine.)

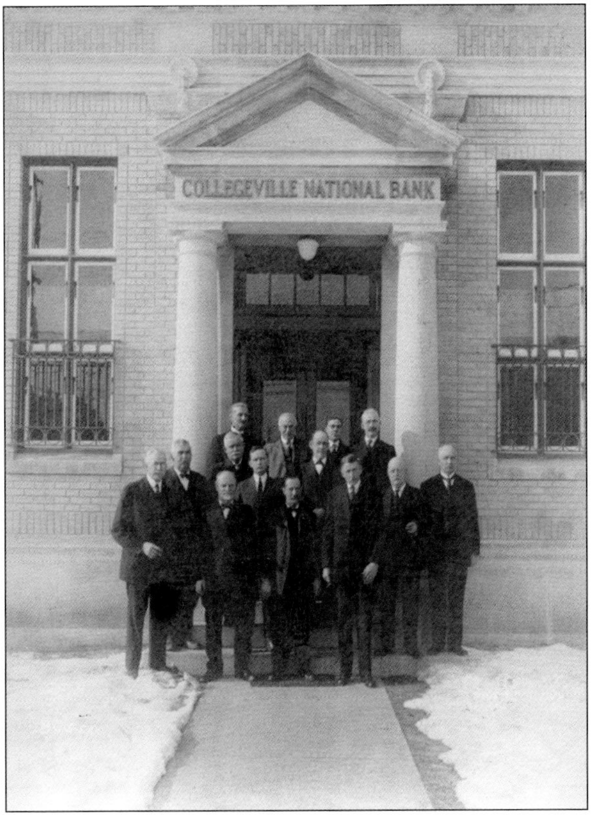

COLLEGEVILLE NATIONAL BANK. The Collegeville National Bank was organized on August 20, 1906, and opened for business on February 14, 1907. Abraham D. Fetterolf was the founding president, assisted by Montgomery B. Linderman as vice president and William D. Renninger as cashier. It was founded with $25,000 in capital; on the first day of business, $24,767 was deposited into 60 different accounts. For nearly 30 years, until 1935, the bank printed US currency in eight different types and denominations totaling $994,360. (Courtesy of the Historical Society of Trappe, Collegeville, Perkiomen Valley.)

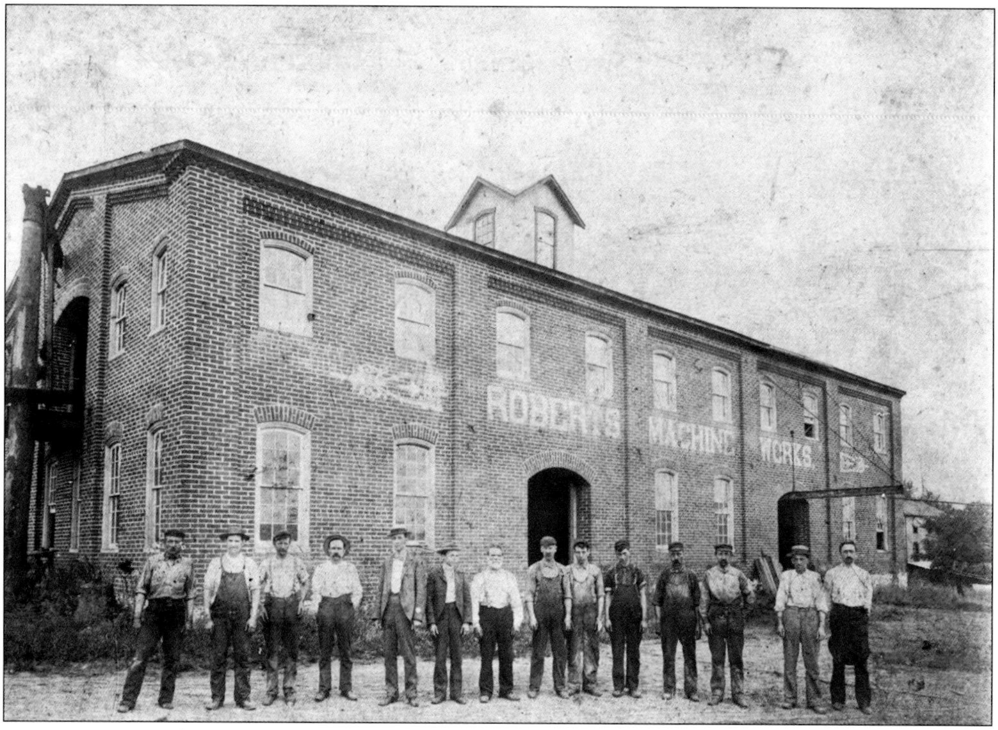

Roberts Machine Works. In 1884, Milton O. Roberts relocated his company from Worcester, Pennsylvania, to Third Avenue and Walnut Street in Collegeville. Roberts Machine Works manufactured and sold a wide range of machines. Among their products were windmills, feed cutters, and one- and two-horsepower versions of New Model Dwarf Threshers and Separators, which a brochure claimed were the "simplest and most complete machines ever built." (Both, courtesy of Jerry A. Chiccarine.)

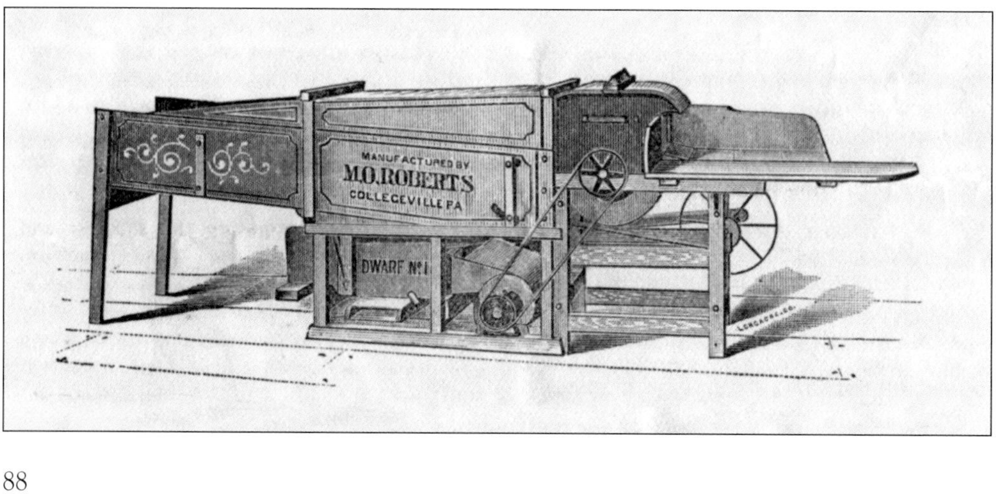

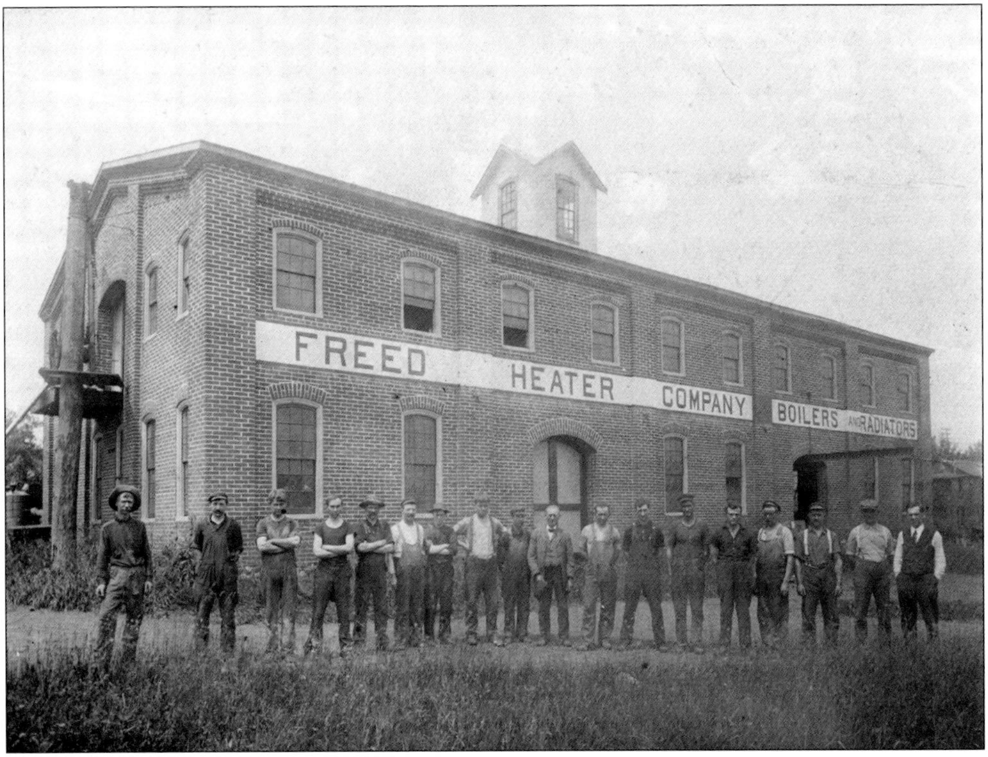

Freed Heater Company. Although Trappe and Collegeville remained a predominantly rural area at the turn of the 20th century, a number of modest manufacturing plants had begun to open by the late 1800s. One of the first was the Freed Heater Company, which took over the former Roberts Machine Works building. Freed made and retailed both feed steam and water boilers and radiators. After 1930, the Klein Stove Company used the building until it was lost in a fire in 1940. Rees Companies now occupies the site. (Courtesy of Jerry A. Chiccarine.)

Collegeville Flag Company. Dr. Samuel D. Cornish founded the Collegeville Manufacturing Company, later known as the Collegeville Flag Company, in 1909. The business initially made aprons but began to make flags in 1910. It operated out of a leased space in the west end of the Freed Heater Company until that structure was destroyed by fire in 1940. Beginning in 1922, the company also made Halloween costumes. A specialty division was then formed under the name Collegeville Costumes, which was a leading national manufacturer of Halloween apparel from the 1960s through the 1980s. (Courtesy of the Historical Society of Trappe, Collegeville, Perkiomen Valley.)

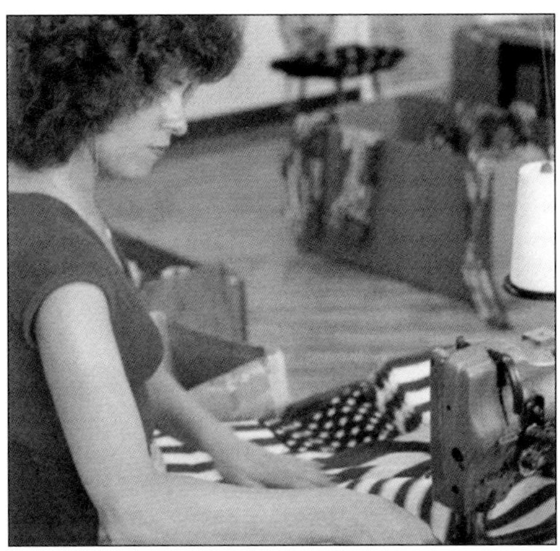

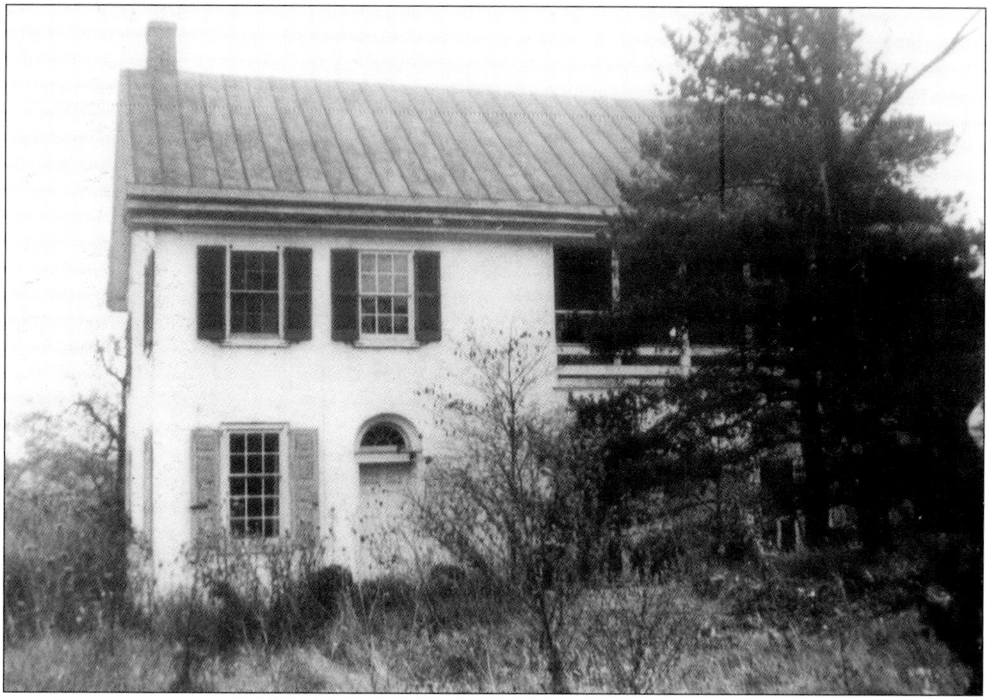

719 Clayhor Avenue. The oldest section of this stone farmhouse was built for Philip Schrack, son of Trappe founder Jacob Schrack Sr. and a tanner by trade. Newspaper advertisements reveal that there was also a quarry on Philip Schrack's property, which likely provided the stone from which his brothers Christian, John, and Jacob Jr. built their own houses. Later owned by artist Walter Stuempfig and then by Paul Davis, the house was in deteriorated condition when the present owners bought the property in 1978, but it has since been lovingly restored. The barn had already been torn down by that time; note the wooden beams used to shore it up in the photograph below. In the 1940s and 1950s, the barn was used to shelter steers raised by Harold and Iona (Souder) Weaver, who owned a 122-acre farm at 345 West Second Avenue. (Both, courtesy of the Historical Society of Trappe, Collegeville, Perkiomen Valley.)

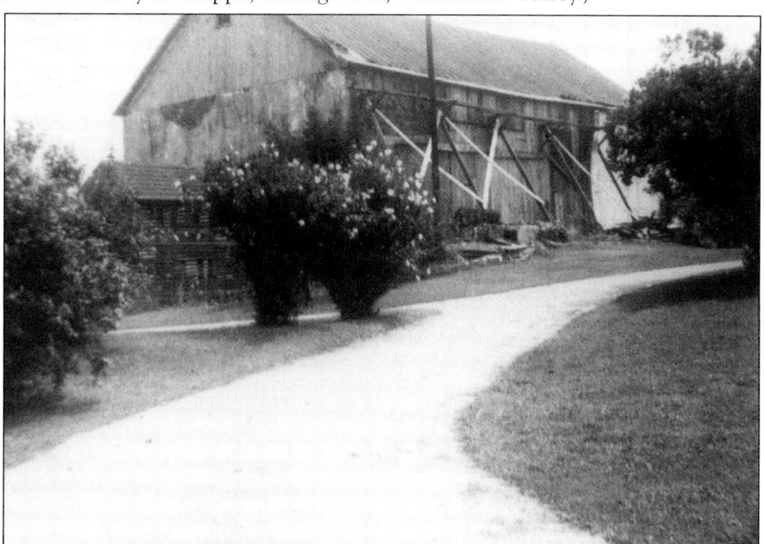

Six

SCHOOLS

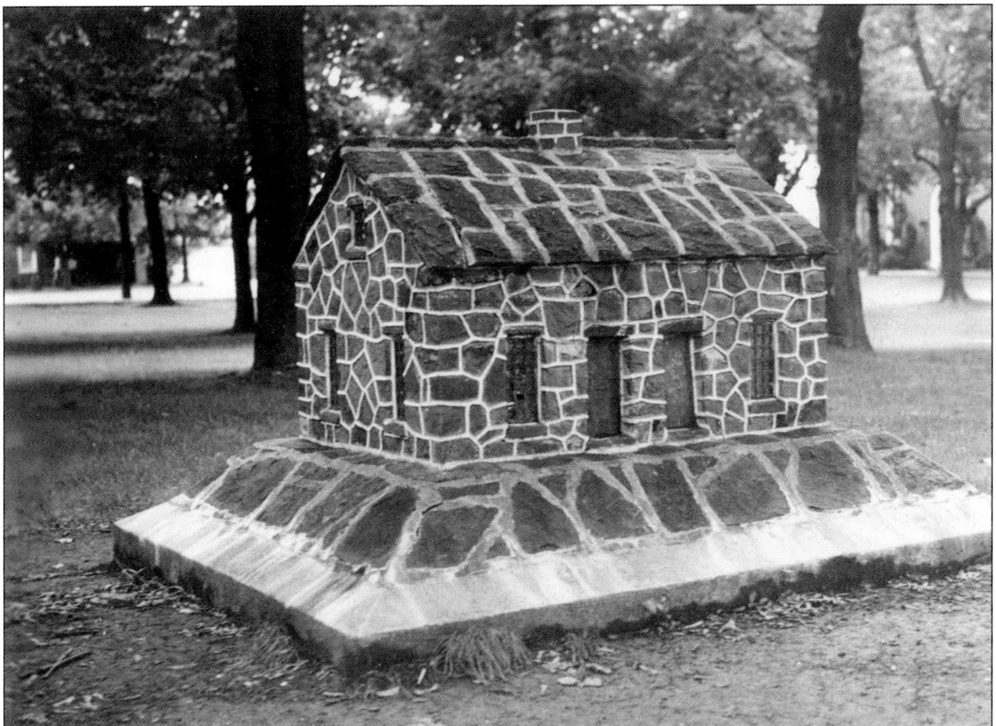

AUGUSTUS LUTHERAN CHURCH SCHOOL MODEL, C. 1988. The earliest-known schoolhouse in Trappe was a log structure built near Augustus Lutheran Church in 1743; it was replaced with another log building in 1750, then with one made of stone that also included dwelling quarters for a resident schoolmaster in 1793. From 1808 to 1811, future governor Francis Shunk was the schoolmaster. The last parochial schoolmaster was Abraham Miller in 1845, after which the building was rented to the directors of the local public school. The schoolhouse was torn down in September 1851. It is memorialized by this stone model, erected in 1931. (Courtesy of the Historical Society of Trappe, Collegeville, Perkiomen Valley.)

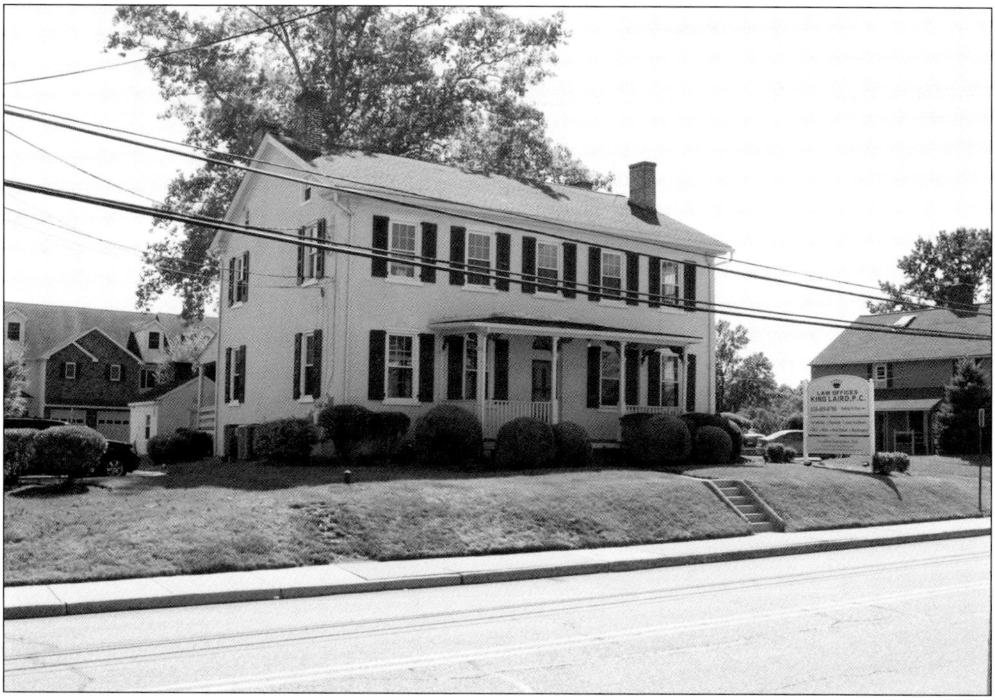

360 West Main Street. In the mid-1700s, this property was home to a tavern known as the Duke of Cumberland. It was acquired by schoolmaster Henry Prizer in 1833, then remodeled, and finally opened as the Trappe Boarding School in 1838. The school, later known as the Washington Hall Collegiate Institute, was moved to a large four-story brick building erected at 550 West Main Street in 1853. (Photograph by Denae A. Zvarick.)

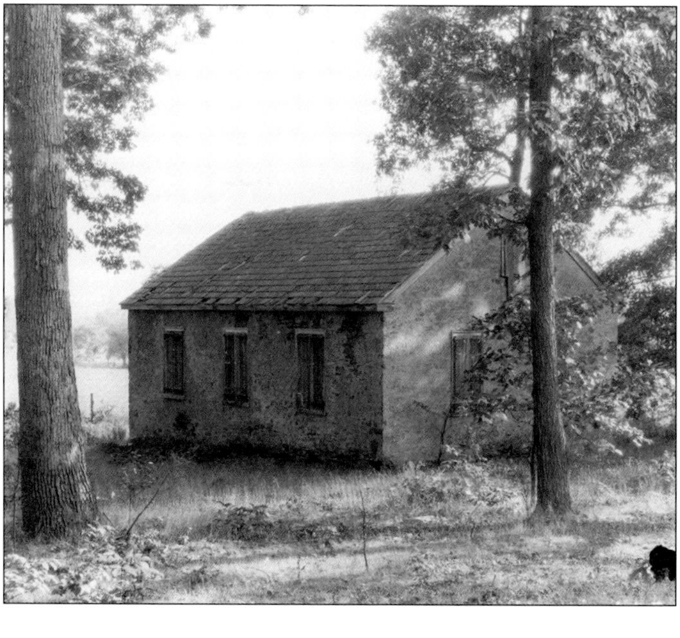

Todd's School. In 1832, Andrew Todd donated the land on which a one-room stone schoolhouse, known as Todd's School, was built in place of an earlier log schoolhouse. The founding trustees were David Beard, John Berk, Abraham Hunsicker, John Prizer, and John Todd. In 1844, when the township accepted the state's Free Public Schools Act of 1834, it became the Freeland Public School and served as such for about 30 years. (Courtesy of the Ursinus College Archives.)

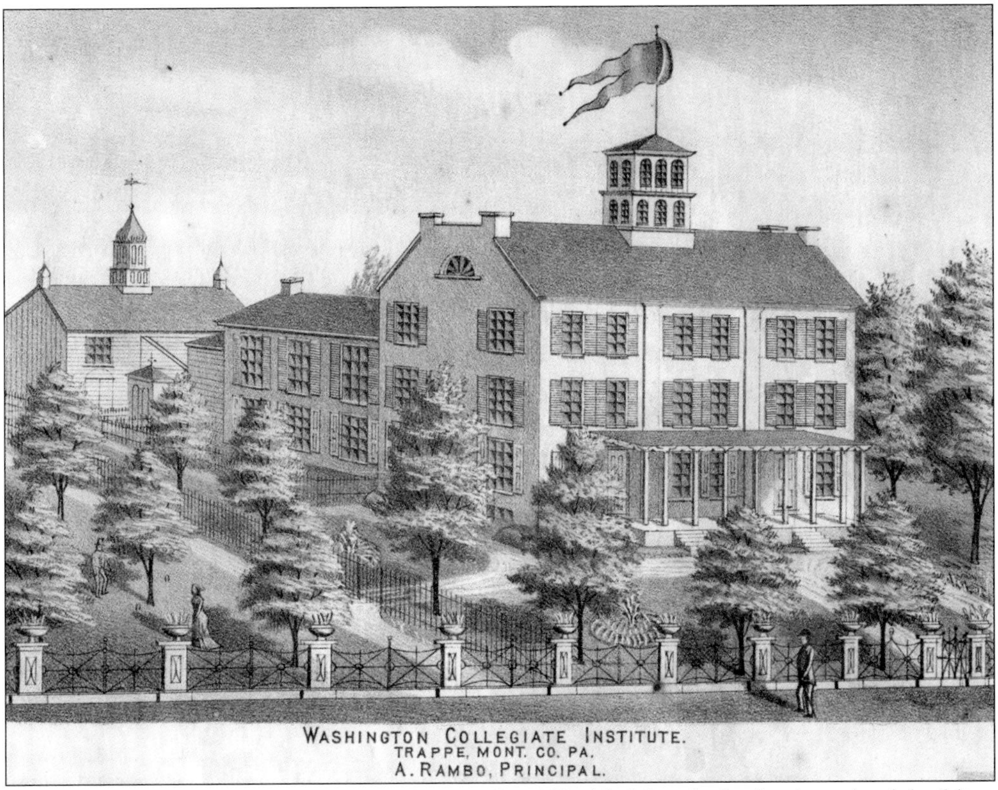

WASHINGTON HALL, 550 WEST MAIN STREET. In 1853, Abel Rambo built a large brick building to house the Washington Hall Collegiate Institute, originally established as the Trappe Boarding School at 360 West Main Street in 1830. The school closed after Rambo's death in 1887, and its contents were dispersed at auction in 1935. Still owned by the Rambo family, the former school has been converted into apartments. (Both, courtesy of the Historical Society of Trappe, Collegeville, Perkiomen Valley.)

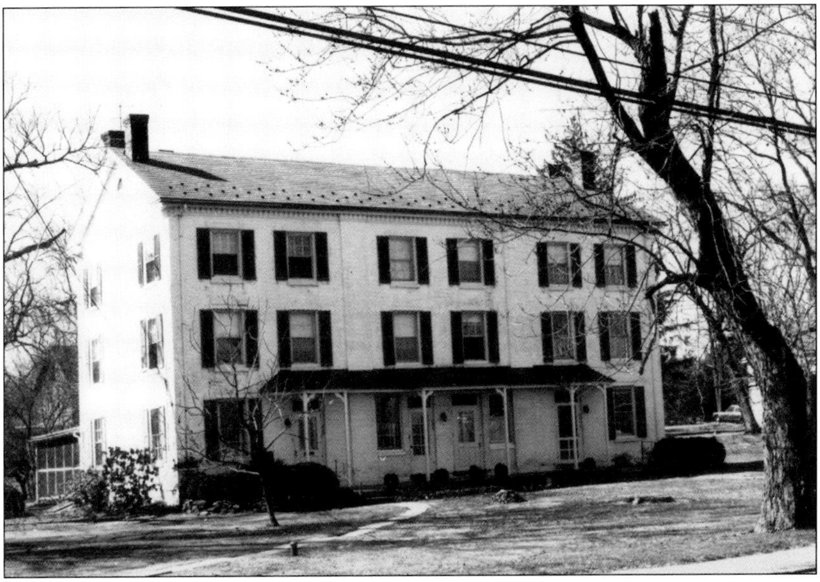

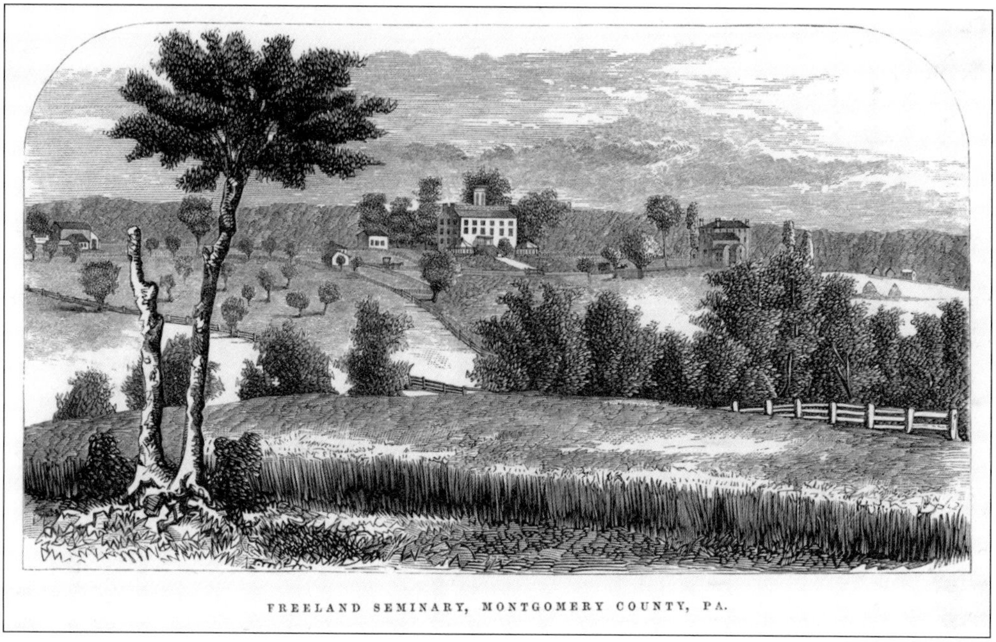

FREELAND SEMINARY, 1853. In 1848, Rev. Abraham Hunsicker established Freeland Seminary in what is now Collegeville. This rendering from the school's 1853 catalog suggests how rural the area was at the time, depicting the seminary buildings surrounded by acres of farmland and trees. More than 2,000 young men studied at Freeland Seminary during the 21 years the school was in operation. (Courtesy of the Ursinus College Archives.)

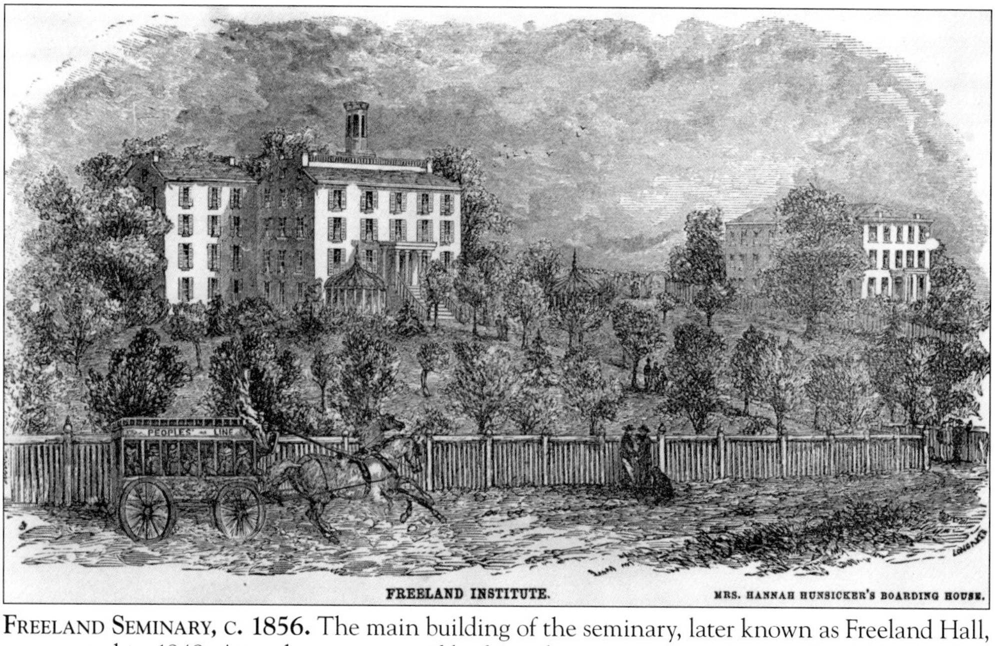

FREELAND SEMINARY, C. 1856. The main building of the seminary, later known as Freeland Hall, was erected in 1848. Attendance grew swiftly, from three to seventy-nine pupils within the first year. By 1856, a wing had been added, later known as Stine Hall, on the north side of Freeland. It is depicted in this engraving along with a building to the east identified as "Mrs. Hannah Hunsicker's Boarding House," later known as Prospect Terrace. (Courtesy of the Ursinus College Archives.)

Freeland Seminary Receipt, 1856. This receipt shows that John E. Spare paid $40 for his son Charles's tuition and boarding expenses at the Freeland Seminary in 1856. It is signed by principal Henry A. Hunsicker, son of the seminary's founder Rev. Abraham Hunsicker. (Courtesy of the Historical Society of Trappe, Collegeville, Perkiomen Valley.)

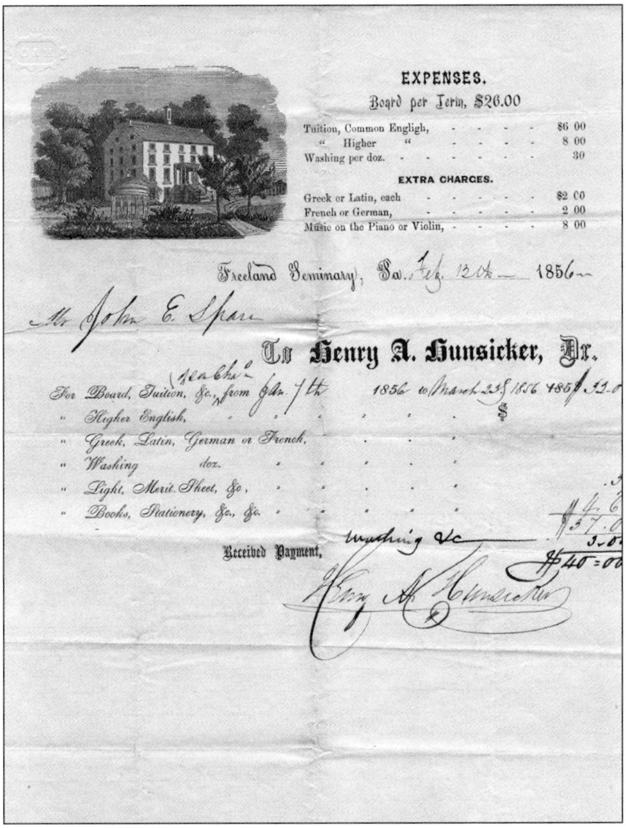

EXPENSES.

Board per Term, $26.00

Tuition, Common English,	$6 00
" Higher "	8 00
Washing per doz.	30

EXTRA CHARGES.

Greek or Latin, each	$2 00
French or German,	2 00
Music on the Piano or Violin,	8 00

Freeland Seminary, Pa. Feb. 13th 1856

Mr John E. Spare

To Henry A. Hunsicker, Dr.

For Board, Tuition, &c., from Jan. 7th 1856 to March 23 1856

" Higher English,

" Greek, Latin, German or French,

" Washing doz.

" Light, Merit Sheet, &c.

" Books, Stationery, &c., &c.

Received Payment, washing &c

$40=00

Henry A. Hunsicker

Freeland Seminary Reunion, 1910. More than 60 Freeland Seminary alumni gathered on the steps of the old Freeland Seminary building in 1910 for the 62nd anniversary of the institution's founding. Three years later, the building was remodeled and became known as Freeland Hall. (Courtesy of the Ursinus College Archives.)

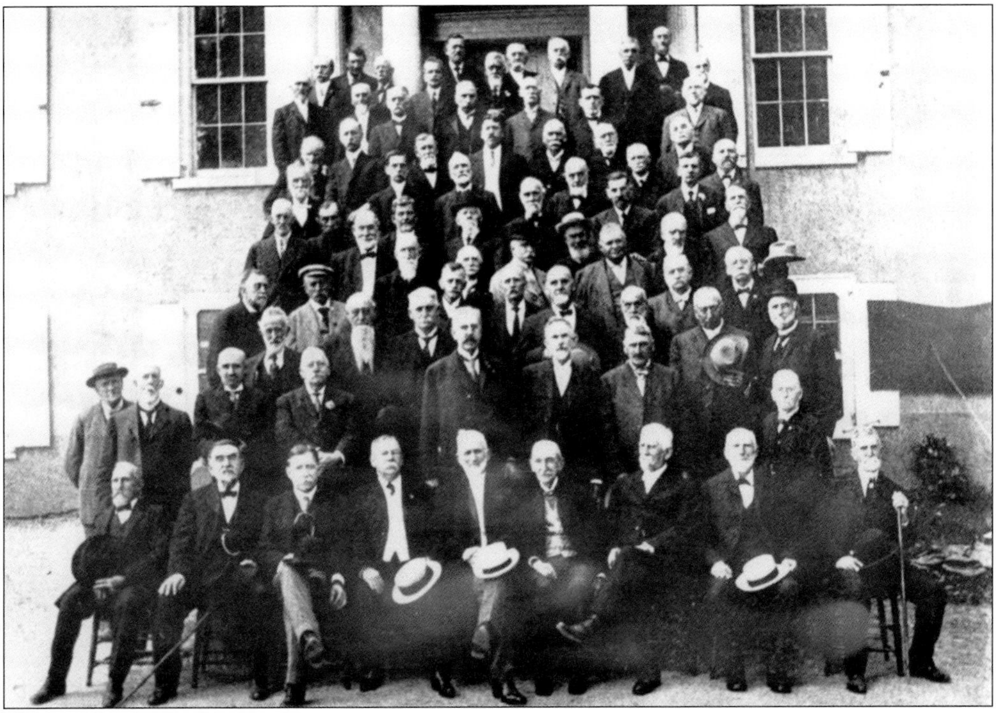

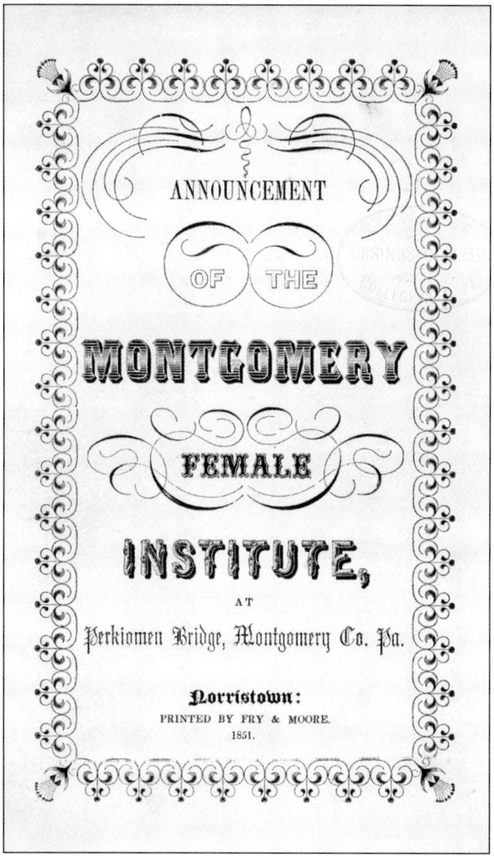

MONTGOMERY FEMALE INSTITUTE ANNOUNCEMENT, 1851. Founded by Dr. and Mrs. J. Warrene Sunderland in 1851, the Montgomery Female Institute was financed by Rev. Abraham Hunsicker. In 1853, it was chartered by the state legislature as the Pennsylvania Female College. A pioneer in liberal arts education for women, it offered "facilities for the education of young ladies, not inferior to any other Institution in the country," according to an 1855 advertisement. (Courtesy of the Ursinus College Archives.)

PENNSYLVANIA FEMALE COLLEGE, 1866. This image of the Pennsylvania Female College appeared on the back cover of its 1866 catalog. A list of instructors within included college president J. Warrene Sunderland ("professor of moral, mental, and physical science"), Luanna Sunderland ("teacher of drawing, painting, and fancy work"), Elizabeth Chatham ("teacher of the Latin and Greek languages"), and Sarah Longstreth ("teacher of botany"). Others taught mathematics, penmanship, music, French, and German. (Courtesy of the Ursinus College Archives.)

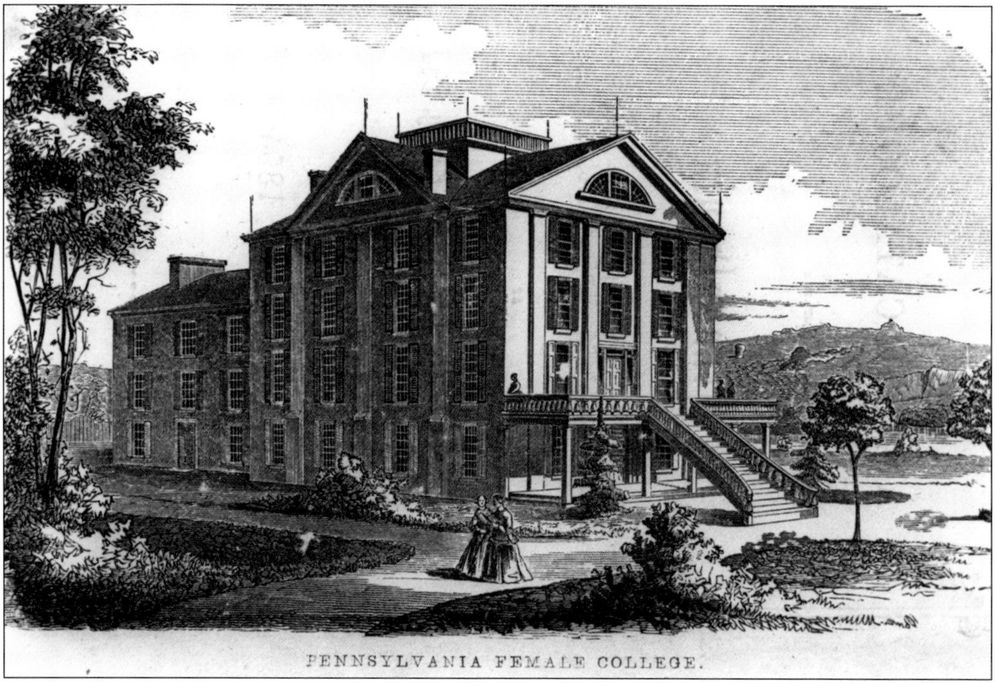

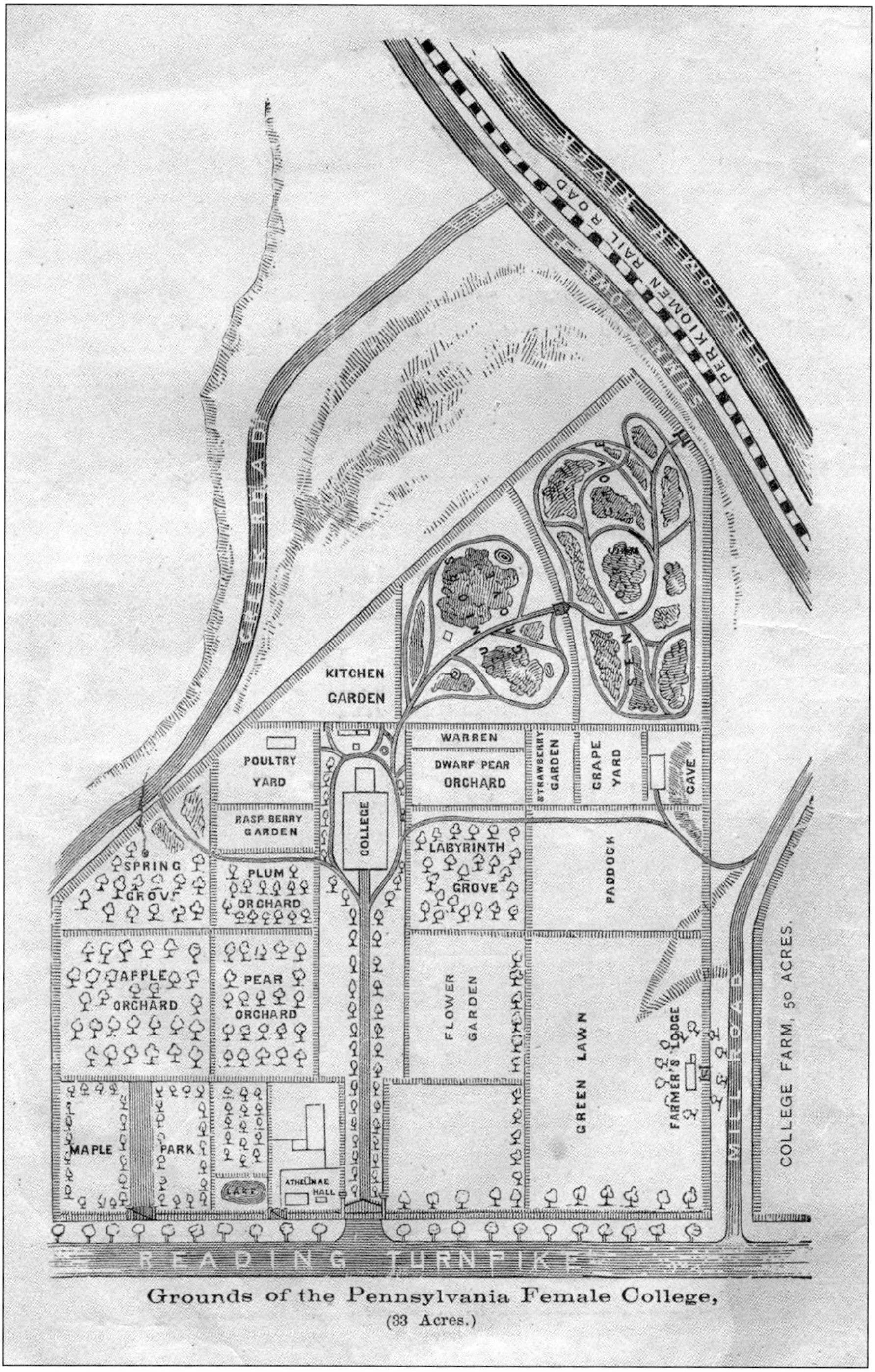

Grounds of the Pennsylvania Female College,
(33 Acres.)

GROUNDS OF THE PENNSYLVANIA FEMALE COLLEGE. Glenwood Hall, an impressive four-story building accessed via a 900-foot-long avenue lined with stately trees, was the focal point of the 33-acre campus. The parklike grounds included an expansive lawn, flower and kitchen gardens, fruit orchards, a poultry yard, a paddock, and a collection of marble statuary. (Courtesy of Jerry A. Chiccarine.)

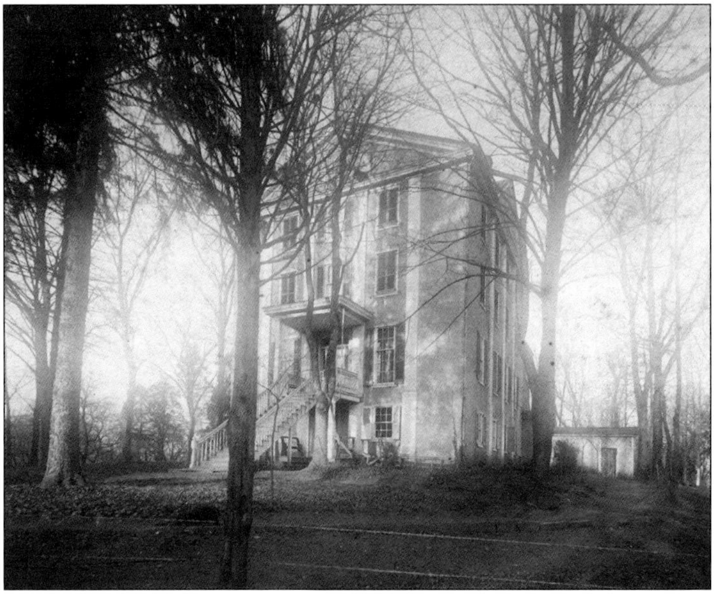

Pennsylvania Female College, 1897. Surviving photographs of the Pennsylvania Female College reveal that it was as impressive as the engravings suggest. The main building was accessed via a grand exterior staircase. After the college closed in 1880, it was bought by Francis J. Clamer, remodeled, and leased for use as a boardinghouse. (Courtesy of the Historical Society of Trappe, Collegeville, Perkiomen Valley.)

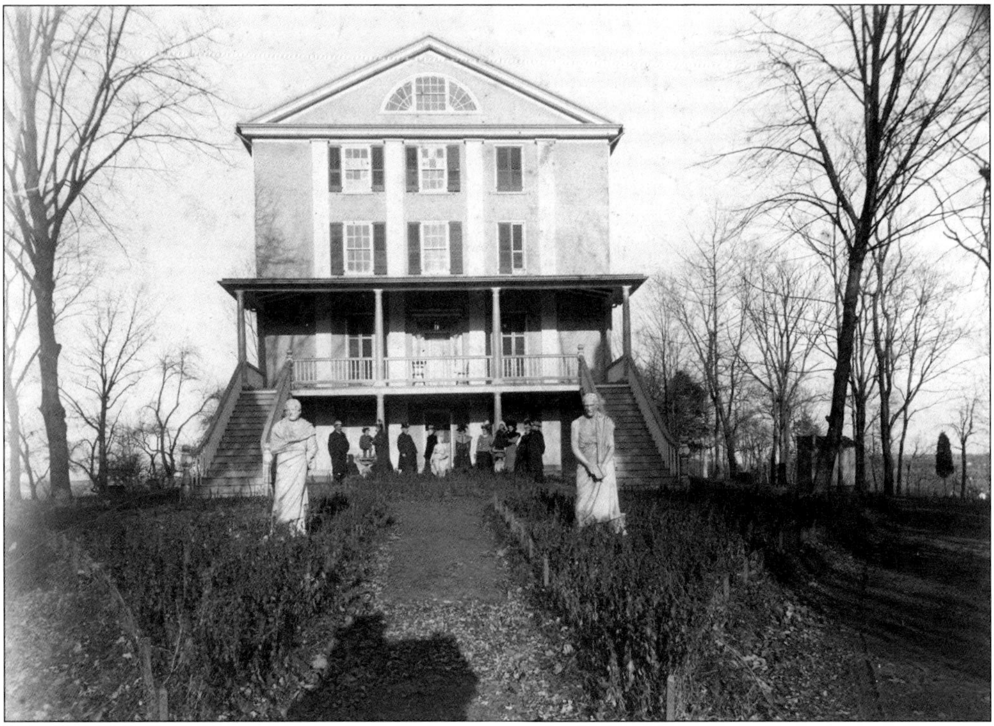

Pennsylvania Female College, 1900. The rear elevation of Glenwood Hall, which overlooked a sloping hillside, was a popular gathering place to enjoy views of the gardens, as seen by this group under the porch. Note the pair of classical statues facing toward the Perkiomen Creek in the foreground. (Courtesy of the Historical Society of Trappe, Collegeville, Perkiomen Valley.)

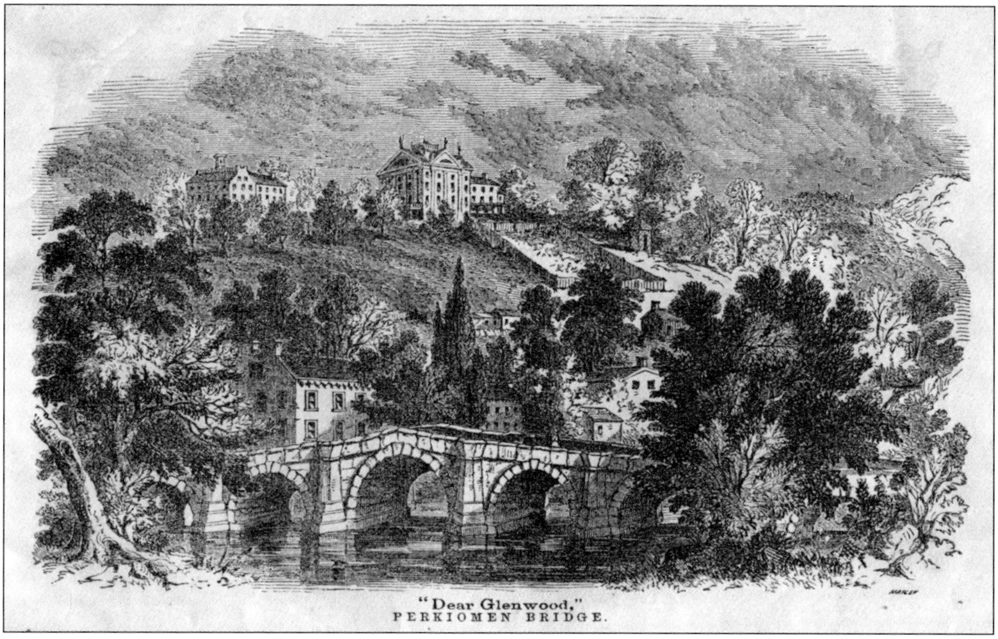

"DEAR GLENWOOD." Built at the end of what is now Glenwood Avenue in Collegeville on a bluff overlooking the Perkiomen Creek, the Pennsylvania Female College was affectionately referred to as "Dear Glenwood" by students and alumnae. The four-story, 40-room building was demolished in 1919; salvaged architectural components were later used in the construction of houses on Glenwood Avenue. (Courtesy of Jerry A. Chiccarine.)

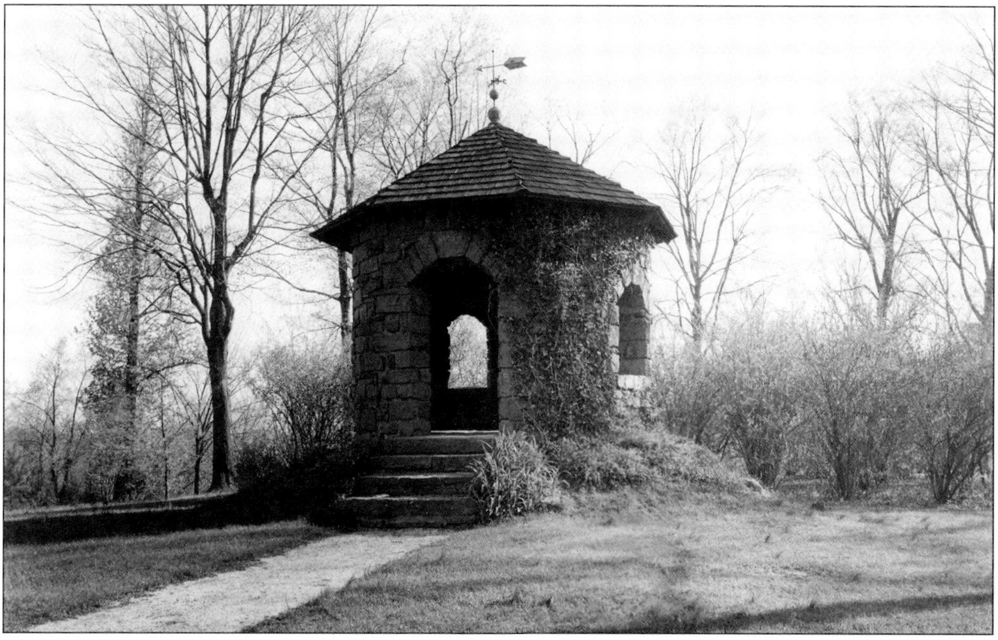

GLENWOOD MONUMENT, 1962. The Clamer family built this circular stone gazebo on Glenwood Avenue in 1920 to mark the site of the Pennsylvania Female College. More than 1,000 young women were educated at the college before it closed in 1880. (Courtesy of the Ursinus College Archives.)

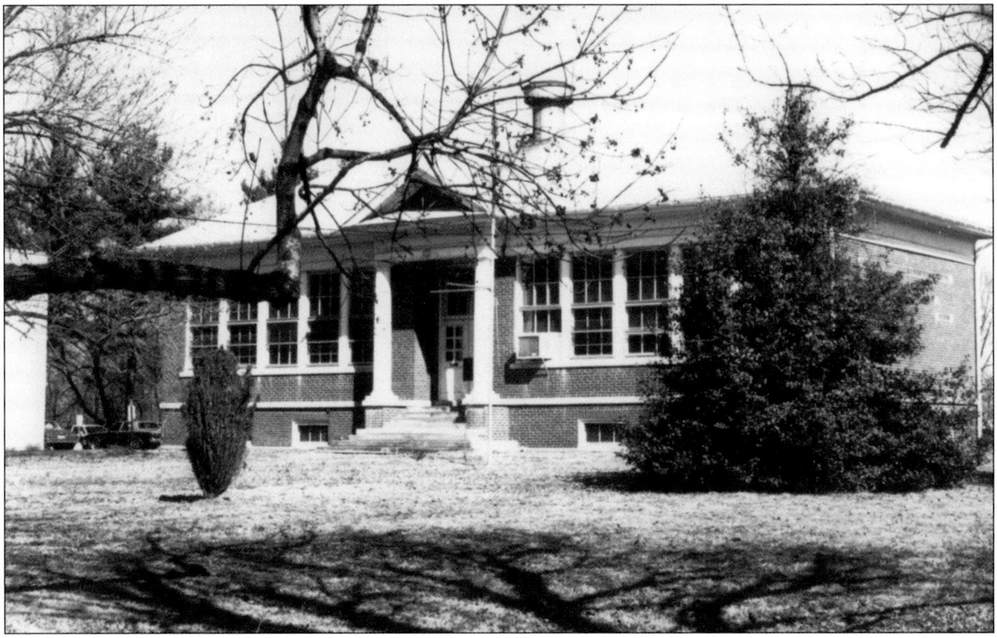

TRAPPE ELEMENTARY SCHOOL. On February 23, 1880, the Trappe Independent School District was officially established. The district included Trappe, Freeland, and Collegeville, but was abolished in 1896 when Trappe and Collegeville were incorporated as separate boroughs. In 1922, a new elementary school consisting of two rooms was constructed at 525 West Main Street. It was used as a school until 1958, then acquired by the Borough of Trappe in 1965 for use as a town hall. (Both, courtesy of the Historical Society of Trappe, Collegeville, Perkiomen Valley.)

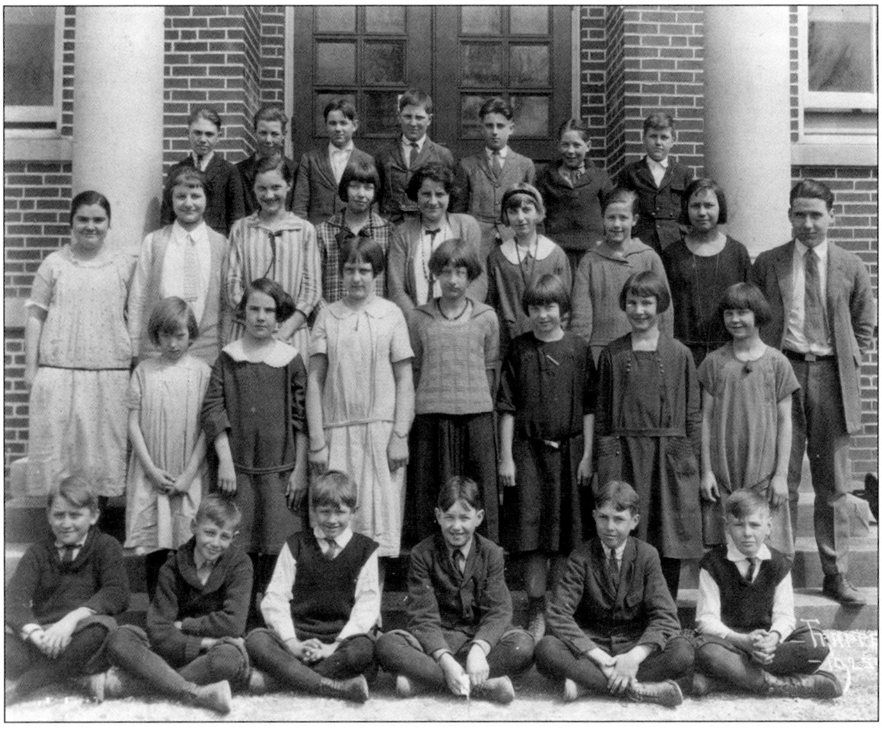

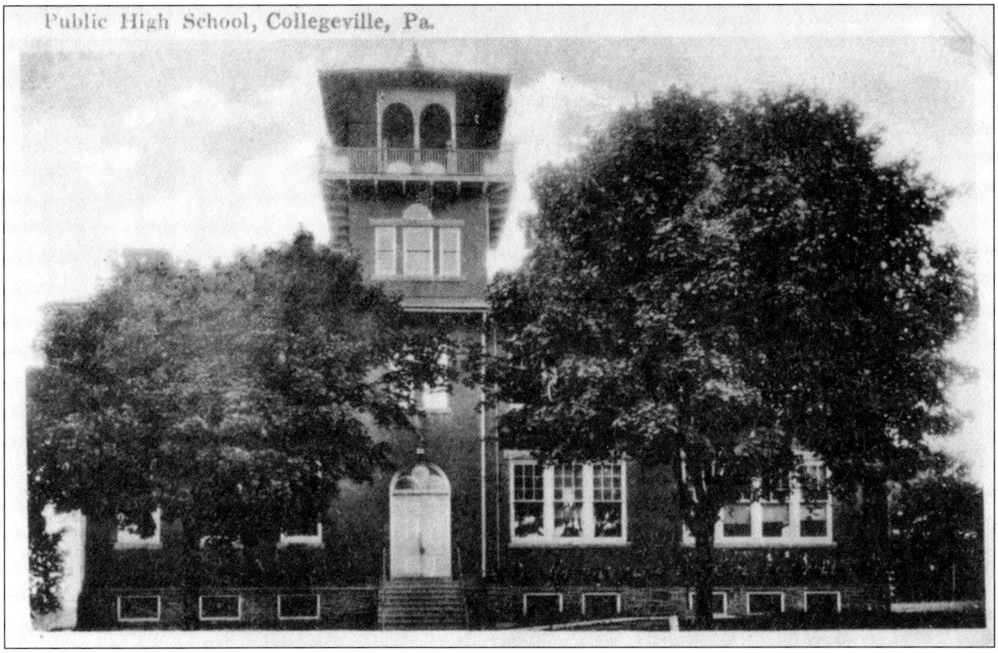

COLLEGEVILLE HIGH SCHOOL, 95 WEST FIFTH STREET. In 1897, the Borough of Collegeville erected a new public high school. An addition was built in 1914 to provide more classroom space, but the school was soon overcrowded. In 1938, Collegeville and Trappe voted to create a joint school board and construct a new high school, leaving this building for first through sixth grades. The school ceased operations in June 1958, then was sold and remodeled into the College Court Apartments. (Courtesy of Jerry A. Chiccarine.)

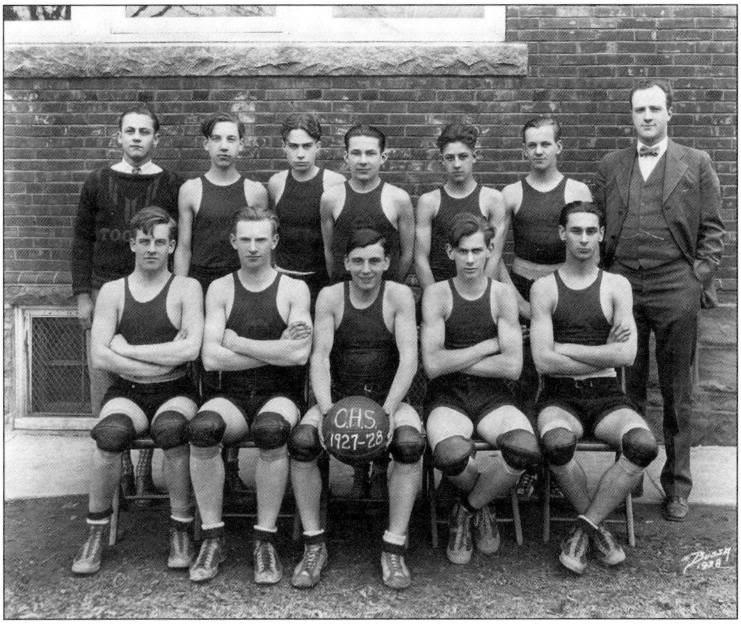

MEN'S BASKETBALL TEAM, 1928. The Collegeville High School had both men's and women's basketball teams by the late 1920s. This photograph depicts the men's team of 1927–1928. (Courtesy of the Historical Society of Trappe, Collegeville, Perkiomen Valley.)

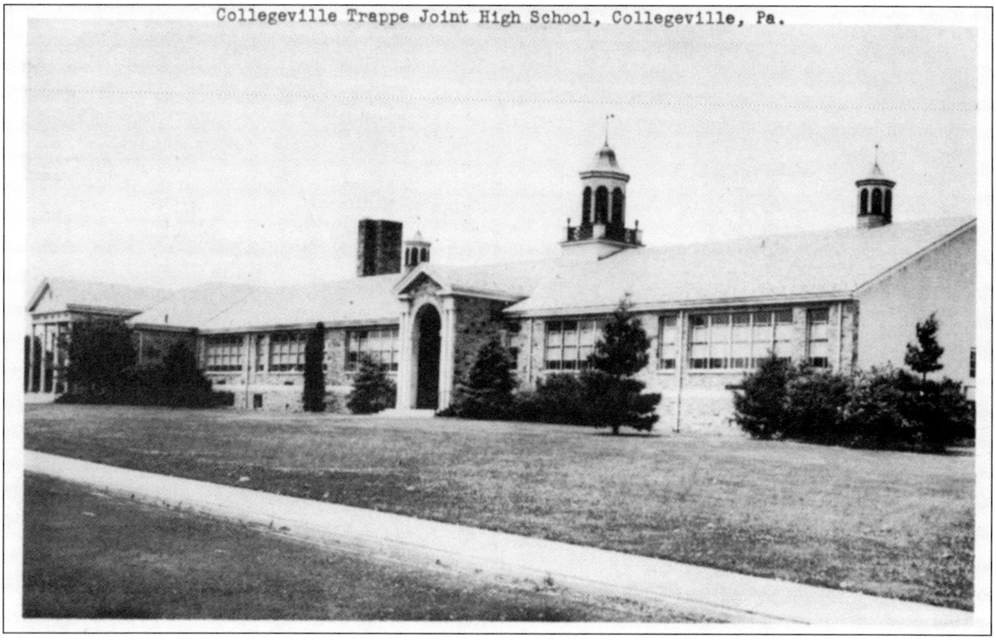

COLLEGEVILLE-TRAPPE HIGH SCHOOL, 29 EAST FIRST AVENUE. On November 11, 1938, a groundbreaking ceremony was held for a new Collegeville-Trappe High School to be built under the auspices of the federal government's Public Works Administration. The postcard above depicts the school in its original form; in 1953, an addition was built on the right side to match the Colonial Revival style of the school, as seen in the postcard below. Howard B. Keyser, a 1905 graduate of Collegeville High School and a 1910 graduate of Ursinus College, was the supervising principal of the newly consolidated school district. The project architect was W. Marshall Hughes of Reading, Pennsylvania, and the general contractor was Warren B. Zern of Pottstown, Pennsylvania. Most of the land for the new school was provided by Ursinus College through a bargain sale in which the former Frederick Muhlenberg property at 151 West Main Street was subdivided. The former school is currently being converted into condominiums. (Both, courtesy of Jerry A. Chiccarine.)

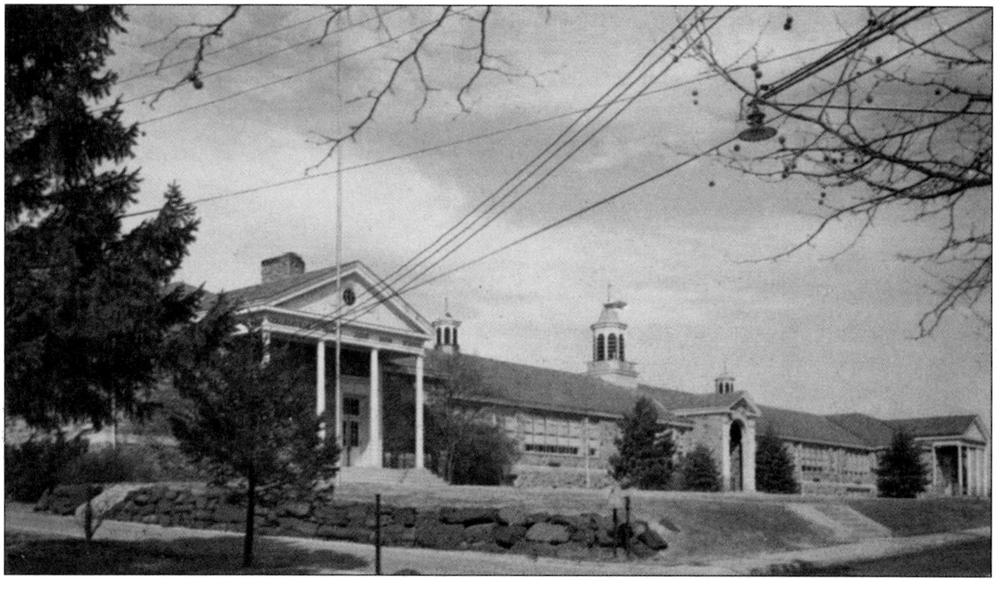

Seven

Ursinus College

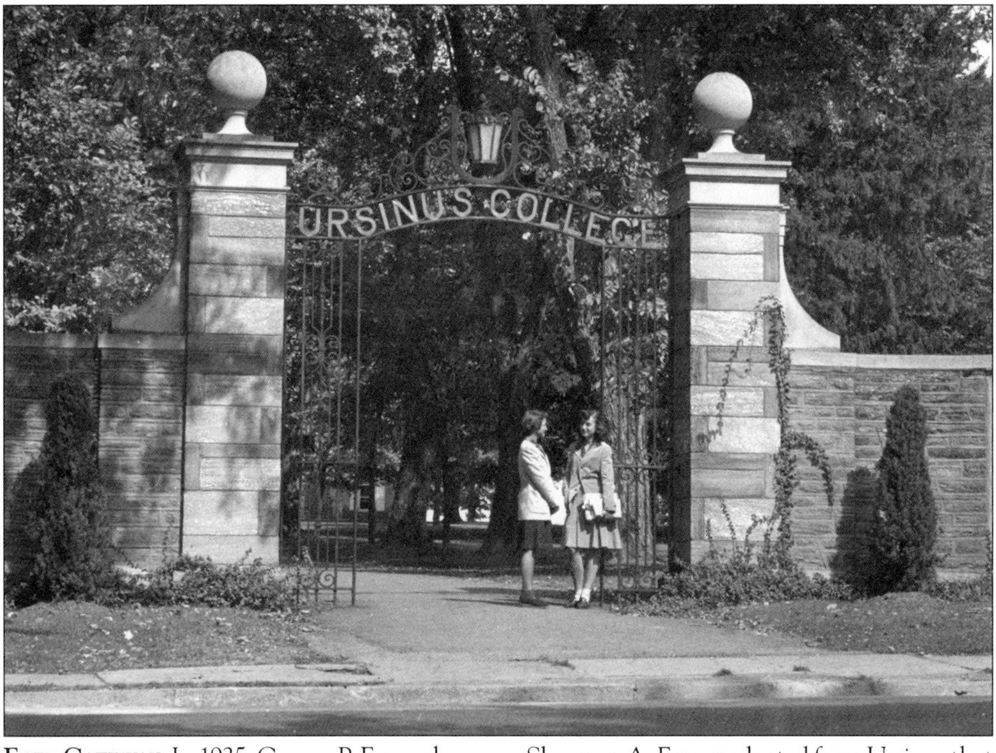

Eger Gateway. In 1925, George P. Eger, whose son Sherman A. Eger graduated from Ursinus that year, donated this iron and stone gateway inset with tablets that tell the history of education on the campus since the founding of Todd's School in 1832. The gateway marks the campus entrance on Main Street, where a walking path once led back to Freeland Hall. (Courtesy of the Ursinus College Archives.)

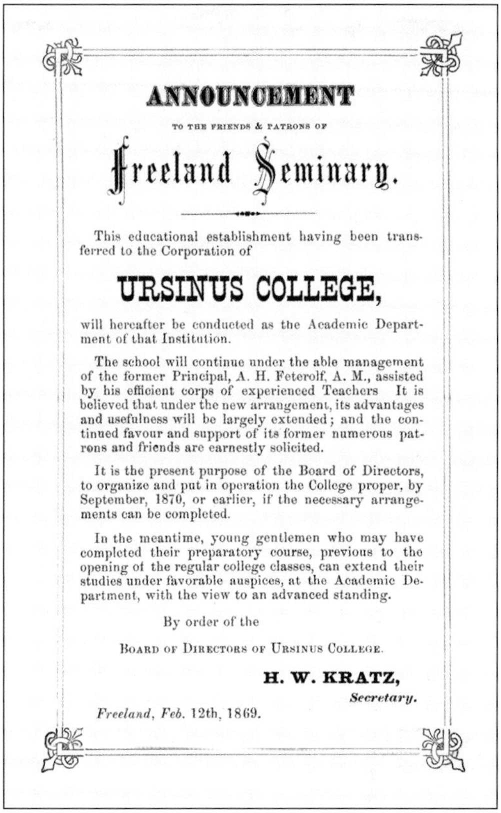

ANNOUNCEMENT

TO THE FRIENDS & PATRONS OF

Freeland Seminary.

This educational establishment having been transferred to the Corporation of

URSINUS COLLEGE,

will hereafter be conducted as the Academic Department of that Institution.

The school will continue under the able management of the former Principal, A. H. Feterolf, A. M., assisted by his efficient corps of experienced Teachers It is believed that under the new arrangement, its advantages and usefulness will be largely extended; and the continued favour and support of its former numerous patrons and friends are earnestly solicited.

It is the present purpose of the Board of Directors, to organize and put in operation the College proper, by September, 1870, or earlier, if the necessary arrangements can be completed.

In the meantime, young gentlemen who may have completed their preparatory course, previous to the opening of the regular college classes, can extend their studies under favorable auspices, at the Academic Department, with the view to an advanced standing.

By order of the

BOARD OF DIRECTORS OF URSINUS COLLEGE.

H. W. KRATZ,
Secretary.

Freeland, Feb. 12th, 1869.

FOUNDING OF URSINUS COLLEGE, 1869. On February 5, 1869, the Pennsylvania legislature granted the charter of Ursinus College. Seven days later, this broadside was issued announcing the transfer of Freeland Seminary to the newly incorporated college. For $20,000, Ursinus acquired the seminary's buildings and seven-plus acres of land. (Courtesy of the Ursinus College Archives.)

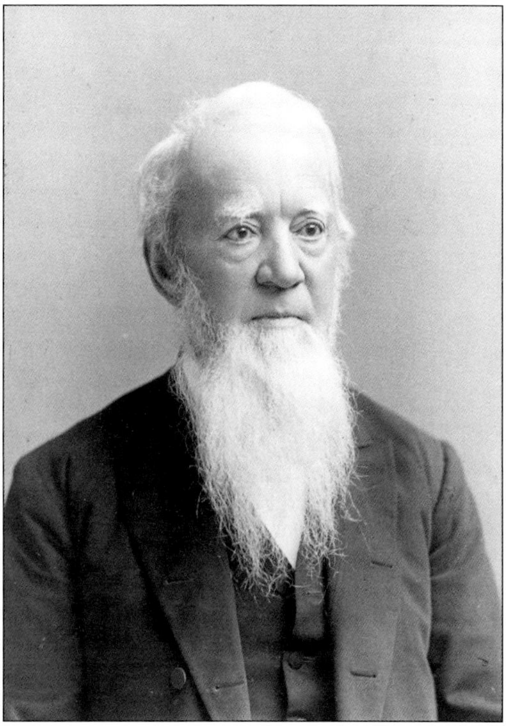

DR. JOHN H.A. BOMBERGER. The college's founder and first president, Dr. John Henry Augustus Bomberger (1817–1890), was a minister and leader of the "low church" party within the Reformed Church. In 1867, his supporters decided to establish their own college, leading to the founding of Ursinus in 1869. The college was named after Zacharias Ursinus (1534–1583), a Reformed Church theologian who coauthored the Palatine Liturgy and was the principal author of the Heidelberg Catechism. (Courtesy of the Ursinus College Archives.)

Freeland Hall, c. 1872. For the first 20 years after its founding, Ursinus College operated on the Freeland Seminary campus, including the main building (later known as Freeland Hall) and its adjacent west wing (later known as Stine Hall). This photograph was taken shortly before construction of the east wing (later known as Derr Hall), which was dedicated on October 1, 1872. (Courtesy of the Ursinus College Archives.)

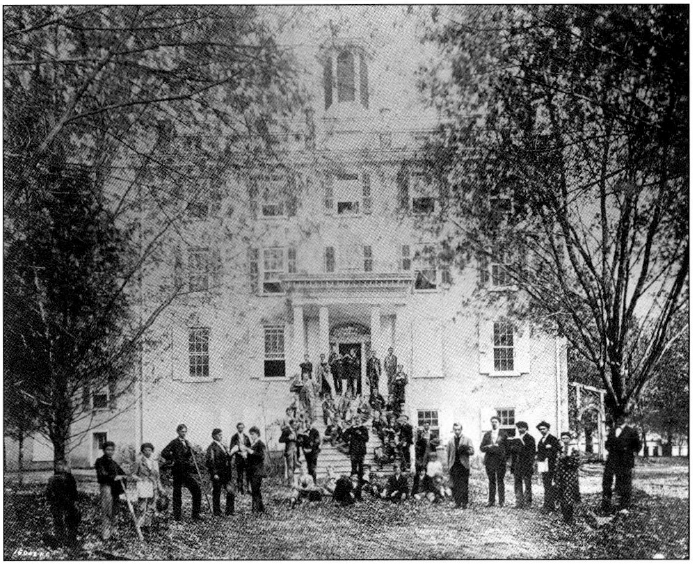

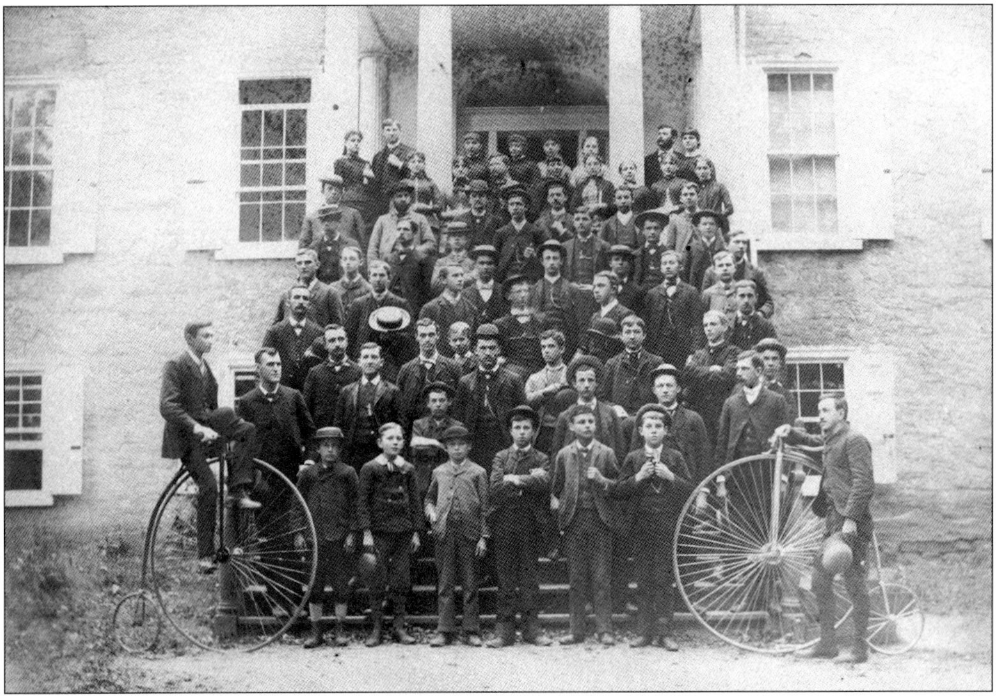

Freeland Hall, 1882. Judging by their frequent appearance in early photographs, the steps of Freeland Hall were the most popular place on campus to pose for the camera, as this group of young men did in 1882. Two of them even brought their penny-farthing bicycles along for the occasion. (Courtesy of the Ursinus College Archives.)

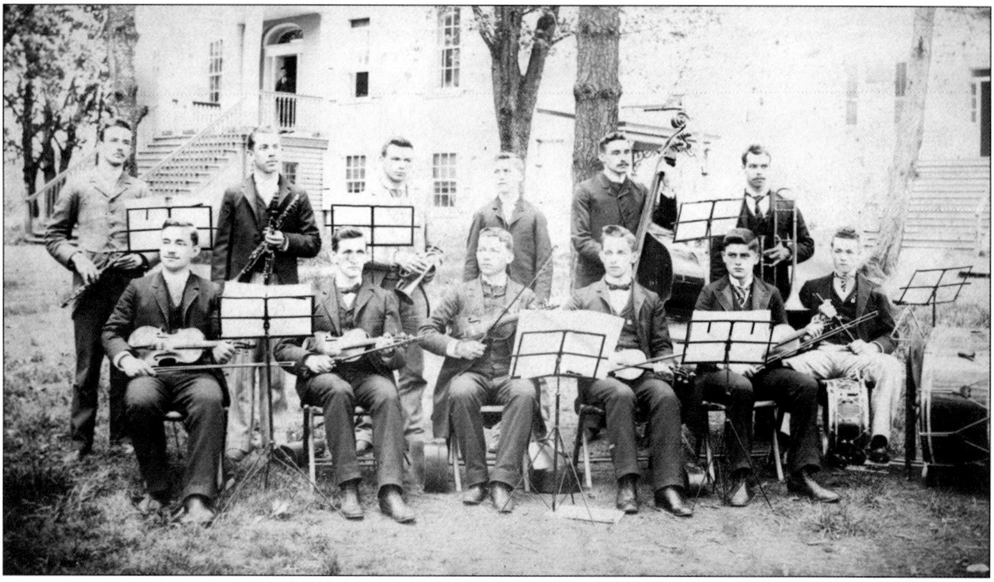

Orchestra, 1889. Extracurricular activities included literary and debating societies, drama clubs, and music groups. By 1889, when this photograph was taken, Ursinus students had even formed an orchestra. (Courtesy of the Ursinus College Archives.)

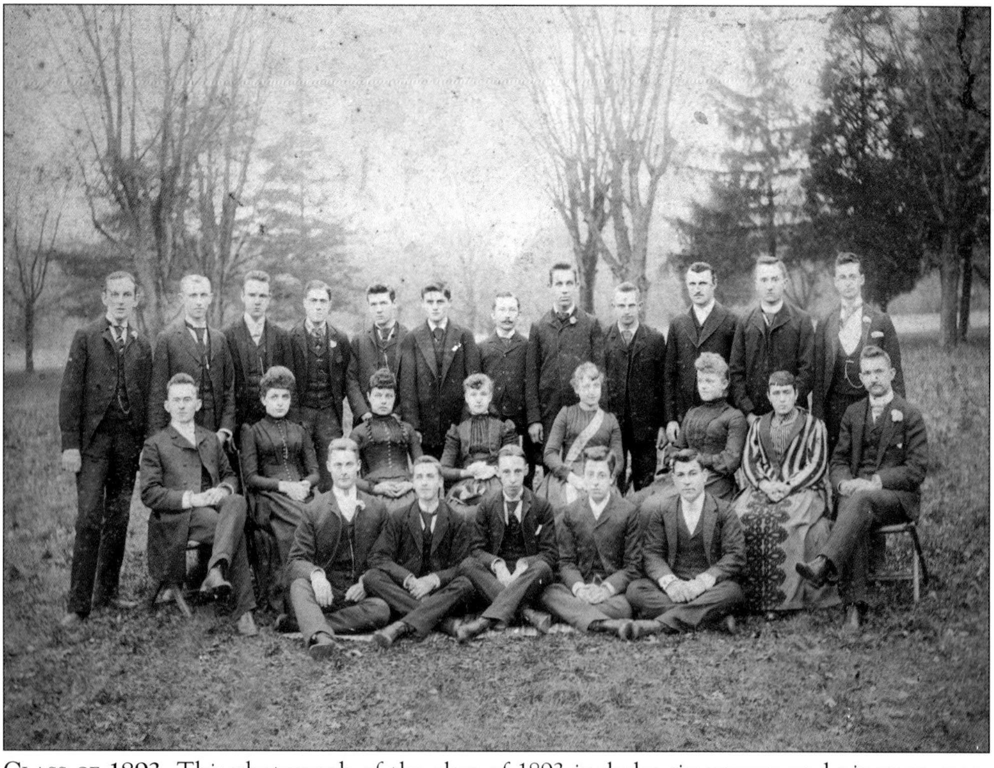

Class of 1893. This photograph of the class of 1893 includes six women and nineteen men. Ursinus College was a pioneer in coed education and began admitting women in 1881, with Minerva Weinberger and Bertha Hendricks as the first female students. Three years later, Minerva graduated as valedictorian of the class. (Courtesy of the Ursinus College Archives.)

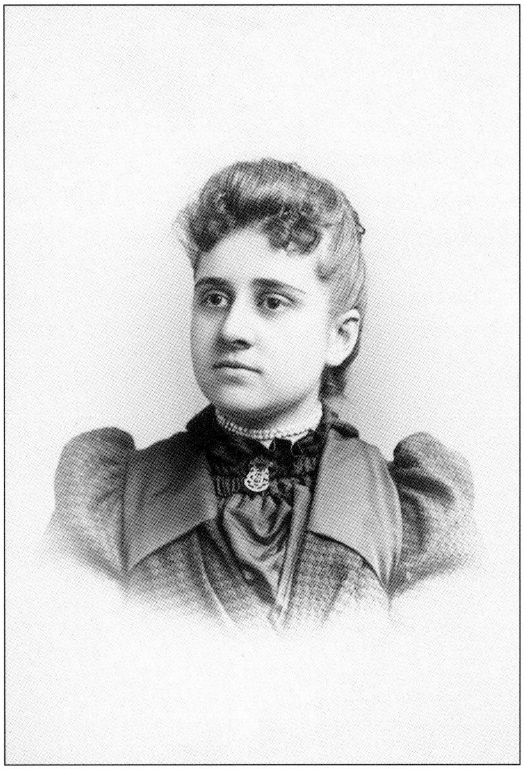

Hallie R. Vanderslice, c. 1891. Collegeville native Hallie R. Vanderslice graduated from Ursinus College in 1891. She was an active member of Augustus Lutheran Church, serving as vice president of the Pastor's Aid Society and secretary of the Sunday school program. (Courtesy of the Ursinus College Archives.)

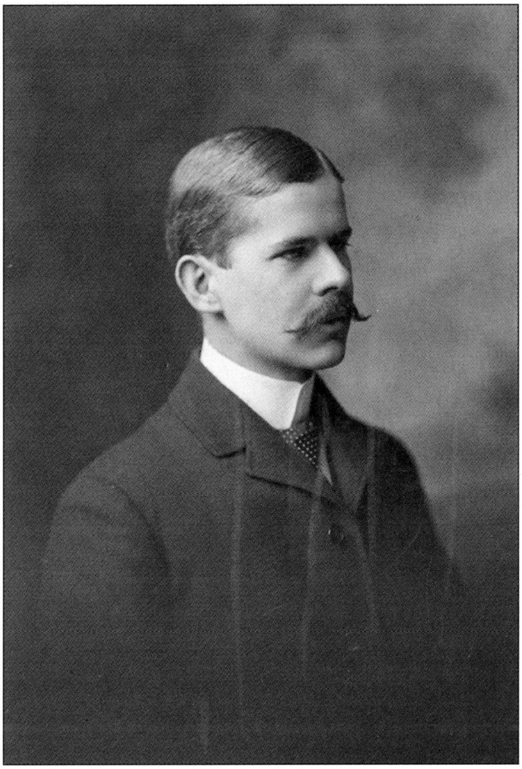

Mayne R. Longstreth, c. 1889. Trappe native Mayne R. Longstreth (1869–1935) graduated from Ursinus College in 1889. After his death in 1935, the college acquired nearly 30 acres of land from his estate along the northern and western sides of the campus, providing much-needed space for soccer, baseball, and other athletic fields. (Courtesy of the Historical Society of Trappe, Collegeville, Perkiomen Valley.)

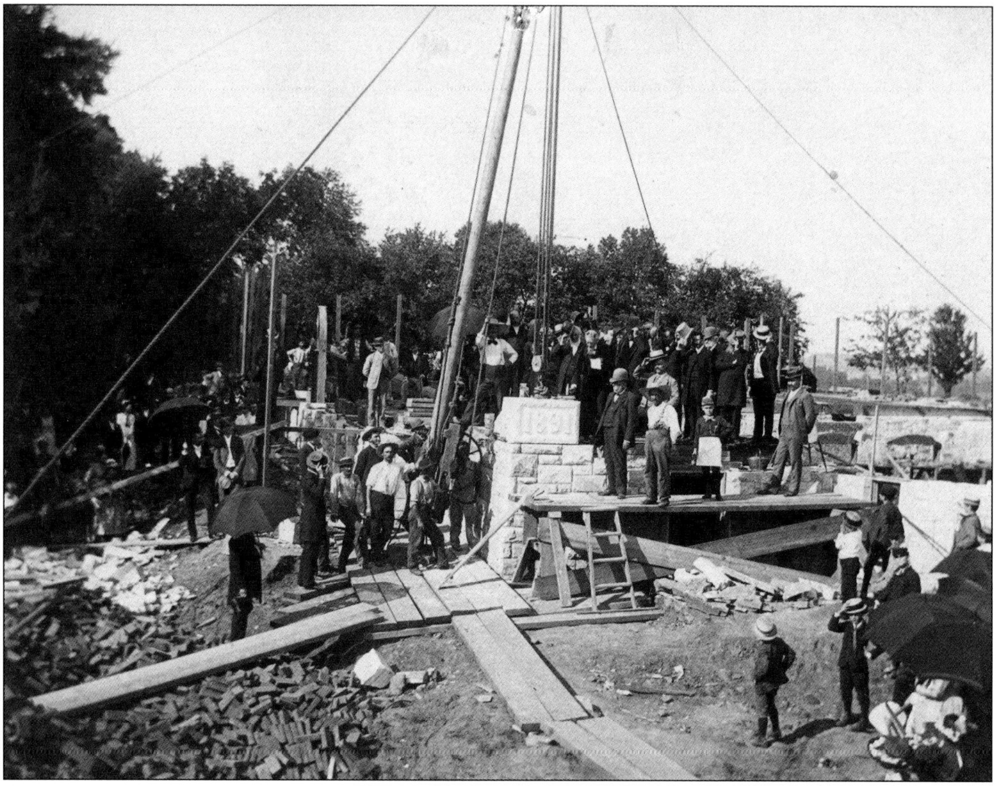

Cornerstone Laying of Bomberger Hall, 1891. As the college's enrollment rose during the 1880s, it quickly outgrew the old Freeland Seminary buildings. With the financial support of Robert Patterson, a wealthy iron manufacturer, a large new building was planned, and a groundbreaking ceremony was held on April 22, 1891. Several months later, the cornerstone was laid on Commencement Day, June 25, 1891. Patterson appears in this photograph standing beside the cornerstone; he died only two years later and was buried at St. Luke's cemetery in Trappe. The building was named Bomberger Memorial Hall after Dr. John H.A. Bomberger, who died on August 19, 1890. (Courtesy of the Ursinus College Archives.)

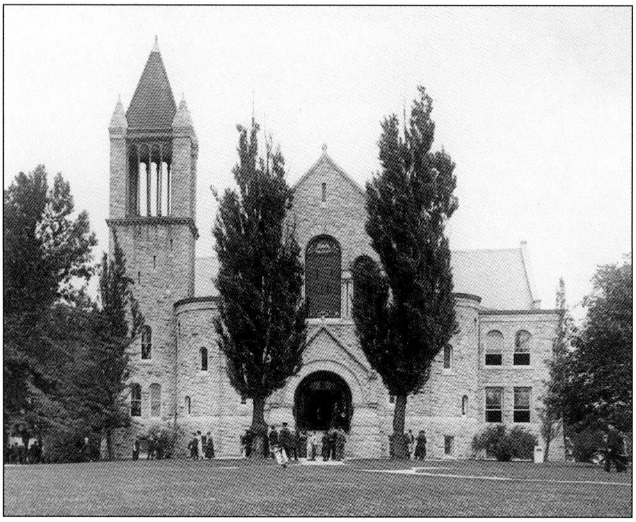

Bomberger Hall. Designed in the Romanesque style by architect Frank R. Watson of Philadelphia, Bomberger Memorial Hall was dedicated on June 23, 1892. Much of the stone was quarried in nearby King of Prussia, Pennsylvania. The hall provided the college with much-needed space for modern classrooms, laboratories, offices, a library, and a chapel. (Courtesy of the Ursinus College Archives.)

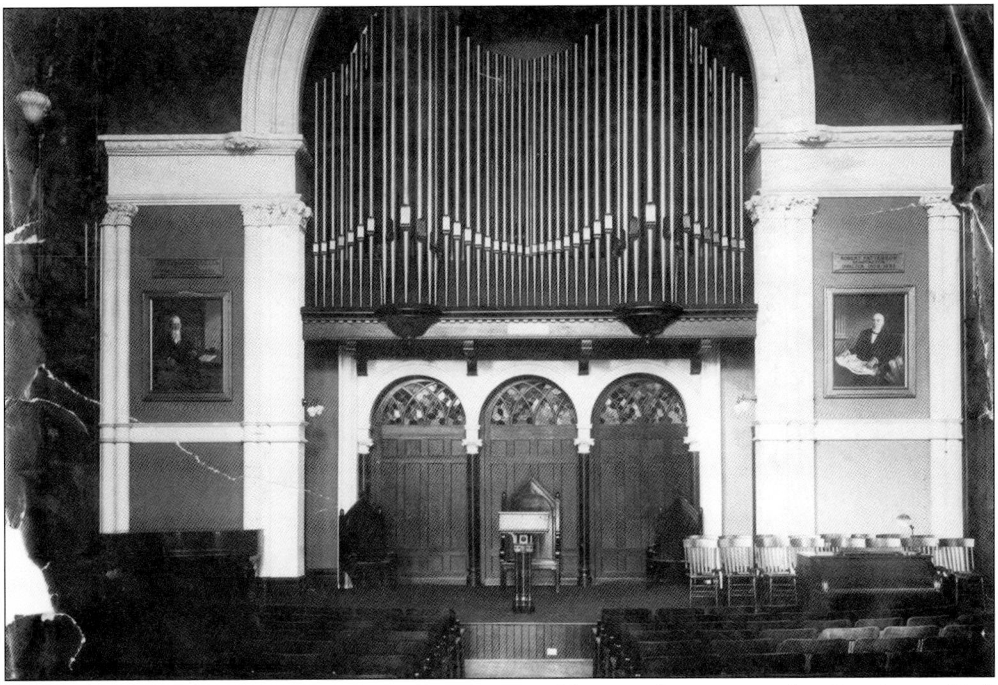

Bomberger Chapel and Clark Memorial Organ. The grandest space within Bomberger Hall is the chapel. This photograph was taken soon after the installation of the Charles Heber Clark Memorial Organ, a two-manual Haskell organ dedicated in 1916. Portraits of president John H.A. Bomberger and benefactor Robert Patterson flank the organ pipes to the left and right. (Courtesy of the Ursinus College Archives.)

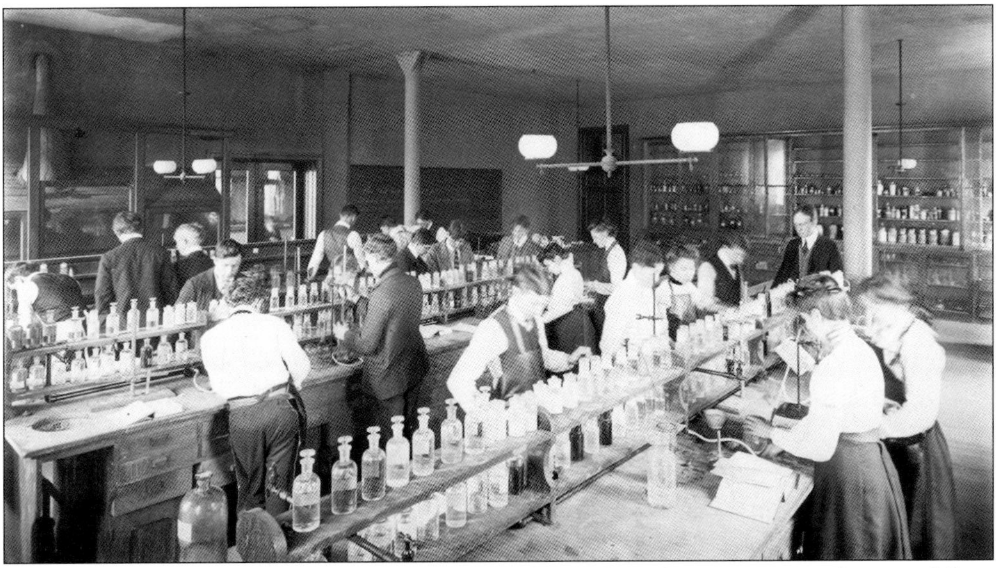

Chemistry Laboratory, c. 1905. Large rooms in the north and east corners on the second floor of Bomberger Hall were used as chemistry and physics laboratories, enabling the college to offer an up-to-date science curriculum. A biology laboratory was added on the first floor in 1895. Female students worked alongside male students in the laboratories, as seen in this c. 1905 photograph. (Courtesy of the Ursinus College Archives.)

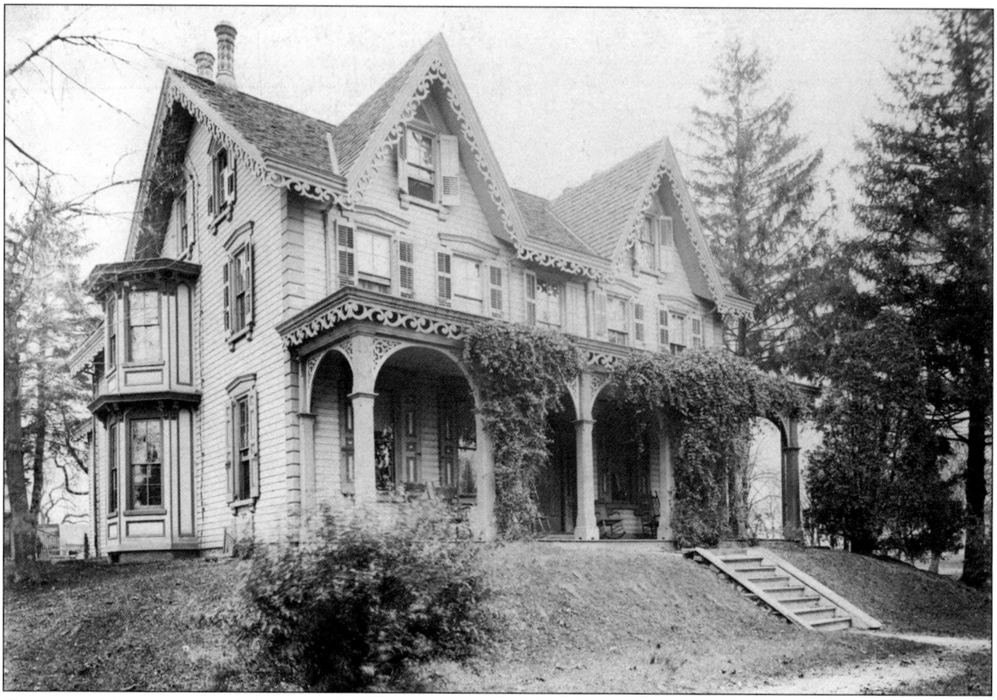

OLEVIAN HALL, 1891. This ornate Victorian house, built in 1865 for Henry A. Hunsicker on land that he acquired from the widow of Samuel Townsend in 1860, stood to the west of the Freeland Seminary campus. Together with a barn and 20 acres of land, Ursinus purchased the house in 1891 as the college's first dormitory for women, initially known as the Ladies Boarding Hall. In 1896, it was named Olevian Hall after Caspar Olevian, a German Reformed theologian. Due to the strict supervision of the young ladies who lived there, students nicknamed it the "nunnery." On February 20, 1931, the house was burned to the ground to make way for the construction of a new science building, now known as Pfahler Hall. (Courtesy of the Ursinus College Archives.)

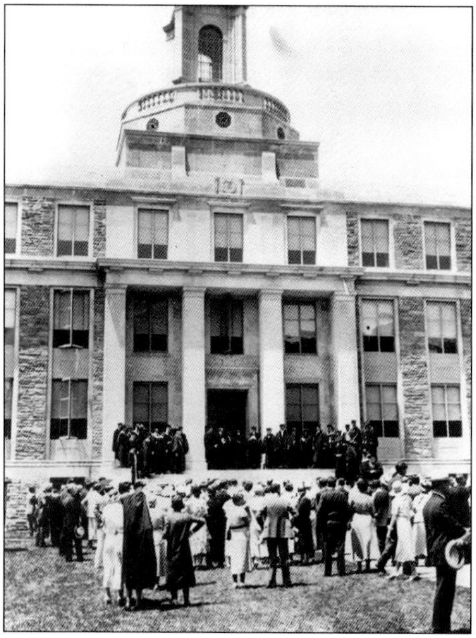

PHALER HALL, 1933. Ursinus dedicated a new science building in 1933—the occasion of this photograph. In 1942, it was renamed the Phaler Hall of Science after Dr. George E. Pfahler, a pioneer in the field of radiology. The building contained a large lecture hall, thirteen teaching laboratories, two research laboratories, and nine professors' laboratories. Here, Dr. John W. Mauchly, professor of physics from 1933 to 1941, began research that would lead him to co-invent the ENIAC (Electronic Numerical Integrator and Computer), the first electronic general-purpose computer. In the 1950s, Walter W. Marsteller (class of 1949) built an astronomy observatory atop the building using surplus military parts and aircraft aluminum. The observatory, which housed a telescope on loan from the Franklin Institute for several decades, was dismantled in 1997–1998. (Courtesy of the Ursinus College Archives.)

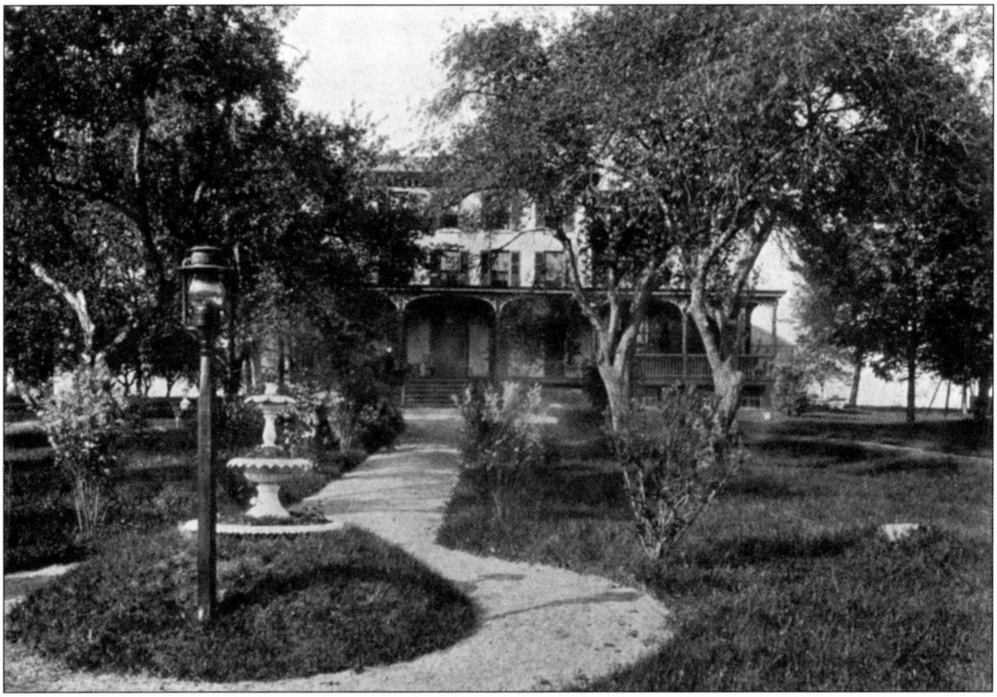

PROSPECT TERRACE, C. 1890. Located just east of the Freeland Seminary campus, Prospect Terrace was a large boardinghouse erected by Benjamin and Hannah (Detweiler) Hunsicker in 1854. Benjamin's father, Rev. Abraham Hunsicker, was the founder of Freeland Seminary. After Benjamin's death in 1855, it became known as Mrs. Hannah Hunsicker's boardinghouse. It was later owned by Dr. James Palmer. The building was lost in a fire in February 1900; it stood in front of where the Alumni Memorial Library was built in 1923. (Courtesy of the Ursinus College Archives.)

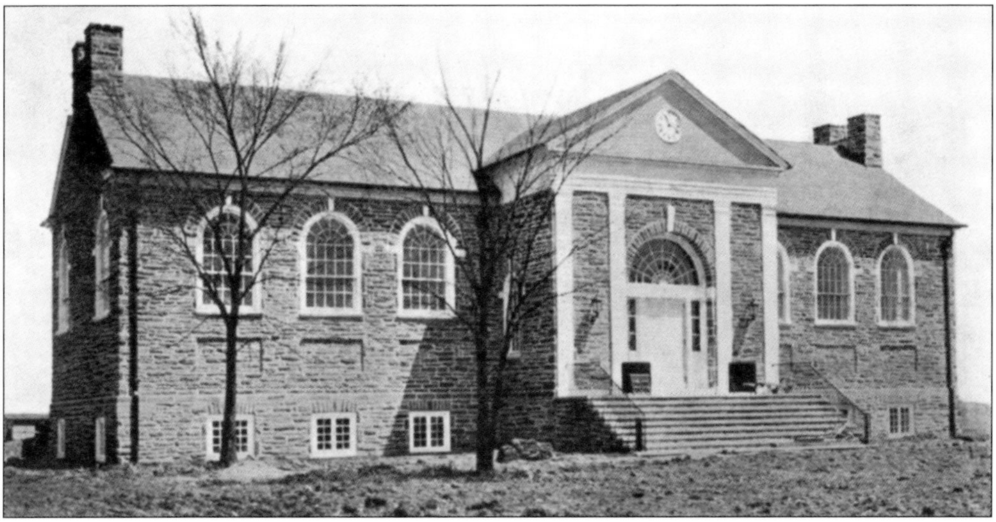

ALUMNI MEMORIAL LIBRARY, C. 1930. Opened in 1923, the Alumni Memorial Library was built to commemorate the 271 Ursinus students and alumni who served in World War I and particularly the eight who died in service. It closed in October 1970, following the completion of Myrin Library, and was then used as a student union building before it was remodeled as the Philip and Muriel Berman Museum of Art. (Courtesy of Jerry A. Chiccarine.)

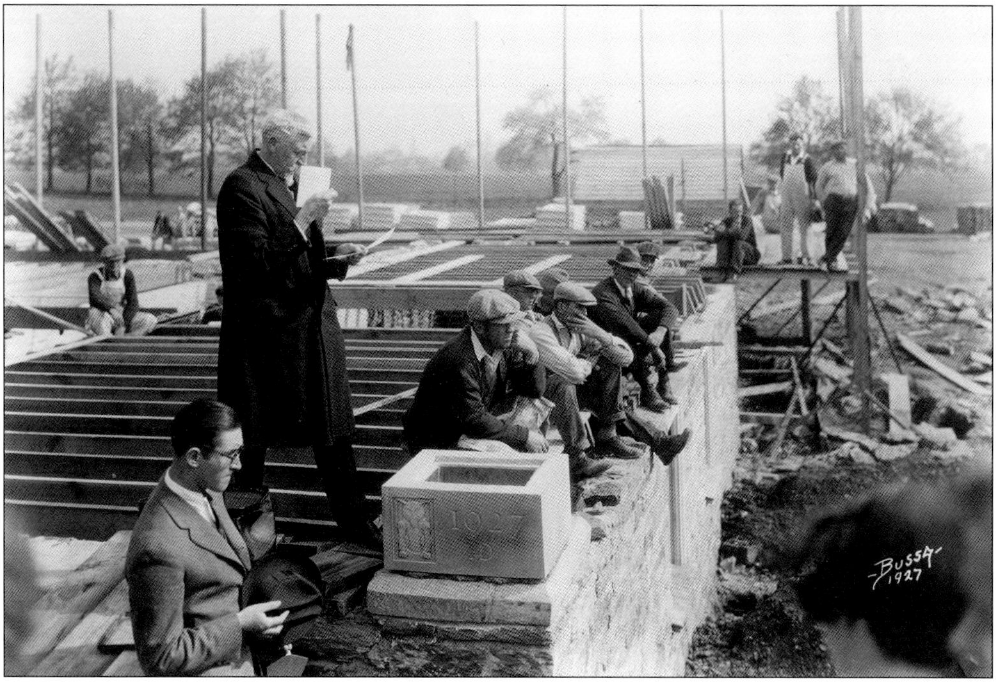

Cornerstone of Curtis and Brodbeck Halls, 1927. As the Ursinus student body expanded, it outgrew the capacity of the existing dormitories and repurposed Victorian houses along Main Street. In 1927, the college embarked on the construction of two identical men's dormitories, each to house 54 students. The cornerstones of Curtis and Brodbeck Halls were laid on May 9, 1927; remarkably, the buildings were officially opened less than seven months later. In 1966, a third dormitory unit, named Wilkinson Hall, was constructed between Curtis and Brodbeck. (Courtesy of the Ursinus College Archives.)

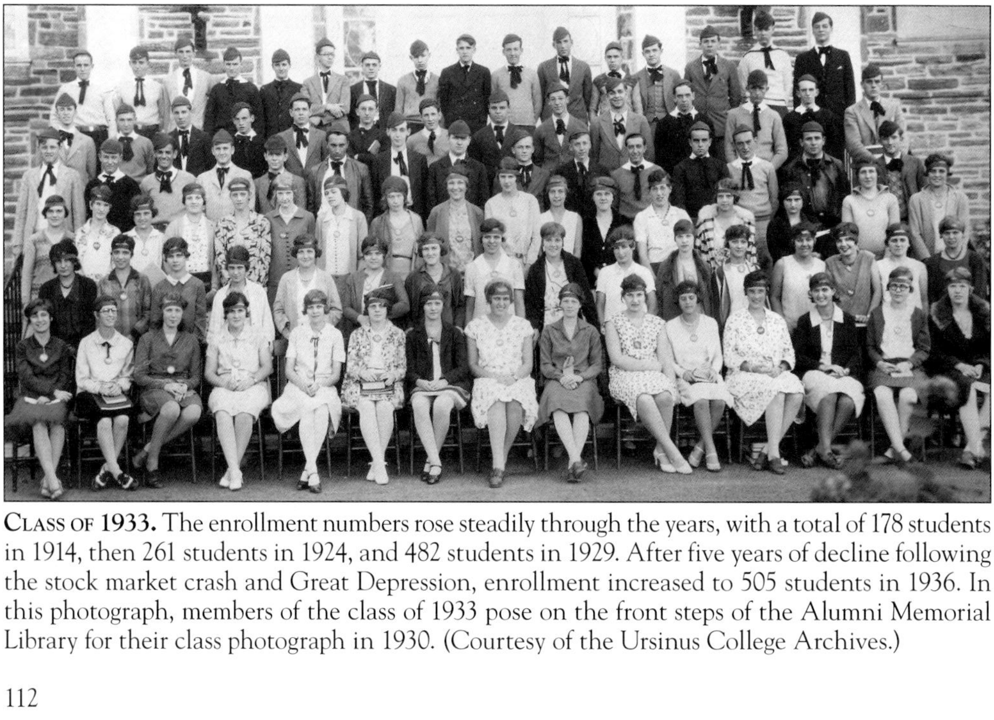

Class of 1933. The enrollment numbers rose steadily through the years, with a total of 178 students in 1914, then 261 students in 1924, and 482 students in 1929. After five years of decline following the stock market crash and Great Depression, enrollment increased to 505 students in 1936. In this photograph, members of the class of 1933 pose on the front steps of the Alumni Memorial Library for their class photograph in 1930. (Courtesy of the Ursinus College Archives.)

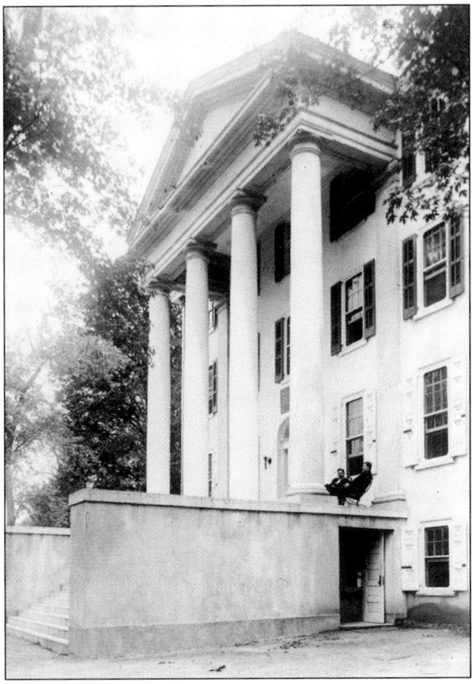

FREELAND HALL PORTICO. In 1910, the college made plans to renovate the old Freeland Seminary complex; this work was not carried out until 1913 under Pres. George Leslie Omwake's administration. The three buildings were extensively remodeled to provide new dormitory and dining facilities, as well as electricity and modern plumbing. On the exterior, a new cupola and colonnaded portico were constructed. The buildings were also renamed: the original Freeland Seminary building in the center became known as Freeland Hall, with the east wing as Derr Hall and the west wing as Stine Hall. (Courtesy of the Ursinus College Archives.)

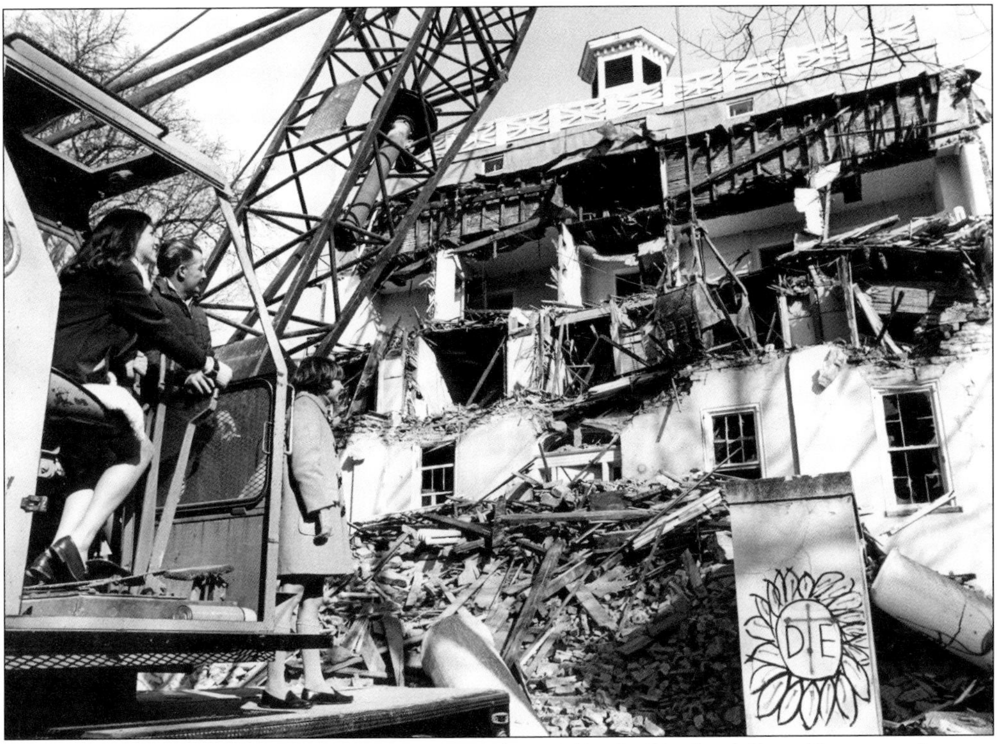

FREELAND HALL DEMOLITION, 1968. In November 1968, the Freeland-Stine-Derr complex was demolished to make way for the construction of Myrin Library. Students were permitted to try their hand at knocking down the historic buildings. Here, the crane operator looks on while one student operates the crane and another watches. (Courtesy of the Ursinus College Archives.)

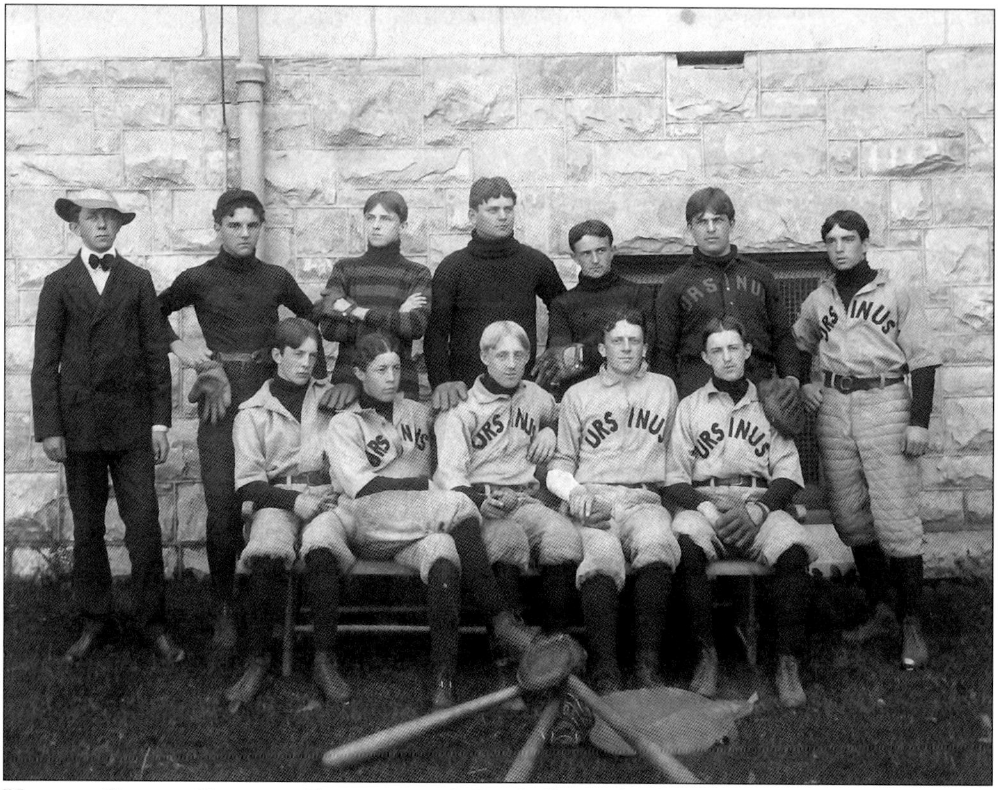

URSINUS COLLEGE BASEBALL TEAM, C. 1895. Baseball was the first organized sport to emerge at the college. By 1886, the Ursinus College Base Ball Club had been established and competed against Muhlenberg College. Four years later, the student-led Ursinus Athletic Association implored the college to improve its baseball diamond, but their request was denied. The students improvised by leasing land from Dr. James Hamer, building a new diamond, and organizing a concert—the proceeds of which were used to purchase team uniforms. (Courtesy of the Ursinus College Archives.)

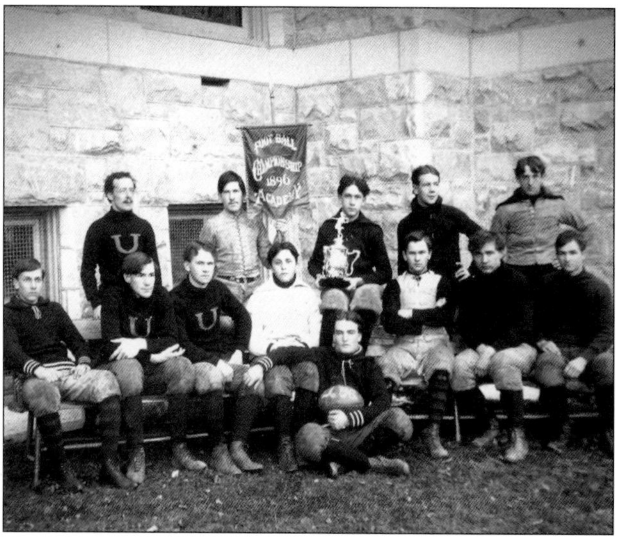

URSINUS FOOTBALL TEAM, 1896. By the fall of 1890, a football team had been established, much to the initial dismay of the Ursinus faculty. The team did not play against another college until 1893, when Ursinus was crushed 62-0 by the Pennsylvania Military College. Despite this loss, it was reported that the "football craze has struck Ursinus now that our students have actually seen a game played." In 1894, a football coach was hired, and sweaters with a large gold "U" on the front were ordered. (Courtesy of the Ursinus College Archives.)

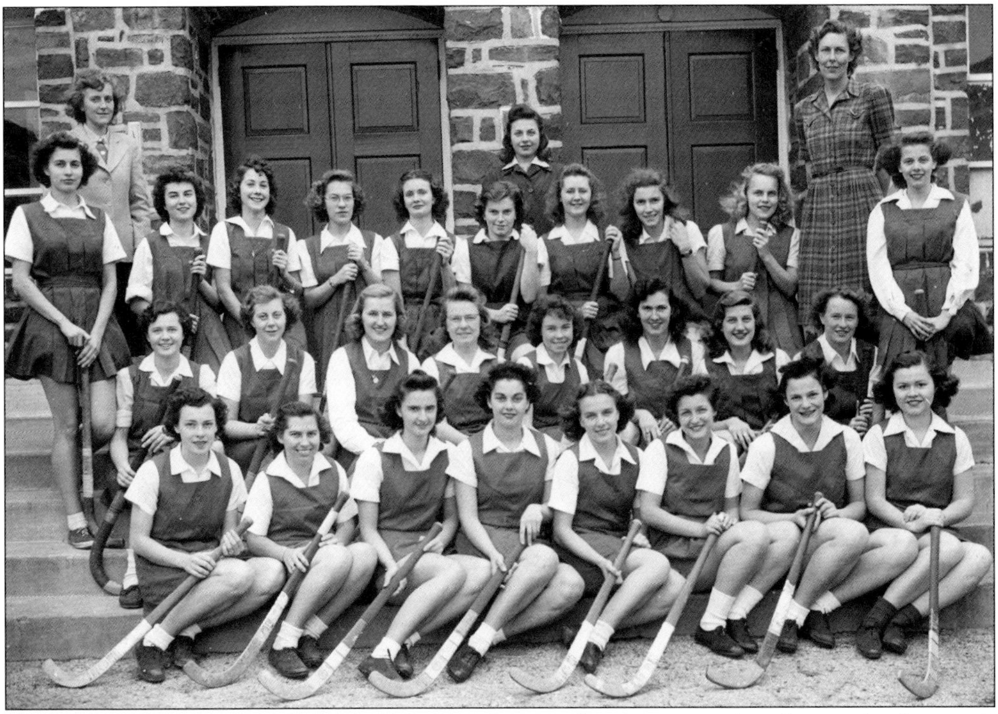

Field Hockey Team, 1944. In 1931, Eleanor Frost Snell was appointed as the coach of women's athletics and as an instructor of physical education. She led the field hockey team, later nicknamed "Snell's Belles," to a 7-1-1 record in her first year. Snell became the most successful coach in Ursinus history, with a lifetime record of 191-60-29. In this photograph of the undefeated 1944 field hockey team, Coach Snell stands at upper right in a plaid dress. (Courtesy of the Ursinus College Archives.)

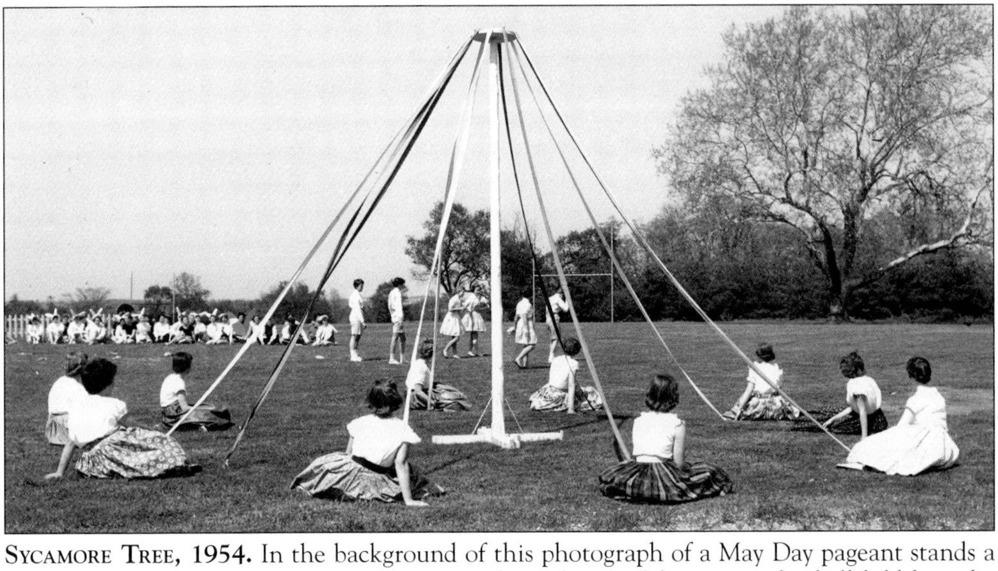

Sycamore Tree, 1954. In the background of this photograph of a May Day pageant stands a mighty sycamore tree, which famously stood in the end zone of the Ursinus football field from the 1920s, when Dean Whorten Kline refused to let the tree be cut down when the land was cleared for Patterson Field, until it was felled by a windstorm in 1984. The tree stood only 20 feet from the goalposts in the end zone. (Courtesy of the Ursinus College Archives.)

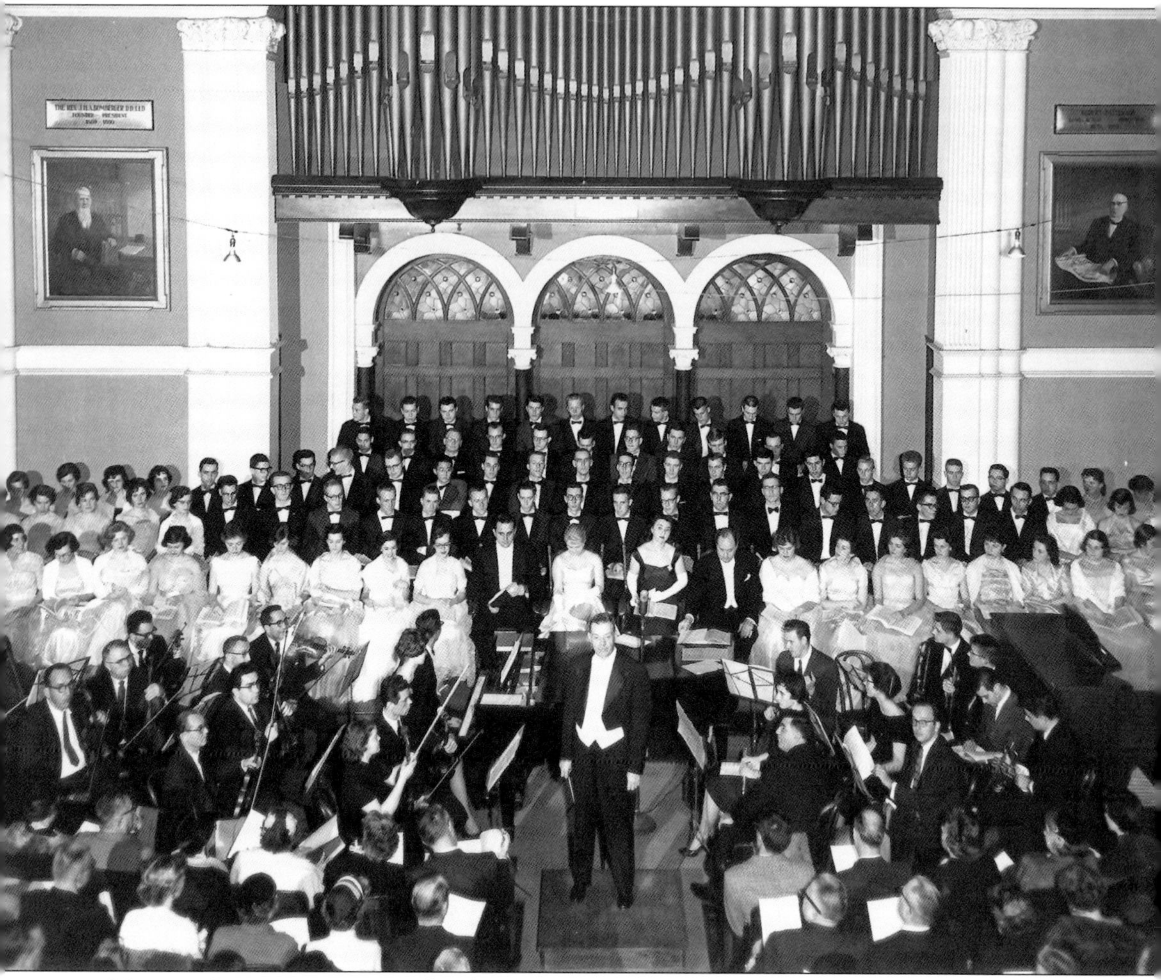

MESSIAH CONCERT, 1959. Under the direction of Dr. William F. Philip, the first performance of Handel's *Messiah* at Ursinus was given before a full house in Bomberger Hall on December 8, 1938. Ever since then, it has been a beloved Christmas tradition attended by students, alumni, and community residents alike. This photograph shows Dr. Philip conducting the concert on December 10, 1959. (Courtesy of the Ursinus College Archives.)

Eight

Community Life

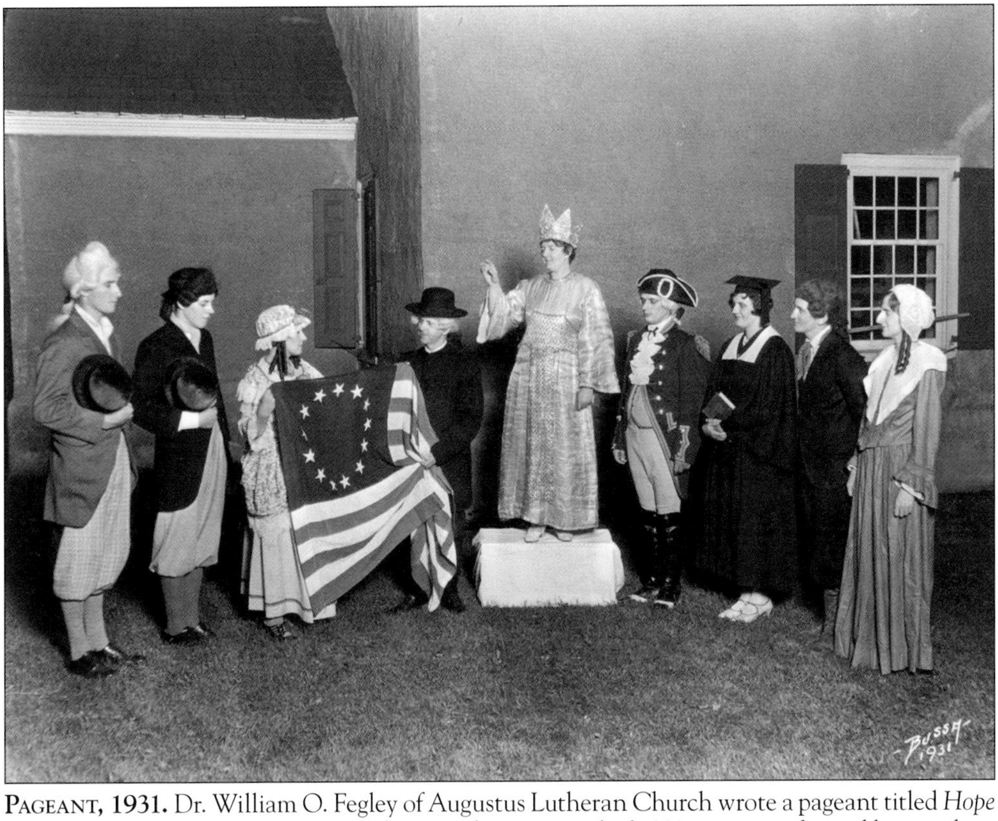

Pageant, 1931. Dr. William O. Fegley of Augustus Lutheran Church wrote a pageant titled *Hope Fulfilled* to celebrate the George Washington bicentennial of 1932; it was performed by members of the congregation. A note accompanying this photograph describes the scene as follows: "Betsy Ross extends the protection of the flag to the church while the army guarantees it, and education perpetuates the teaching of the gospel. The spirit of civilization blesses all." (Courtesy of Augustus Lutheran Church.)

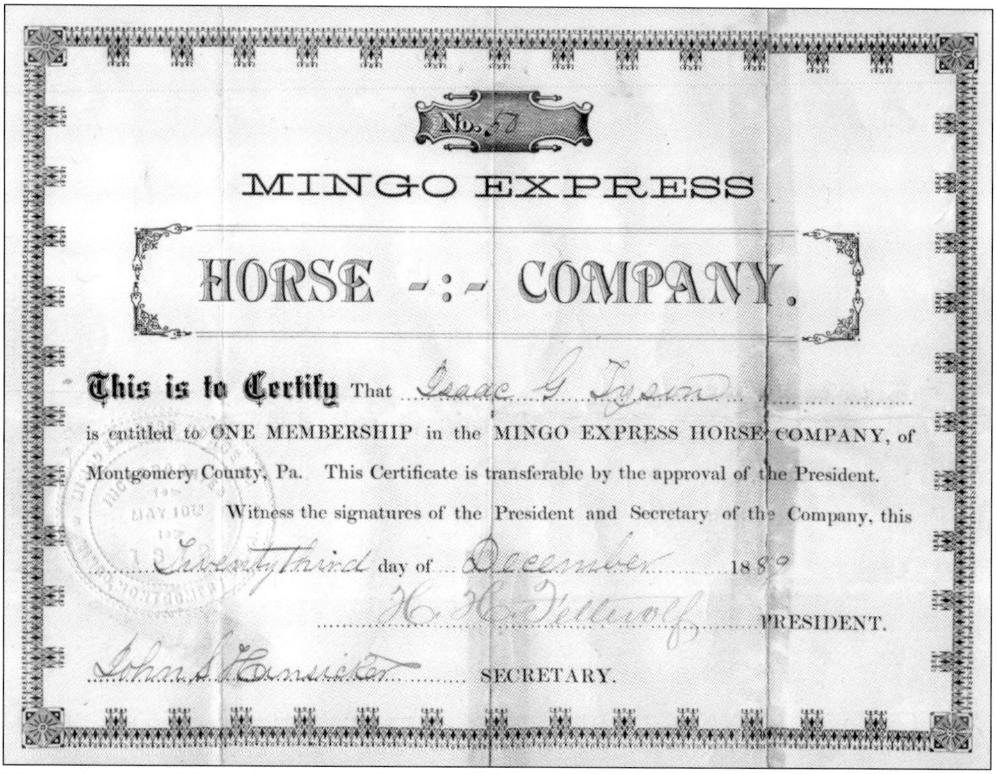

No. 50

MINGO EXPRESS

HORSE -:- COMPANY.

This is to Certify That Isaac G. Tyson is entitled to ONE MEMBERSHIP in the MINGO EXPRESS HORSE COMPANY, of Montgomery County, Pa. This Certificate is transferable by the approval of the President.

Witness the signatures of the President and Secretary of the Company, this Twenty third day of December 1889

H. H. Fetterolf PRESIDENT.

John S. Hunsicker SECRETARY.

MINGO EXPRESS HORSE COMPANY. The Mingo Express Horse Company was founded in 1836 to help members recover stolen horses and bring horse thieves to justice. Its jurisdiction covered the townships of Upper and Lower Providence, Limerick, and Perkiomen. Certificates were issued as proof of membership; this example, No. 50, was issued to Isaac G. Tyson on December 23, 1889. The company continues to meet annually on the first Saturday in January. (Courtesy of the Historical Society of Trappe, Collegeville, Perkiomen Valley.)

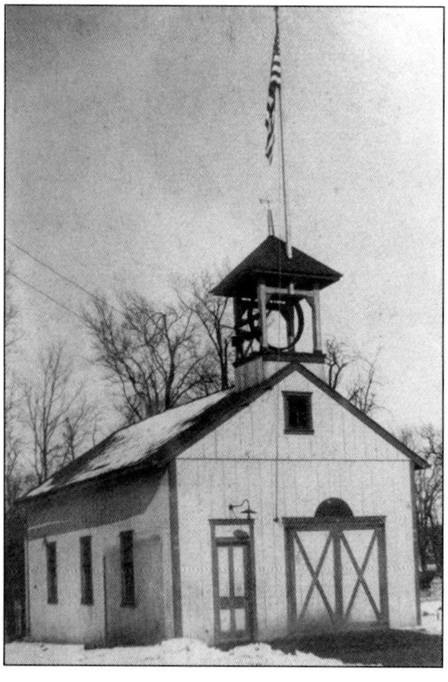

COLLEGEVILLE AND TRAPPE FIRE COMPANIES. On July 14, 1891, a tremendous fire nearly burned down two contiguous businesses—the Roberts Machine Works and the Collegeville Ice Manufacturing Company. Local citizens rallied to purchase firefighting equipment, and on November 6, 1891, Collegeville Fire Company No. 1 was organized. In 1892, the first fire hall was built where the Masonic Hall now stands at 324 East Main Street, but in 1905, it was moved to an empty lot on East Fifth Avenue. A new fire hall was erected there in 1950 and enlarged in 1959. After a bad house fire at 324 West Main Street in 1911, local residents organized Trappe Fire Company No. 1. The following year, a two-story brick building was erected at 20 West Fifth Avenue and later expanded. The Trappe Fire Company Ambulance was founded in 1947. (Courtesy of the J. Howard Fenstermacher Collection at the Historical Society of Trappe, Collegeville, Perkiomen Valley.)

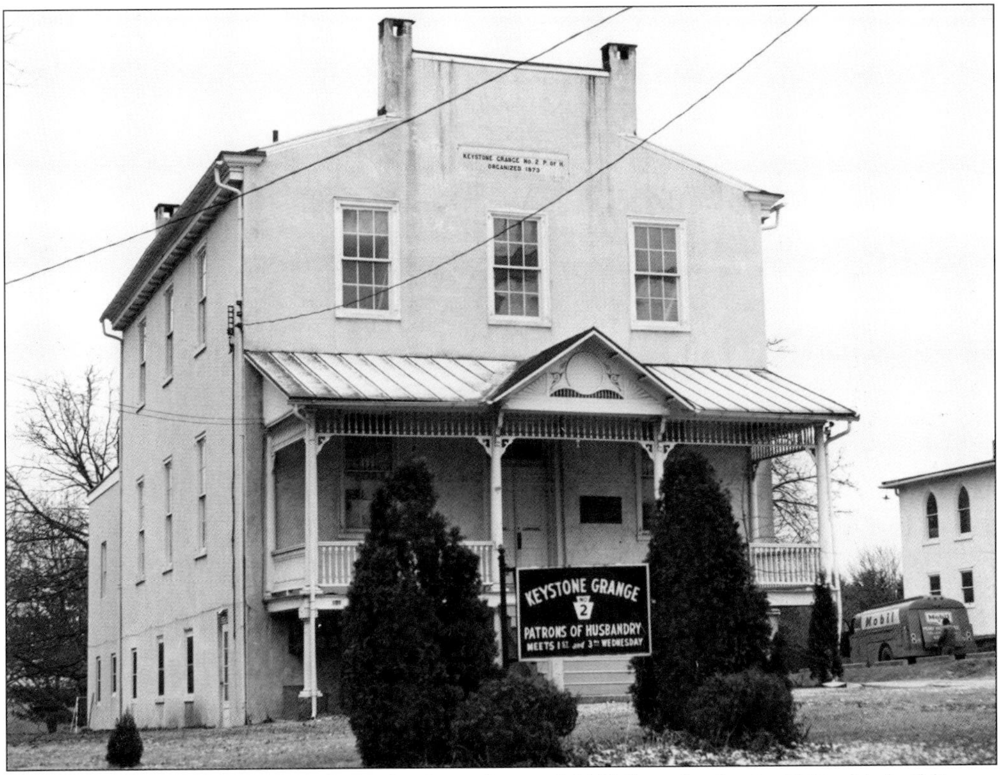

Keystone Grange No. 2. Built for the Providence Odd Fellows Lodge in 1849, this building at 192 West Main Street in Trappe was sold to Horace Royer in 1865. Royer then leased it to the Warren Masonic Lodge, which bought it in 1872. Later, it became the headquarters of Keystone Grange No. 2 in 1913. From 1919 to 1950, the lower level of the building was used as a store that sold farm supplies and groceries. Organized in 1873, Keystone Grange No. 2 is the second-oldest grange in Pennsylvania, and in 1973, its 100th anniversary was celebrated with a Centennial Fair. This inaugurated a decades-long tradition of the annual Grange Country Fair, a local summertime highlight held in Water Works Park. Fairs included demonstrations of old-time farm equipment, historic trades, and baking contests. (Courtesy of Matthew G. Wismer.)

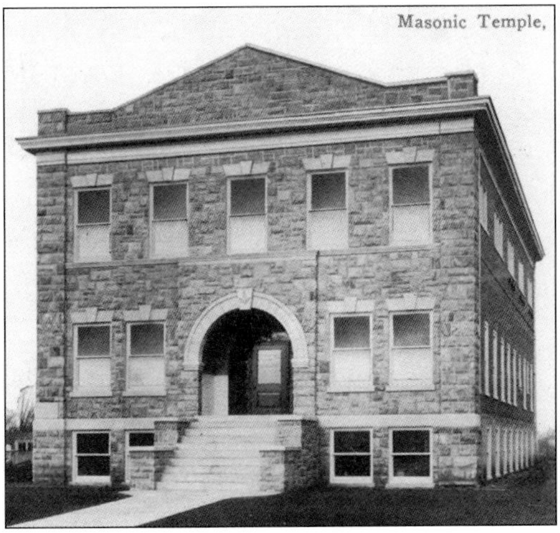

Warren Masonic Lodge. Warren Lodge No. 310 of the Free and Accepted Masons was chartered on September 5, 1857. Dr. Joseph Warren Royer of Trappe was the first worshipful master. In 1913, the lodge erected a new building at 324 East Main Street in Collegeville on a tract of land donated by Francis J. Clamer. The construction was overseen by Abraham D. Fetterolf, who served as chairman of the building committee. Lodge meetings have been held there ever since. They are scheduled for the Saturday night on or before the full moon, a tradition harkening back to the days when moonlight aided those traveling after dark. (Courtesy of Jerry A. Chiccarine.)

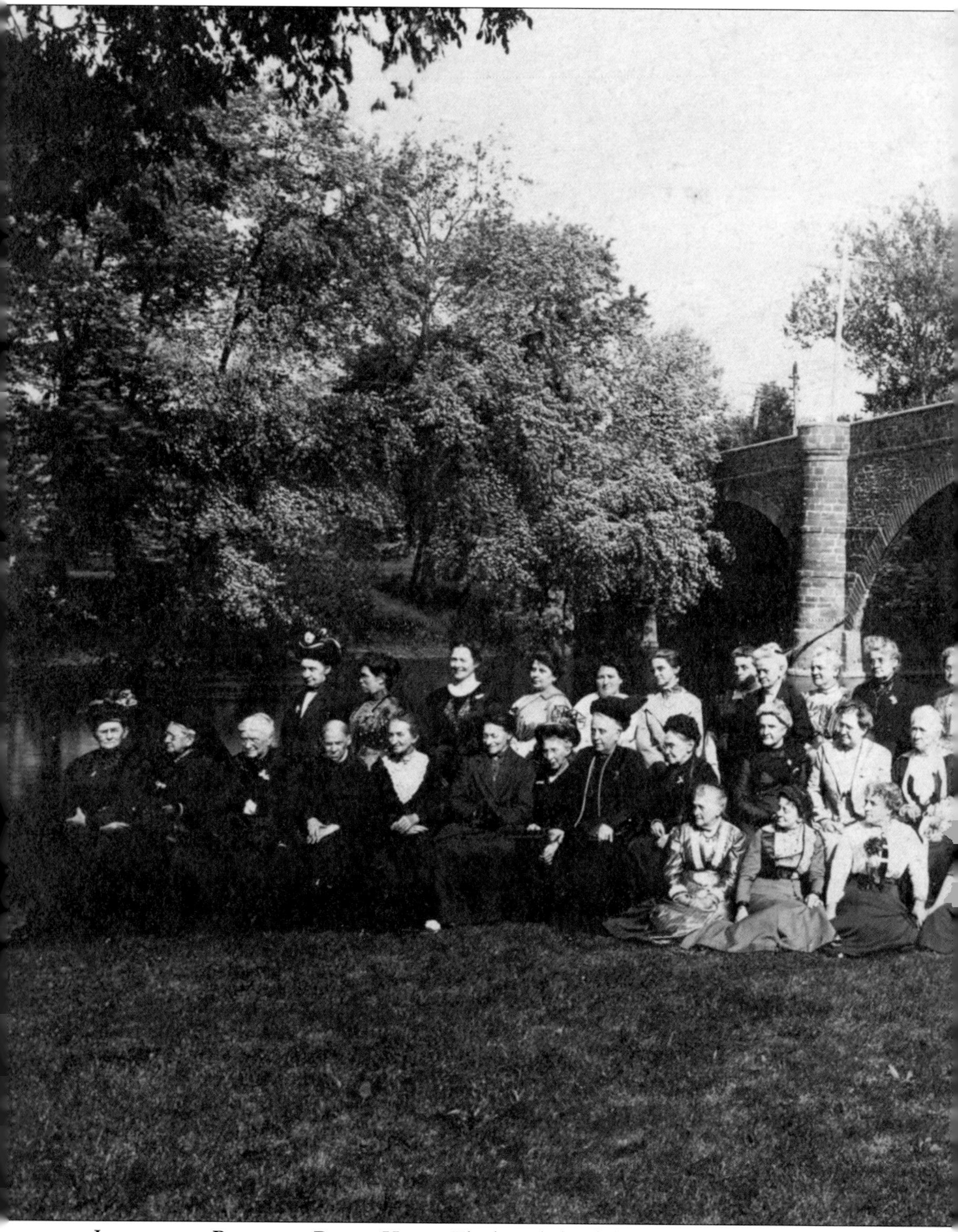

Lawn of the Perkiomen Bridge Hotel. The lawn behind the Perkiomen Bridge Hotel, which bordered the west bank of the Perkiomen Creek, was a popular gathering place. Here, 58 women

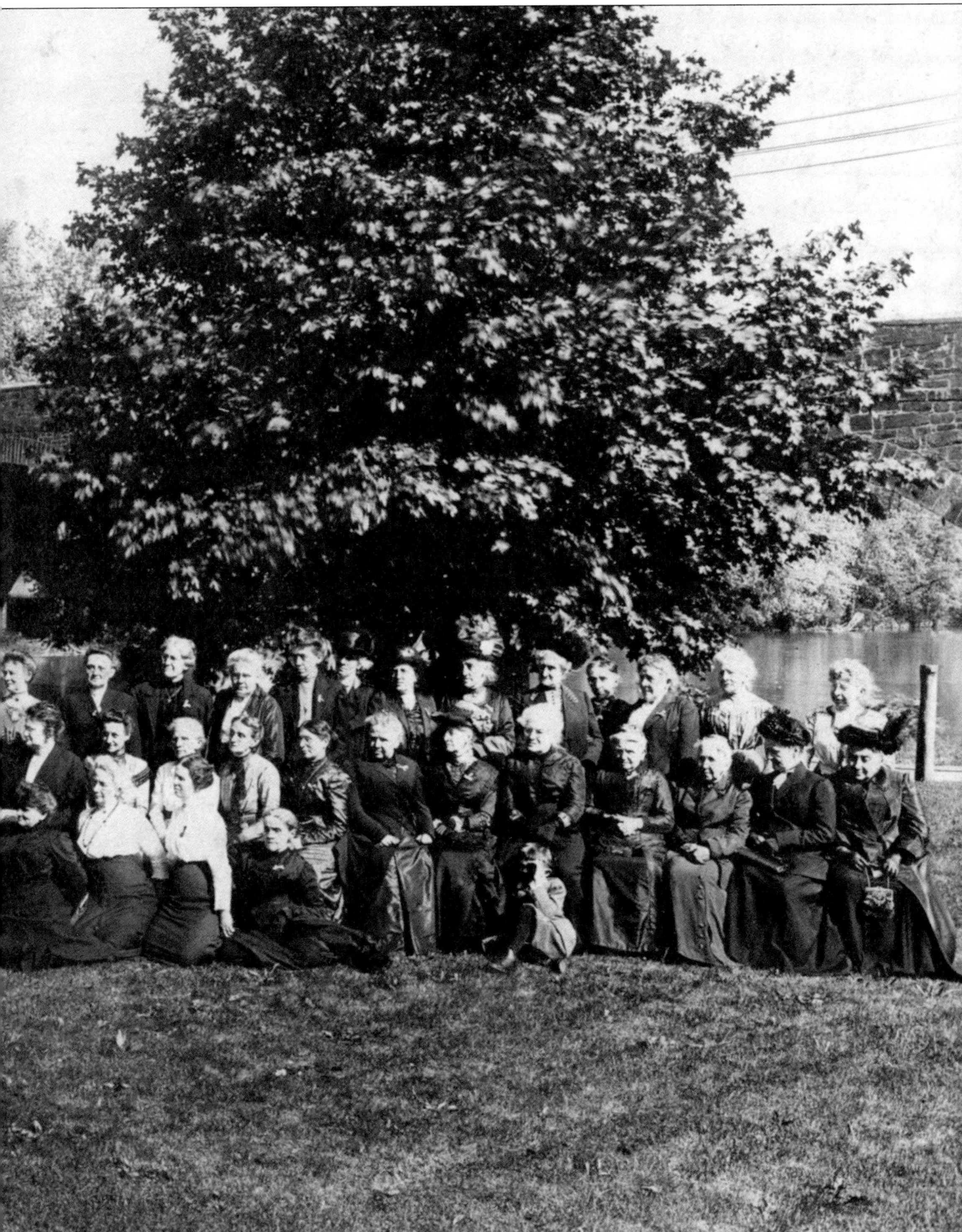

from Augustus Lutheran Church pose for a group photograph, with the stone arches of the Perkiomen Bridge as a backdrop. (Courtesy of Augustus Lutheran Church.)

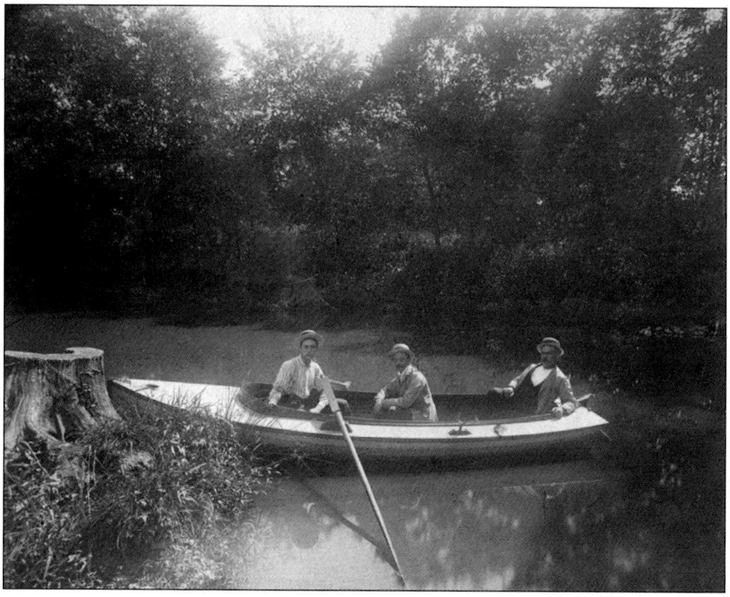

Clamer Family Canoers, 1891. Taken in 1891, this photograph shows Francis J. Clamer at right with his son Guilliam and an unidentified young man in a canoe on the Perkiomen Creek. The Clamer family had their own boat launch known as the Glen Farm Wharf, located near the Clamer Mill Dam. (Courtesy of the Historical Society of Trappe, Collegeville, Perkiomen Valley.)

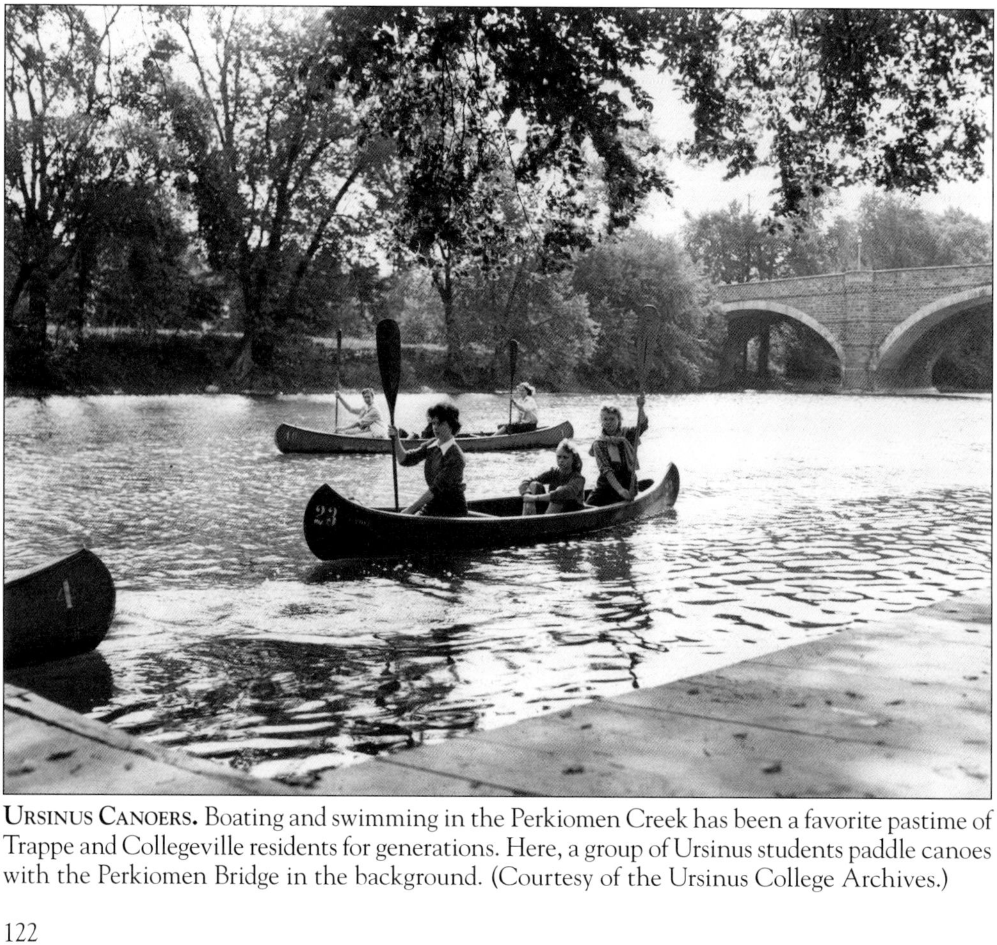

Ursinus Canoers. Boating and swimming in the Perkiomen Creek has been a favorite pastime of Trappe and Collegeville residents for generations. Here, a group of Ursinus students paddle canoes with the Perkiomen Bridge in the background. (Courtesy of the Ursinus College Archives.)

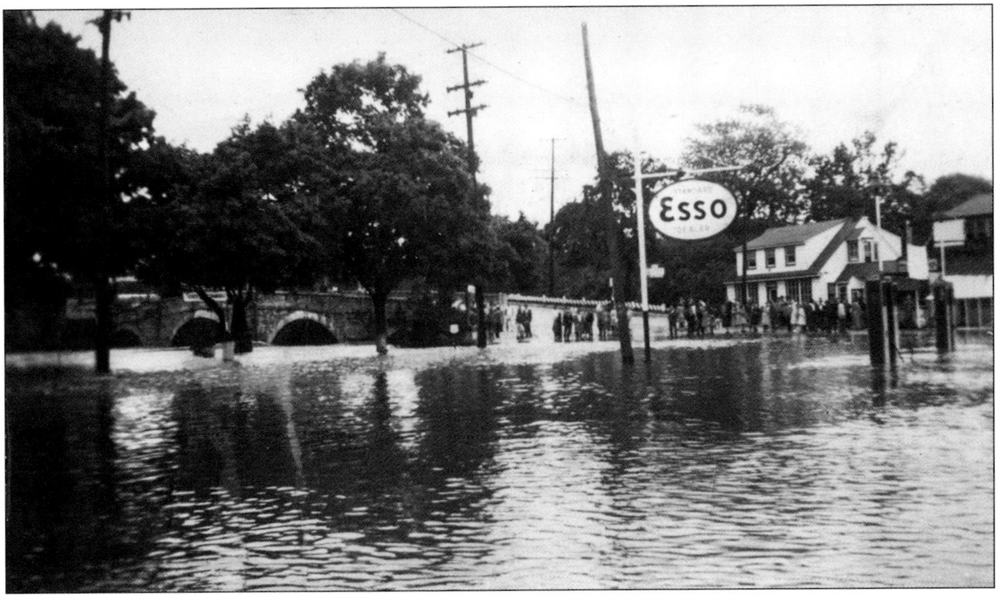

Perkiomen Creek Flooding. Checking out floods when the Perkiomen Creek overflows its banks is a long-standing community pastime. On August 23–24, 1933, tremendous rains caused the creek to rise 20 feet above normal in the vicinity of the Perkiomen Bridge. It was the second-highest flood in local history, coming within two feet of the great flood of October 4, 1869. Since the completion of the Green Lane Reservoir in 1957, the flooding has been less severe. The reservoir is located about 16 miles north of Collegeville. (Both, courtesy of the J. Howard Fenstermacher Collection.)

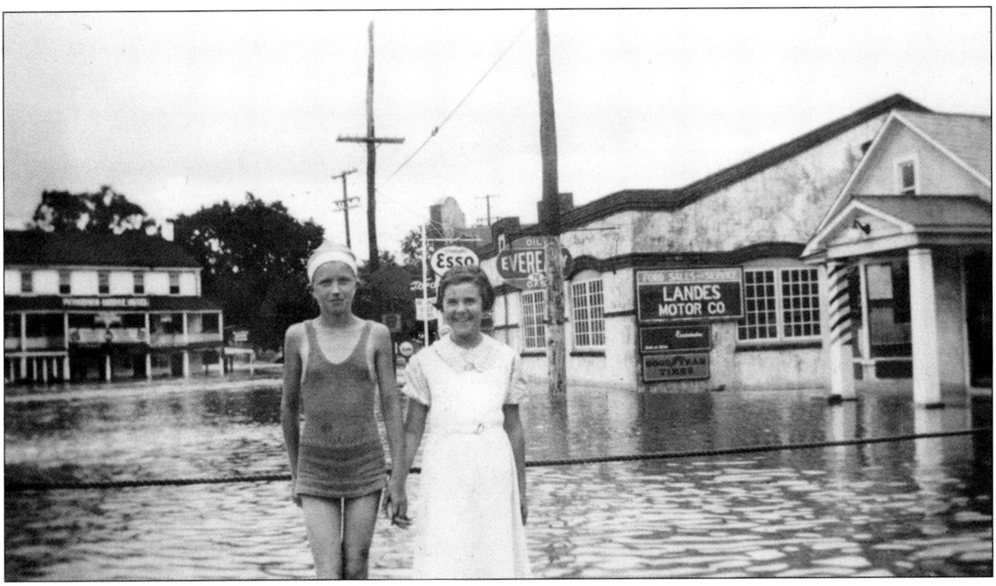

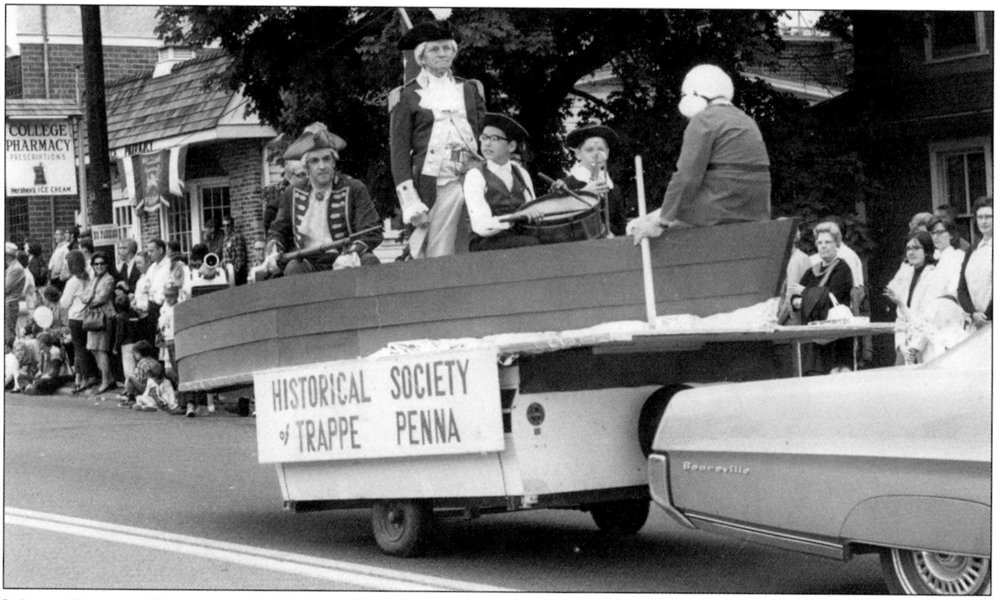

Main Street Parade, 1967. Local residents put on a parade to celebrate the 250th anniversary of Trappe's founding. Frederick W. Grimison, first president of the historical society, dressed as George Washington on a float reenacting the crossing of the Delaware River during the night of December 25, 1776. The College Pharmacy at far left still stands at 321 East Main Street. (Courtesy of the Historical Society of Trappe, Collegeville, Perkiomen Valley.)

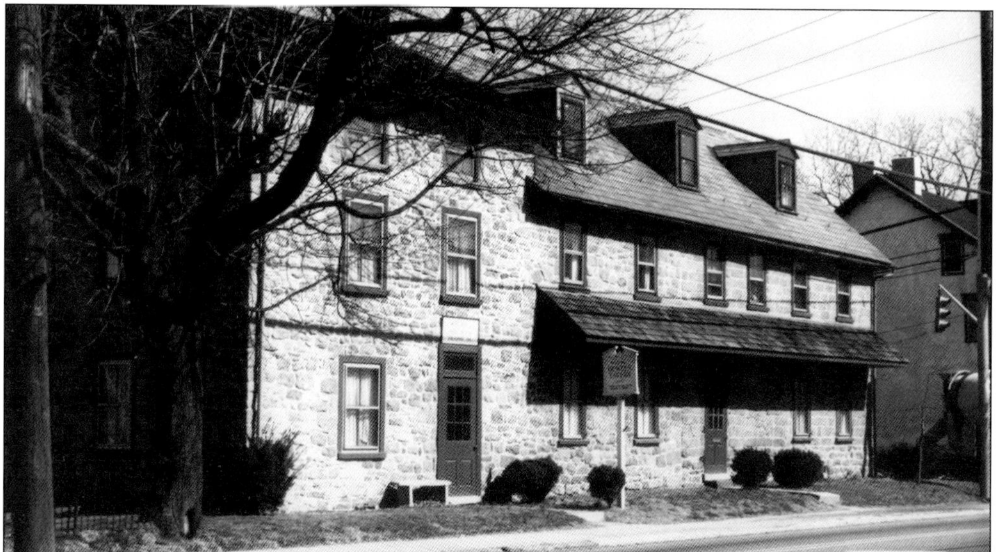

Dewees Tavern Museum. Led by Frederick W. Grimison, a local historical society was founded in 1964. It initially met in the west end of the Dewees Tavern at 301 West Main Street, owned by St. Luke's Church. In 1973, the church was considering razing the deteriorated tavern. The building was saved in 1974 when the society signed a 99-year lease with the proviso that they restore and maintain the building. A goal was set to restore the tavern by 1976, and work commenced under the direction of Frank Eld. The restored building was dedicated on June 13, 1976. (Courtesy of the Historical Society of Trappe, Collegeville, Perkiomen Valley.)

HENRY MUHLENBERG HOUSE, 201 WEST MAIN STREET. After moving from Trappe to Philadelphia in 1760, Henry and Mary Muhlenberg returned in 1776 and settled in this house, built for Jacob Schrack Jr. between 1750 and 1755. The house was later remodeled, but it was acquired by the local historical society in 1989 and restored to its c. 1776 appearance. (Photograph by Glenn Holcombe; courtesy of the Historical Society of Trappe, Collegeville, Perkiomen Valley.)

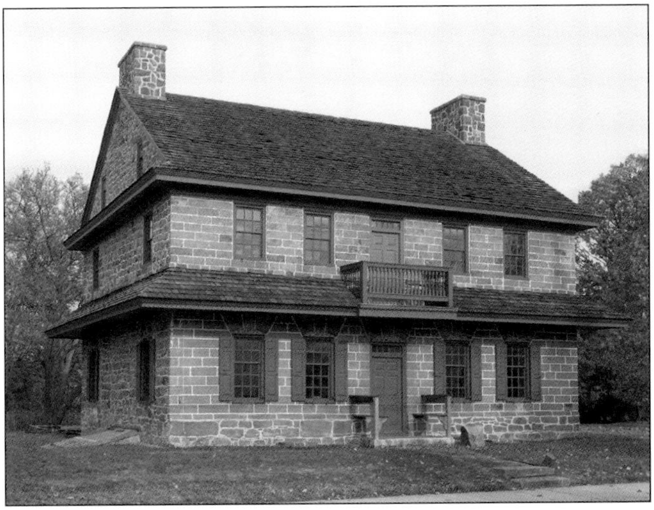

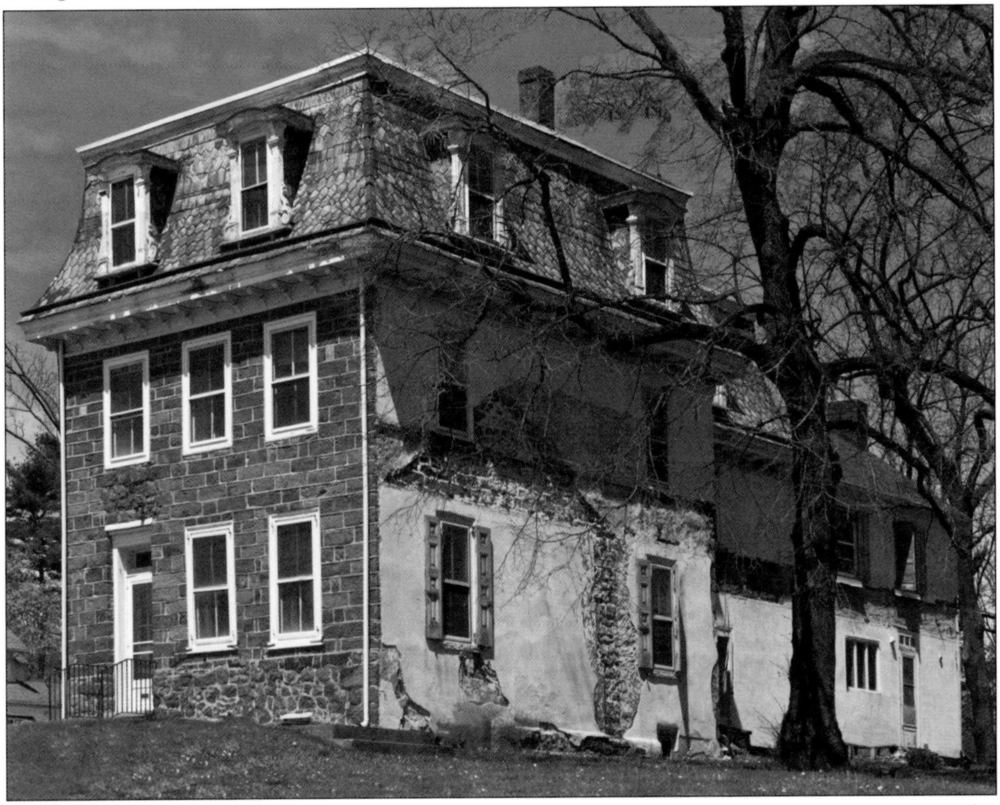

FREDERICK MUHLENBERG HOUSE, 151 WEST MAIN STREET. Local citizens rallied to save the Frederick Muhlenberg house from demolition in the early 2000s. Now owned by a nonprofit organization known as The Speaker's House, the building is undergoing an intensive effort to restore its appearance to the period of the Muhlenberg family's ownership, from 1781 to 1803. The Victorian-era mansard roofs will be removed, and pitched roofs will be rebuilt per the original architectural evidence. Visible on the east gable wall in this photograph is the outline of Muhlenberg's general store, which he operated during the 1780s. (Photograph by Gavin Ashworth; courtesy of The Speaker's House.)

BIBLIOGRAPHY

Bean, Theodore W., ed. *History of Montgomery County, Pennsylvania.* Philadelphia, PA: Everts & Peck, 1884.

Chiccarine, Jerry A. *Along the Perkiomen.* Charleston, SC: Arcadia Publishing, 2005.

Hoover, Margaret Hocker. *Concerning Collegeville: A History of that Community and Somewhat of Its Neighbor Trappe.* Philadelphia, PA: self-published, 1966.

Hunsicker, Clifton S. *Montgomery County, Pennsylvania: A History*, vol. 2. New York, NY: Lewis Historical Publishing Co., 1923.

Hunsicker, Henry A. "Sketches of Local History." *The Independent*, 18 October 1906. Reprinted in *History Sketches of Trappe and Collegeville: 1812–1912*, edited by William T. Parsons, 41–90. Collegeville, PA: Chestnut Books, 1990.

Kretschmann, Ernest T., ed. *The Old Trappe Church: A Memorial of the Sesqui-Centennial Services of Augustus Evangelical Lutheran Church, Montgomery County, Pennsylvania.* Philadelphia, PA: 1893.

Minardi, Lisa. *Pastors & Patriots: The Muhlenberg Family of Pennsylvania.* Collegeville, PA: Philip and Muriel Berman Museum of Art at Ursinus College, 2011.

Montgomery County deeds, probate records, and tax records. Montgomery County Archives and the Historical Society of Montgomery County, Norristown, PA.

Roberts, Ellwood, ed. *Biographical Annals of Montgomery County, Pennsylvania.* New York, NY: T.S. Benham & Co., 1904.

Scott, J.D. *Combination Atlas Map of Montgomery County, Pennsylvania.* Philadelphia, PA: self-published, 1877.

Shetler, John C. "The Historical Society of Trappe and the Restoration of the Muhlenberg House, 1964–2002." *The Bulletin of the Historical Society of Montgomery County*, 33, no. 3 (Fall 2002): 154–191.

Swenk, Thomas. "Recollections of Col. Thomas Swenk, Octogenarian." *The Perkiomen Region* 2, nos. 1–8 (1899). Reprinted in *History Sketches of Trappe and Collegeville: 1812–1912*, edited by William T. Parsons, 10–24. Collegeville, PA: Chestnut Books, 1990.

Toll, Jean Barth, and Michael J. Schwager, eds. *Montgomery County: The Second Hundred Years.* 2 vols. Norristown, PA: Montgomery County Federation of Historical Societies, 1984.

Yost, Calvin D. *Ursinus College: A History of Its First Hundred Years.* Collegeville, PA: Ursinus College, 1985.

About the Organization

The Trappe 300 Steering Committee is a collaborative initiative of numerous Trappe and Collegeville nonprofit organizations and residents. Led by cochairs Rachael Morrison and Lisa Minardi, its members include Augustus Lutheran Church, Jen Wentworth; Collegeville Economic Development Corporation, Karen McCaslin; Community Music School, Vibha Agrawal; Historical Society of Trappe, Collegeville, Perkiomen Valley, Bridgie Daller, Anne Grasberger, Josh Macel, and Manni McNeil; The Speaker's House, Kate Minardi, Vordea Mingis, and Denae and Gene Zvarick; Borough of Trappe, Scott Martin, Mayor Connie Peck, and Pat Webster; and Fred Schuetz.

Trappe is home to two organizations devoted to researching and maintaining local history. Founded in 1964, the Historical Society of Trappe, Collegeville, Perkiomen Valley's mission is the encouragement of local historical research and community activities and preservation of historic structures and archaeological sites in Trappe and surrounding areas. The organization maintains a museum and research library in the Dewees Tavern at 301 West Main Street, as well as the restored Henry Muhlenberg House at 201 West Main Street. The Speaker's House was founded in 2001 to rescue from demolition the historic home of Frederick Muhlenberg at 151 West Main Street. Its mission is to inspire leadership and civic engagement by bringing to life the home and legacy of Frederick Muhlenberg, first speaker of the US House of Representatives. The house, built in 1763 with later additions, is currently undergoing restoration to its appearance during the Muhlenberg family's ownership, from 1781 to 1803.

All author royalties from this publication benefit the Trappe 300 Steering Committee and its successors. Visit www.historictrappe.org for more images and information about the people and places discussed in this book.

Discover Thousands of Local History Books Featuring Millions of Vintage Images

Arcadia Publishing, the leading local history publisher in the United States, is committed to making history accessible and meaningful through publishing books that celebrate and preserve the heritage of America's people and places.

Find more books like this at
www.arcadiapublishing.com

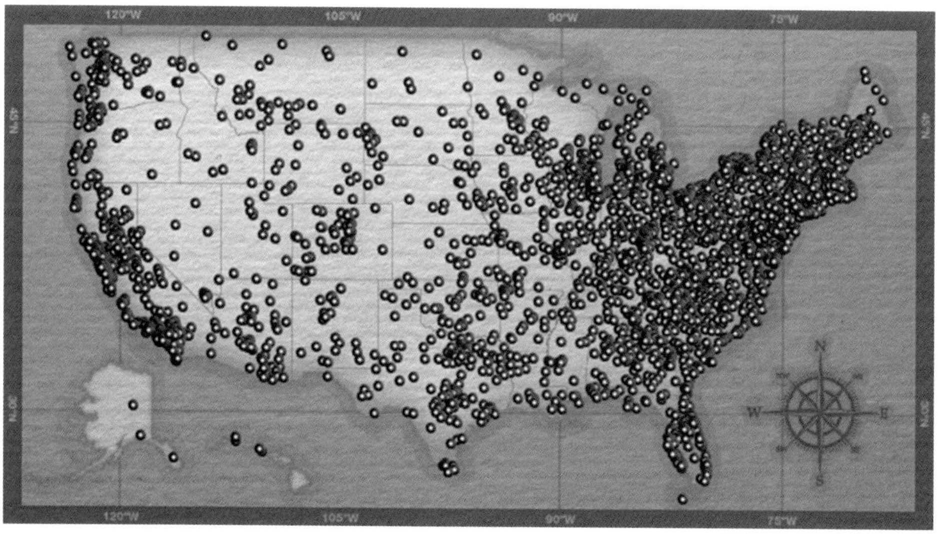

Search for your hometown history, your old stomping grounds, and even your favorite sports team.

Consistent with our mission to preserve history on a local level, this book was printed in South Carolina on American-made paper and manufactured entirely in the United States. Products carrying the accredited Forest Stewardship Council (FSC) label are printed on 100 percent FSC-certified paper.

MADE IN THE USA